Music in the French
Royal Academy of Sciences

Music in the French
Royal Academy of Sciences

A STUDY IN THE EVOLUTION
OF MUSICAL THOUGHT

by

Albert Cohen

PRINCETON UNIVERSITY PRESS

Copyright © 1981 by Princeton University Press
Published by Princeton University Press, Princeton, New Jersey
In the United Kingdom: Princeton University Press, Guildford, Surrey

All Rights Reserved
Library of Congress Cataloging in Publication Data will be
found on the last printed page of this book

Publication of this book has been aided by a grant from the
Paul Mellon Fund of Princeton University Press
This book has been composed in Linotron Bembo
Designed by Barbara Werden

Clothbound editions of Princeton University Press books
are printed on acid-free paper, and binding materials are
chosen for strength and durability

Printed in the United States of America by Princeton
University Press, Princeton, New Jersey

To Eva and Stefan

La Théorie de la Musique est aussi sublime,
que la Pratique en est délicieuse, & l'une
est aussi charmante pour l'Esprit, que l'autre
l'est pour les Sens & pour l'imagination.

[The theory of music is as sublime, as
its practice is delightful; and the one
is as charming for the spirit, as is the other
for the senses and for the imagination.]

—Fontenelle (1704)

Contents

Preface

The Royal Academy of Sciences in Paris is generally conceded to have played a crucial role in the scientific movements of the seventeenth and eighteenth centuries. Supported by the Crown, its authority grew to be supreme, and it wielded enormous power over developments in science and technology, both in France and abroad. That the Academy included music among the disciplines it considered appropriate to scientific study is not surprising. The close relationship of music to science had long been recognized, and it formed a natural part of the traditional knowledge on which the Academy built its new structure. What is noteworthy, however, is the extent to which the Academy developed its interests in musical subjects, and the evolving nature of those interests throughout its activity.

The present study seeks to make a contribution to understanding the role played by the scientific movements of the time in the evolution of musical thought prior to the Revolution, through an investigation of the precise character of the place assigned to music in France's preeminent scientific institution, the Paris Academy. It is based in large part on documents only recently uncovered that bear on the subject, and it supplements the author's earlier article in the *Stanford French Review* (1977). The French provincial academies also played a role, though relatively minor, in this evolution, but additional study is needed before that role can be properly assessed; a brief review of the nature of their activity is appended to Chapter IV.

The format adopted in this work is intended to provide a narrative text, reserving full documentation for the footnotes. In the interest of consistency and wider use, citations of complete dates are given in their French forms. Quotations from original sources retain their spelling, but accent marks have been modernized; translations have been provided where needed to clarify meaning in the text, but not for titles. Spellings of proper names have been standardized, as possible, with reference to the Institut de France's *Index biographique de l'Académie des Sciences* (1979). It should be noted that the collection of *pochettes des séances* in the Archives of the Académie des Sciences in Paris is currently being catalogued, and that occasional documents are being reclassified in the process; in the present study, references to the *pochettes* are to be understood as reflecting the organization of that collection at this writing.

In the Academy's broad view, the "science" of music (as opposed to its "practice") comprised three principal facets, which serve as the central subjects for Chapters II, III, and IV of this study. There is no intent here to retell the story of the Academy or of the intellectual and aesthetic movements of which it formed a part; these have been covered elsewhere. Rather, details will be drawn from this history as they pertain directly to music. It is a history that traces the boundaries of a critical period in the development of Western man, one in which music and science are partners in a great adventure.

Acknowledgments

This study would not have been possible without access to the rich archives of the Académie des Sciences in Paris. I am most grateful to MM. *les secrétaires perpétuels* of the Académie for permitting me this access, and to its archivist, M. Pierre Berthon, and his staff for helpful cooperation during my visits. Courtesies were also extended to me at many other libraries and archives during the course of the project, of which the following are deserving of special mention: in Paris—Bibliothèque de l'Institut de France, Bibliothèque Nationale, Bibliothèque Mazarine, Bibliothèque du Conservatoire National des Arts et Métiers, Archives de l'Académie des Beaux-Arts, and Archives Nationales; in the provinces—Bibliothèque Municipale de Bordeaux, Archives Municipales de Lyon, and Archives de l'Hérault in Montpellier; in London—the British Library, and the Library of the Royal Society; and in the United States—the libraries of Stanford University and of the University of California at Berkeley.

Illustrations are reproduced with the kind permission of the Académie des Sciences (figs. 2, 3, 4, 9, 10, 11, 12, and 13), the Bibliothèque Nationale (fig. 1), the Conservatoire National des Arts et Métiers (fig. 6), the British Library (fig. 7), the University of California at Berkeley (fig. 14), and the Sibley Library of the Eastman School of Music (fig. 8).

Finally, I am pleased to acknowledge support by the National Endowment for the Humanities and the American Council of Learned Societies, which facilitated research abroad.

Stanford, California   ALBERT COHEN
August 1980

List of Illustrations

following page 76

(xv)

Abbreviations

AdS	Paris, Académie des Sciences, Archives
AN	Paris, Archives Nationales
BI	Paris, Bibliothèque de l'Institut de France
BN	Paris, Bibliothèque Nationale
DBF	*Dictionnaire de Biographie Française*
DSB	*Dictionary of Scientific Biography*
Histoire	*Histoire de l'Académie Royale des Sciences*
Machines	*Machines et Inventions approuvées par l'Académie Royale des Sciences*
Mémoires	*Mémoires de Mathématique et de Physique*
MGG	*Die Musik in Geschichte und Gegenwart*
Reg.	Paris, Académie des Sciences, Archives, *Registres des procès-verbaux*
RISM	*Répertoire International des Sources Musicales*

Complete references to printed sources are found in the Bibliography.

Music in the French
Royal Academy of Sciences

≈ I ≈

THE EARLY YEARS:
MUSIC AS DISCIPLINE

Background

THE Académie Royale des Sciences (established 1666, suppressed 1793) was enormously influential in fostering a new spirit for a period that became known as the Enlightenment. The rise of the scientific attitude was central to this spirit: an openness to inquiry, an interest in experimentation, and general encouragement for the exchange of ideas. It was not alone in its work, to be sure; throughout the seventeenth and eighteenth centuries, other academies having similar interests and goals were established in the West. But the Paris Academy was unlike the others in that it was subsidized by and became an agent for an entire nation. Indeed, it was through the Academy that science became a national policy in France, and one can trace the evolution of the social and political order there in the development and ultimate demise of its Académie Royale.[1]

Music played a visible role in that development. Generally understood as constituting a dual nature, comprising both a science (or theory) and an art (or practice)—d'Alembert's "double

---

[1] There is a large literature covering the rise of the scientific movement and the creation of the Paris Academy, of which the following are especially useful to the present study: Ernest Maindron, *L'Académie des Sciences* (Paris: Félix Alcan, 1888); Martha Ornstein, *The Rôle of Scientific Societies in the Seventeenth Century* (Chicago: Univ. of Chicago Press, 1928), chap. V; Harcourt Brown, *Scientific Organizations in Seventeenth Century France (1620-1680)* (Baltimore: Wilkins and Wilkins, 1934); Institut de France, *Académie des Sciences, Troisième centenaire, 1666-1966* (Paris: Gauthier-Villars, 1967), T. I; and Roger Hahn, *The Anatomy of a Scientific Institution: The Paris Academy of Sciences, 1666-1803* (Berkeley: Univ. of California Press, 1971).

point de vue":[2] the one addressing its underlying principles of organization, and the other its effects on the senses—music was considered then, as in earlier times, an integral part of the mathematical and physical sciences. It quite naturally formed an area for scientific inquiry at the Academy.[3]

Even prior to the formal establishment of the Academy, music was already assigned a place in discussions held at the informal meetings of learned men that took place in France early in the seventeenth century. Chief among these were the gatherings organized by Marin Mersenne (1588-1648), the Minorite friar in whose cell at the Place Royale—and through whose correspondence—ideas were exchanged by some of the most eminent thinkers of the time, some of whom later became members of the scientific academy.

A true intermediary between the humanism of an earlier age and the developing scientific attitude of his own time, Mersenne believed in the universality of knowledge and in the reason of man. He fostered an empirical approach to scientific methodology, based on experimentation and mechanics, and strove for cooperation in pursuit of learning, championing the establishment of an international academy.

Having derived his thinking from the platonic traditions of the Renaissance (in which music was considered "the image of the whole encyclopaedia"), Mersenne assigned a special role to music in his own system, where it formed an essential part of mathematics, "utile à toutes les sciences."[4] Certainly, this view of music reflects its place in the quadrivium of the medieval *artes liberales* (the four mathematical disciplines that had their common basis in numerical ratio and proportion: "arithmetic—pure number, music—applied number, geometry—stationary number, astronomy—number in motion"),[5] which continued to form the foundation for

[2] Jean Le Rond d'Alembert, *Elémens de musique théorique et pratique*, new ed. (Lyon: Jean-Marie Bruyset, 1766), "discours préliminaire," p. i.

[3] For a general review of this point, see the author's "Music in the French Scientific Academy before the Revolution," *Stanford French Review*, I/1 (1977), 29-37.

[4] Marin Mersenne, "Livre de l'utilité de l'harmonie et des autres parties des mathématiques," *Harmonie universelle* (Paris: Cramoisy and Ballard, 1636-1637), p. 1: "useful to all the sciences." See Frances A. Yates, *The French Academies of the Sixteenth Century* (London: The Warburg Institute, 1947), p. 285.

[5] Dayton C. Miller, *Anecdotal History of the Science of Sound* (New York: Macmillan, 1935), p. 19.

university studies through the Renaissance and into early modern times. However, whereas Mersenne notes that the "knowledge of music is necessary or at least of value to the understanding and the perfection of the other arts and sciences," he also stresses the importance of science to "the complete musician"—a view he shares with other French theorists of the time.[6] While he accepts the bipartite division of music into theory and practice, he argues for maintaining an ideal balance between the two.

Mersenne's understanding of music—as both science and practice—and the prominence he assigns to it in his voluminous publications and correspondence were influential in promoting a particular interest in the field among the many scientists who profited from contact with him, and from whom he in turn learned. Among them, those who wrote on music include, in France: René Descartes, Pierre Gassendi, Gérard Desargues, Claude Hardy, Ismaël Boulliau, Jean de Beaugrand, Pierre de Fermat, Claude Bredeau, Gabriel de La Charlonye, Etienne Pascal, Gilles Personne de Roberval, and de La Voye-Mignot; and outside of France: Constantijn Huygens, Galileo Galilei, Isaac Beeckman, J.-B. van Helmont, and Theodore Haack.[7]

These scientists, trained broadly in the liberal arts, as was Mersenne, generally prove to be guided by an equally liberal approach to study that embraced many fields, rather than by a narrow technical competence in any single discipline. They were, in fact, philosopher-scientists whose attitudes pervaded the times and helped provide a very special base for the establishment of the Paris Academy. A. E. Bell[8] describes the quality of "the early scientific societies" as exhibiting

> an enthusiasm and universal interest which scarcely characterizes the professional societies into which they have developed. Specialization was virtually unknown and through Latin the members had a means of communication with foreign societies and

[6] See Herbert Schneider, *Die französische Kompositionslehre in der ersten Hälfte des 17. Jahrhunderts* (Tutzing: Hans Schneider, 1972), p. 194.

[7] *Correspondance du P. Marin Mersenne*, ed. C. de Waard, R. Pintard, B. Rochot, and A. Beaulieu, 1932—.

[8] Arthur E. Bell, *Christian Huygens and the Development of Science in the Seventeenth Century* (London: E. Arnold, 1947), p. 47. See also, Abraham Wolf, *A History of Science, Technology, and Philosophy in the 16th and 17th Centuries* (London: G. Allen and Unwin, 1935), p. 1.

I. THE EARLY YEARS

with a learned world which had existed before the new studies had begun.

The Founding Generation

Building on the base of informal scientific meetings that took place in France under differing auspices during the earlier part of the seventeenth century, and on the experiences of scientific societies already established in Italy and in England,[9] the Paris Academy was formally organized under the patronage of Colbert in 1666. Its founding members comprised "three astronomers, three anatomists, one botanist, two chemists, seven geometers, one mechanic, three physicians, and one unclassified member."[10] Several of them had already written on music by the time of their appointments, notably Roberval, Claude Perrault, Christian Huygens, and La Voye-Mignot.

Of these, only Huygens and La Voye-Mignot do not appear in surviving records as having occupied themselves with music as members of the Academy, although references are found to work done by the former on the physics of sound (see below). The absence of known musical references to the latter, however, is especially curious, since La Voye-Mignot (admitted as a geometer and junior member, d. 1684) published a thorough and systematic *Traité de musique* (Paris, 1656), which had a second, enlarged edition in 1666, the very year of the Academy's founding.[11] It is a practical guide for beginners in the elements of music and in mus-

[9] For the influence of the Accademia del Cimento in Florence and the Royal Society of London on the founding and the work of the Paris Academy, see René Taton, *Les origines de l'Académie Royale des Sciences* (Paris: Univ. de Paris, 1966), pp. 10-11; and Hahn, *The Anatomy*, p. 6. In music, that influence appears to have been restricted largely to acoustics. The Paris Academy had access to French translations of experiments conducted by both the Florentine and the London Academies (these are referred to below, as pertinent). The early acoustical work of the Royal Society is summarized in Ll. S. Lloyd, "Musical Theory in the Early *Philosophical Transactions*," in *Notes and Records of the Royal Society of London*, III/2 (1941), 149-157; see also, the listings in François de Brémond, *Table des mémoires imprimés dans les Transactions philosophiques* (Paris: Piget, 1739), pp. 209-210. For the relevant work of the Academy in Florence, see W. E. Knowles Middleton, *The Experimenters* (Baltimore: Johns Hopkins Press, 1971), pp. 151-154, 212-214, 237-240, and passim.

[10] Ornstein, *The Rôle of Scientific Societies*, p. 146.

[11] Repr. 1972, in facs. ed. (Geneva: Minkoff) and in English trans. by A. Gruber (Brooklyn, N.Y.: Institute of Medieval Music).

ical composition, current in its day, and still referred to in 1724 as "un excellent traitté" (by Sébastien de Brossard, the lexicographer-musician).[12] Earlier still, La Voye-Mignot had published a *Commentaire bref des éléments d'Euclide* (Paris, 1649). However, his work at the Academy principally concerned natural science; in the words of Condorcet: "observations curieuses sur les vers luisants des huitres, sur ceux que vivent dans la pierre, et sur des insectes qu'il a vus dans le mortier."[13]

The earliest reference to music at the Paris Academy among surviving records occurs in 1676. To be sure, early record keeping was not systematic or complete at the Academy, and, in fact, large portions of the *procès-verbaux* that cover proceedings before 1699 appear to be lost.[14] Any attempt to sketch a chronology of musical interest at the Academy before the reforms of 1699 must be considered tentative; nevertheless, those references that are available do project a pattern that helps provide perspective for later developments.

The *Registres des procès-verbaux* (Reg.) for 21 novembre 1676[15] include an inventory of papers left at his death by Gilles Personne de Roberval (1602-1675), prepared by a committee comprised of François Blondel, Jean Picard, and Jacques Buot. In the *second paquet* of these papers are listed two musical items: "feuilles Elementa musicae leçons" and "Traitté de Musique." It is unclear whether these items were ever presented to the Academy by Roberval. Nevertheless, at least one sheet of the first of these appears to have survived at the Archives of the Academy (AdS)—a single, half-folio sheet entitled "musicae . . . Le diapason musical diatonique, et chromatique; avec le tempérament pour le monocorde, le lut, la viole, et autres instruments à cordes, où on se sert de

---

[12] In Sébastien de Brossard, *Catalogue des livres de musique théorique et pratique* (1724), BN, Rés. Vm⁸ 20, p. 22. In the 2d ed. of his treatise, La Voye-Mignot refers to musical compositions that he was preparing for publication. The only music of his that survives may be the *allemande* attributed to "Lavoÿ" in a manuscript source; see further, Jaroslav J. S. Mráček, *Seventeenth-Century Instrumental Dances in Uppsala University IMhs 409* (Ph.D. dissertation, Indiana Univ., 1965), I, 82.

[13] A. C. O'Connor and F. Arago (eds.), *Oeuvres de Condorcet* (Paris: Firmin-Didot, 1847-1849, 12 vols.), II, 87-88: "curious observations on glow-worms of oysters, of those that live in rock, and on insects he has seen in mortar."

[14] See Taton, *Les origines*, p. 41.

[15] Reg., T. 7, f. 65-67v.

(7)

touches."[16] It describes the division of a double-octave (labeled A-a-aa) into 24 equal parts, of which the numerical proportions given prove to be in the ratio of semitone $= \sqrt[12]{2}$, which is exactly that of equal temperament.

The "Traitté de Musique," however, does not appear to have survived, unless it is the manuscript treatise by Roberval found among a collection of his writings (dated 1651) currently at the Bibliothèque Nationale in Paris (BN), entitled *Elementa musicae*.[17] In fact, the similarity in title of the surviving treatise with the first musical item listed in Roberval's inventory, suggests the possibility that the one sheet marked "musicae" may originally have comprised part of a series of "leçons" intended to either supplement or illustrate the treatise, *Elementa musicae* (which is, however, entirely in Latin). In any event, the work is a conservative exposition of the elements of music and traditional rules for counterpoint based on earlier models.[18]

Roberval, a friend of Mersenne (who, in fact, published essays by Roberval among his own printed works, but none on music) and a founding member of the Paris Academy (admitted as a geometer) was active there chiefly as a mathematician and physicist. His interests ranged widely, and his activity in music, while not extensive, is nevertheless of note.

Early interest in the transmission of sound is recorded by Jean-Baptiste Du Hamel in his history of the Academy, published in 1698.[19] He briefly describes an open-air experiment undertaken on 23 juin 1677 by G. D. Cassini, Jean Picard, and Olof Roemer, to determine the speed of sound. Shortly before, the Accademia del Cimento in Florence had addressed this very problem,[20] which

[16] *Dossier Roberval*, carton 9, chemise 6: "*musicae* . . . The diatonic and chromatic musical diapason, together with the temperament for the monochord, the lute, the viol, and other string instruments on which frets are used."

[17] BN, MS fr. 9119, f. 374-407v.

[18] See the analysis of this treatise in Schneider, *Die französische Kompositionslehre*, pp. 180-184. On Roberval, see Léon Auger, *Un savant méconnu: Gilles Personne de Roberval* (Paris: A. Blanchard, 1962).

[19] Jean-Baptiste Du Hamel, *Regiae scientiarum academiae historia* (Paris: S. Michallet, 1698), 2d ed. (Paris: J.-B. Delespine, 1701), p. 161.

[20] Described in the *Saggi di naturali esperienze fatte nell' Accademia del Cimento* (Florence: G. Cocchini, 1667, and later eds.); modern English trans. in Middleton, *The Experimenters*, pp. 237-240. A French trans. of these very experiments appears in *Collection académique*, I (Dijon: F. Desventes, 1755), 168-173. See also the de-

was also to be of interest to members of the Royal Society of London later in the century. Results of the Parisian experiment derived a measurement of 356m/s, in contrast with 361m/s determined by the Florentine experimenters.[21] The question was raised again at the Academy in 1738 (see Chapter II, Later Developments in Acoustics).

Also in 1677, Claude Perrault (1613-1688), one of the Academy's most versatile founding members, is described as having "entreprit d'examiner à fond tout ce qui appartient au sens de l'ouïe."[22] Perrault was admitted as a physicist, but he also contributed as an anatomist, architect, classicist, and natural historian. He is sometimes credited with having provided the incentive for the establishment of the Paris Academy by interesting Colbert in science.

His contributions to music at the Academy span his varied activities: as a physicist, he investigated the nature of sound; as an anatomist, he studied the structure of the ear and the process of hearing; and as a classicist, he left an essay on ancient music. Probably the longest paper he was to present to the Academy, on any subject, was announced on 24 novembre 1677: "Mr. Perrault lira le traitté qu'il a fait du son,"[23] begun on 1 décembre 1677[24] and continued well into the following year (the last reference found to a session of the Academy devoted at least in part to this subject is 18 mai 1678).[25] During this entire period, Perrault's interests extended also to a study of the anatomy of the ear, first presented on 16 février 1678.[26] The results of both investigations were later summarized by Fontenelle in the *Histoire* of 1677 and 1678 (published 1733), and the completed *Traité du bruit* published in Perrault's *Essais de physique* (Paris, 1680 and 1688). In this *Traité*, Perrault rejects the concept of sound waves, and attempts to explain sound as an agitation of air "that occurs in a restricted space and is produced by the impact of particles in a narrow rectilinear

---

scription in Frederick V. Hunt, *Origins in Acoustics* (New Haven: Yale Univ. Press, 1978), pp. 102-104.

[21] See further, Hunt, *Origins in Acoustics*, p. 109.

[22] *Histoire*, 1666-1686, I, 145: "undertaken to investigate in depth all that pertains to the sense of hearing."

[23] Reg., T. 8, f. 142v: "Mr. Perrault will read the treatise he has produced on sound."

[24] Ibid.   [25] Reg., T. 8, f. 173.   [26] Ibid., f. 146.

beam," which affects the ear and causes hearing.[27] The anatomical study, although soon to be superseded by the work of Du Verney (see below), was recognized at the time as an important contribution to the subject.[28]

Perrault's extended essay, *De la musique des anciens* (published in his *Essais de physique*, II), is not referred to in archival documents, and it is doubtful that it ever was formally presented to the Academy. In it, Perrault argues the inferiority of ancient music as compared with that of his own day.[29] A surviving preface to the essay,[30] which appears to have been removed from the original work before publication, concerns questions of aesthetics and proves to be an *apologia* for it.[31] The essay is, at least, of historical value, since it anticipates arguments for and against "ancient music" that were to form an important part of the literature on changing aesthetics in France early in the eighteenth century.[32]

At the same time that Perrault was presenting the results of his study of the ear and hearing, an anatomist-colleague of his, Joseph-Guichard Du Verney (1648-1730), who was appointed to the Academy in 1676, began his own investigations of the same questions, the results of which were to lead to publication of what has widely been considered "the first thorough, scientific treatise on the human ear."[33] In fact, Du Verney's interest in the ear seems to have anticipated that of Perrault, for the *procès-verbaux* of 2 juin 1677 announce: "Mr. Du Verney apportera au l^{er} jour ce qu'il a

[27] DSB, X, 520.

[28] See Wolfgang Herrmann, *The Theory of Claude Perrault* (London: A. Zwemmer, 1973), pp. 194-195.

[29] The arguments are summarized in the *Journal des Sçavans*, 15 juillet 1680 (pp. 202-203).

[30] BN, MS fr. 25,350.

[31] Hubert Gillot, *La querelle des anciens et des modernes en France* (Paris: H. Champion, 1914; repr., Geneva: Slatkine, 1968), pp. 478-481, critiques the essay in light of changing patterns of aesthetics in eighteenth-century France; the MS preface of Perrault is reproduced in Appendix III, pp. 576-591.

[32] For example, Le Cerf de la Viéville's *Comparaison* of 1705 is critical of Perrault's essay. The contributions of Perrault are reviewed in Hermann Scherchen, *Vom Wesen der Musik* (Winterthur: Mondial, 1946), trans. by W. Mann, as *The Nature of Music* (London: H. Regnery, 1950), pp. 20-25. See also DSB, X, 519-521.

[33] DSB, IV, 268. The crucial position of Du Verney in the history of audition is reviewed by Ernest G. Wever and Merle Lawrence, *Physiological Acoustics* (Princeton: Princeton Univ. Press, 1954), pp. 6-9.

découvert sur la structure de l'oreille. . . ."[34] On 30 mars 1678,[35] he read a short essay, "De l'oreille" as part of "Plusieurs écrites . . . touchant les organes des sens" (notice of which is summarized in the *Histoire* for 1678). Having warmed to his subject, Du Verney continued to present findings of his investigations on the hearing mechanism of humans, animals and fish—illustrating his presentations with charts, scale drawings, and dissected organs—over a period of several years. In 1681, he was given permission by the Academy to publish his treatise, and finally, on 17 février 1683,[36] he read to the assembly a preface to the work just prior to its publication later that year, *Traité de l'organe de l'ouïe*[37]—his only work to see publication during his lifetime. Of special interest in the treatise is his examination and description of the distribution and function of auditory nerves in the hearing process. Although he brought new thoughts on the study of the ear to the Academy's attention afterward,[38] his later work chiefly addressed other anatomical problems, especially as they related to vertebrates.[39]

It should be noted that except for the passing interest in the structure of the ear by Du Verney's fellow anatomist at the Academy Jean Méry (1645-1722, admitted 1684), described in 1692,[40] there appears to have been no new contribution to the anatomical study of that organ there until 1714, when Raymond Vieussens (1641-1715) published a treatise on this subject.[41] Méry's interest in the ear may well have been provoked by Perrault and especially by Du Verney, with both of whom Méry worked in projects involving comparative anatomy.[42]

[34] Reg., T. 8, f. 117: "Mr. Du Verney will bring in at the earliest opportunity that which he has discovered on the structure of the ear."

[35] Ibid., f. 161-162.   [36] Reg., T. 10, f. 121v.

[37] Paris: E. Michallet, 1683, and Leyden: J. A. Langerak, 1731; Latin ed., Nurnberg: J. Ziegeri, 1684; Engl. eds., London: S. Baker, 1737, 1748.

[38] 16 mai 1705 (Reg., T. 24, f. 155; *Histoire*, 1705, p. 58).

[39] See Fontenelle's *éloge*, in *Histoire*, 1730, pp. 123-131; and the notice in Antoine L.-J. Bayle and Auguste J. Thillaye, *Biographie médicale* (Paris: A. Delahays, 1855), II, 18-20.

[40] 23 avril 1692 (Reg., T. 13, f. 94v).

[41] Notice in *Histoire*, 1715, p. 14. Vieussens had earlier communicated his views on the structure of the ear and the nature of hearing to the Royal Society of London; see the *Philosophical Transactions* for 1699, vol. 21 (London: S. Smith and B. Walford, 1700), 370-397.

[42] See DSB, IX, 323.

I. THE EARLY YEARS

Indeed, the work of Perrault and Du Verney on hearing and the ear appears to have been largely responsible for a rise in general interest at the Academy in the auditory process and the nature of sound just prior to the publication of Du Verney's *Traité*. Several reports are noted among the *procès-verbaux* during the years 1681-1682. On 9 avril 1681, Edme Mariotte (c. 1620-1684) is listed as having read "ce qu'il a composé de l'organe de l'ouïe."[43] Mariotte, admitted as a physicist to the Academy shortly after its formation in 1666, soon became a leading and influential member of the group, active in a wide range of subjects. It is not known what information on the ear he contributed to the session noted above (since he was not an anatomist). However, on 26 novembre 1681,[44] he is referred to as having made the following observation: "dans la trompette quand le son est grave, on sent le tremblement dans le pavillon, dans la quinte les tremblements se font vers le milieu, et dans l'octave les tremblements se font plus haut."[45] This remark, which deals with the nature of vibrating bodies, appeared together with one made on the same topic by a fellow academician: "Mr. Blondel a fait observer qu'ayant fait bouillir l'eau dans un verre en pressant ses bords avec le doigt, quand le son vient à l'octave les petits cercles se redoublent dans l'eau."[46]

Mariotte's observation may be considered to be one made by an interested and curious contributor to a series of "Diverses obser-

[43] Reg., T. 10, f. 63v-64: "that which he has composed on the organ of hearing."

[44] Ibid., f. 80.

[45] Ibid.: "in the trumpet, when the sound is low, one feels the vibration in the bell; at the fifth, the vibrations occur toward the center; and at the octave, the vibrations occur [yet] higher." Reported also in *Histoire*, 1666-1686, I, 209; and in Du Hamel, *Regiae*, 2d ed., p. 202.

[46] Reg., T. 10, f. 80: "Mr. Blondel demonstrated that, having agitated water in a glass by rubbing its edges with his finger, when the sound [produced] reaches an octave, the small circles in the water are doubled"; likewise, reported in *Histoire*, 1666-1686, I, 209; and in Du Hamel, *Regiae*, p. 202. Clifford A. Truesdell, "The Rational Mechanics of Flexible or Elastic Bodies, 1638-1788," Intro. to *Leonhardi Euleri Opera Omnia*, Series 2, vol. 11, pt. 2 (Zurich: O. Füssli, 1960), p. 35, assumes that Blondel "appropriated" his observation from a similar one made earlier by Galileo in his *Discorsi* (1638). So, too, had Mariotte, who, as an extension of his work in elastic bodies and "la percussion," developed an interest in the propagation of sound, which led him to consult with Huygens and, at his suggestion, to read Galileo's *Two New Sciences*. See the letter by Mariotte (dated 1 février 1668) in Huygens, *Oeuvres complètes*, VI (1895), 177-178; and the discussion in DSB, IX, 114.

vations de physique générale" presented at the session of 26 novembre 1681. In fact, he is known to have often participated in
general discussions of "subjects discussed at length in the Academy," basing his remarks on the "fundamental results achieved by
others."[47] The observation of Blondel, however, should not be so
considered, given his accomplishments in the field. Nicolas-François
Blondel (1618-1686), admitted as a geometer to the Academy in
1669, was a mathematician and architect of some achievement
(besides being a statesman), of whom his biographers note:
"toutes les sciences l'intéressaient et les lettres également."[48] It is
in both his *Cours d'architecture enseigné dans l'Académie Royale
d'Architecture* (Paris, 1675-1683)[49] and his *Cours de mathématique contenant divers traitez composez et enseignez à Monsieur le Dauphin* (Paris,
1683), that music (both theoretical and practical) figures prominently.

In the former, Blondel describes music as "une des plus belles
parties de mathématique,"[50] and devotes a large portion of the *cin-
quième partie* ("De la proportion des parties de l'architecture") to
a comparison of proportion in architecture to that in music, the
one aiming to please the eye and the other the ear.[51] In the latter,
music is assigned a place in the second of two fundamental divisions into which the mathematical sciences are divided—*mathématique
pure* (essentially, arithmetic and geometry) and *mathématique mixte
ou mêlée* (that is, applied mathematics, comprised of those fields
that make use of mathematics for their understanding). In his presentation, Blondel provides a short primer on music,[52] as on most
of the other fields that comprise *mathématique mixte* (including architecture).

This view of mathematics as the central unifying discipline for
all scientific study, and its division into subunits that include music, is later described also by the mathematician Jacques Ozanam

[47] DSB, IX, 114.

[48] Placide Mauclaire and C. Vigoureux, *Nicolas-François de Blondel, Ingénieur et
Architecte du Roi (1618-1686)* (Paris: A. Picard, 1938), p. 118: "all sciences interested
him and letters as well."

[49] Blondel was director of the architectural Academy.

[50] *Cours d'architecture*, III (Paris: the author and N. Langlois, 1683), 770: "one of
the most beautiful parts of mathematics."

[51] Blondel's point of reference is René Ouvrard's *Architecture harmonique* (Paris,
1679); in the comparison, he restricts himself to intervallic proportions in music.

[52] *Cours de mathématique* (Paris: the author and N. Langlois, 1683), I, 46-50.

(13)

I. THE EARLY YEARS

(1640-1718), a writer on music. Like Blondel, he was a member of the Paris Academy (admitted as a geometer in 1707); unlike Blondel, he is not known to have contributed to presentations or discussions on music at the Academy during his activity there.[53]

On 7 juillet 1682, l'Abbé Jean de Hautefeuille (1647-1724) appeared before the Academy to present "une machine acoustique qui est comme un double cornet qu'on applique aux deux oreilles."[54] He was demonstrating a hearing device that he had developed and described earlier in *Explication de l'effet des trompettes parlantes* (Paris, 1673; 2d ed. 1674) and in *L'Art de respirer sous l'eau* (1680, new ed. 1692). Later, he was to refer to this device in his *Lettre à M. Bourdelot sur le moyen de perfectionner l'ouïe* (1702).[55] His reception at the Academy seems to have had less than the desired effect; the *procès-verbaux* continue:[56] "il prétend que par le moyen de cette machine on entend mieux que sans elle, dont on n'a pu encore estre convaincu par l'expérience." In 1718, Hautefeuille became a member of the Académie des Belles-Lettres, Sciences et Arts de Bordeaux, where he made contributions to astronomy,

---

[53] See Albert Cohen, "*Musique* in the *Dictionnaire mathématique* (1690) of Jacques Ozanam," *The Music Review*, 36/2 (1975), 85-91. See also, Jean-Etienne Montucla, *Histoire des mathématiques*, new ed., 4 vols. (Paris: H. Agasse, 1799-1802), passim, but especially vols. 1 and 4, for a similar view and classification. Further on Ozanam, see DSB, X, 263-265.

[54] Reg., T. 11, f. 2: "an acoustical machine, which is like a double horn applied to the two ears."

[55] Still earlier, the description of a "speaking-trumpet" ("Tuba Stentoro-Phonica"), invented by Samuel Morland in 1670, had been transmitted to the Academy (as well as to the Royal Society of London), provoking interest in such a device. See further, Hunt, *Origins in Acoustics*, pp. 124-130, where development of both the "speaking-trumpet" and the "hearing trumpet" is traced.
Several different "cornets pour les sourds," invented by M. Du Quet in 1706, are described in *Machines*, II, 119-129 (references to presentation and report in Reg., T. 25, f. 235v, 236v, and 259); and on 27 avril 1718 (*assemblée publique*; Reg., T. 37, f. 130v), le père Sébastien (Jean Truchet, 1657-1729) read "un écrit sur une oreille artificielle," apparently lost. Later yet, an enlarged, wooden scale-model of the ear (following Winslow's description) was presented on 9 mars 1743 (Reg., T. 62, p. 154; *Histoire*, 1743, p. 85) by a Sicilian doctor named Mastiani.

[56] Reg., T. 11, f. 2: "he claims that by means of this machine, one hears better than without it, of which one was not able to be convinced even by experiment." The value of Hautefeuille's device appears to have been questionable also to scientists outside the Academy; see the exchange of letters between Leibniz and Oldenburg, in *The Correspondence of Henry Oldenburg*, ed. A. R. Hall and M. B. Hall, vol. XI (London: Mansell, 1977), nos. 2550 and 2576.

clock mechanisms, and optics, while continuing to pursue his interests in sound and hearing. The paper for which he was perhaps most acknowledged during his own day was "Dissertation sur la cause de l'écho." It was "couronnée" as the best submission to the *concours* on the subject of echo, held by the Bordeaux Academy the very year of his appointment to that body.[57]

A full century was to pass after Hautefeuille's initial presentation to the Paris Academy, before at least one influential member of that group would acknowledge his contributions to the field. In a posthumous collection of Hautefeuille's writings, entitled *Problème d'acoustique, curieux et intéressant, dont la solution est proposée aux savans, d'après les idées qu'en a laissées M. l'Abbé de Hautefeuille* (Paris: Varin, 1788),[58] there appears an "Extrait des registres de la Société Royale de Médicine de Paris," dated 31 août 1787 and signed by Félix Vicq d'Azyr (a member of the Paris scientific Academy who had interest in aural perception and the structure of the ear); it pays tribute to Hautefeuille for his contributions to "la théorie des sons," and for his devotion to "la perfection des instruments acoustiques."[59]

The fourth of the founding members mentioned above who wrote on music is Christian Huygens (1629-1695), celebrated in his own time as a mathematician with universal interests, and a prime contributor to the fields of mechanics, optics, and the measurement of time. The only foreigner among the initial appointees of the Paris Academy (admitted as a geometer), as well as its most prominent member, Huygens in many ways helped establish the direction and nature of the work undertaken by that body in its earliest years. His father, Constantijn Huygens (a correspondent of Mersenne) served the House of Orange in the Netherlands and was erudite in literature and the sciences, a poet, artist, and musician—interested in both the science and the practice of the art.

[57] See Pierre Barrière, *L'Académie de Bordeaux* (Paris and Bordeaux: Bière, 1951), pp. 177-178.
[58] The publication contains Hautefeuille's several essays on sound and hearing, including at least portions from those mentioned above.
[59] Hautefeuille, *Problème d'acoustique, extrait*: "the theory of sound" and "the perfection of acoustical instruments." Further on Hautefeuille, see J.-F. Michaud (ed.), *Biographie universelle ancienne et moderne*, new ed., vol. 18 (Paris: C. Desplaces, 1857), 556-557. Early references to musical instruments at the Academy are covered in chap. III, below.

Christian's education included training in music (he "sang well and played the viola da gamba, the lute, and the harpsichord")[60] and his *Journaux* of a later time reflect his continuing interest (as an "amateur musician") in practical music.[61]

Theoretical music, on the other hand, also occupied his thoughts throughout most of his life.[62] Of special interest to him were tuning and temperament, intervals, and the modes. He favored a 31-note cyclical, meantone temperament for musical instruments (which he calculated for the first time by use of logarithms), confirmed the harmonic relationship of music to mathematics in the cosmos (reasoning in his *Cosmotheoros* that music must exist on other planets), and speculated on the "natural" tendency of voices to adjust pitches. According to D. Hayes,[63] Huygens's "musings, experiments, and calculations, taken in historical context, represent a universal human desire to hear music and to study its effects as well as its rational organization." Notwithstanding, his activity at the Academy did not center about sound or music, and references to his work in those areas are found in *mémoires* presented by others.[64]

All told, the philosopher-scientists of the founding generation clearly established the relevancy of music as a discipline for scientific study at the Academy. It remained for the generation that followed to identify more specifically those parts of music most applicable to such study.

[60] DSB, VI, 598.

[61] See Herni-L. Brugmans, *Le séjour de Christian Huygens à Paris* (Paris: P. André, 1935), p. 119 and passim.

[62] See Huygens, *Oeuvres complètes*, especially vol. 20, devoted to "Musique et Mathématique" (La Haye: M. Nijhoff, 1940).

[63] Deborah Hayes, "Christian Huygens and the Science of Music," in Wm. Kearns (ed.), *Musicology at the University of Colorado* (1977), p. 30.

[64] See, for example, La Hire's "Explication des différences des sons de la corde tendue sur la trompette marine," *Mémoires*, 1666-1699, IX, 336; Carré's "Traité sur le son" of 1703 (summarized in *Journal des Sçavans*, supp. 1707), pp. 120 and 124; and especially, Sauveur's "Méthode générale pour former les systèmes tempérés de musique," *Mémoires*, 1707, pp. 203-222, in which Sauveur compares Huygens's division of the octave into 31 parts with his own of 43 *mérides* (see below, chap. II, Contributions of Joseph Sauveur).

☙ II ❧

ACOUSTICS, PHONATION, AND
AUDITION: MUSIC AS SOUND

The Second Generation

THE EARLY INTEREST in music at the Academy appears to have waned during the years 1683-1691; no activity in the subject is recorded in the *procès-verbaux* for that time span. But then, with the death in 1683 of the prime minister Colbert, the organizer and protector of the Academy, a general decline, or at least a period of reevaluation appears to have been undergone by this institution.[1] His successor, Louvois, is held to have been unsympathetic to pure science, stressing the need for the group to direct its attention increasingly to "recherche utile, celle qui peut avoir rapport au service du Roi et de l'Etat."[2] Whatever the cause for the decline, it seems clear that in 1691, when Pontchartrain succeeded Louvois, the Academy entered an epoch of renewed life and purpose. Pontchartrain's nephew and an advocate for science, l'Abbé Jean-Paul Bignon, was named president of the group the following year, and he undertook important organizational reforms that led to its official recognition by the king, through royal statutes issued in 1699. The statutes consolidate customs and rules developed at the Academy during its early years, but they also describe an expanded and highly structured institution, adopting new directions, attitudes, and methods for its work.[3]

[1] See Hahn, *The Anatomy*, pp. 19-20.

[2] Ornstein, *The Rôle of Scientific Societies*, p. 157: "useful research, which can be related to the service of the King and the State."

[3] See Maindron, *L'Académie des Sciences*, chap. II, for the statutes; see also the summary in Lucien Plantefol, "L'Académie des Sciences durant les trois premiers siècles de son éxistence," in Institut de France, *Académie des Sciences*, I, 74.

Under the stewardship of l'Abbé Bignon and his *secrétaire perpétuel*, Bernard Le Bovier de Fontenelle (1657-1757), who replaced Du Hamel in 1697, music too entered an epoch of renewal. Perhaps, as Fontenelle reports,[4] this renewal reflects a change in aesthetic of the time; or perhaps it was but a consequence of the broadened scope of activity developed by the Academy through its process of consolidation. All the same, what is evident is that, from 1692, there is a notable increase in the number of academicians who direct their attention to music and, through their contributions, propel yet a wider curiosity in the field, both in and out of the Paris Academy. Chief among them are Philippe de La Hire, Denis Dodart, Nicolas Malebranche, Louis Carré, and especially Joseph Sauveur.

Philippe de La Hire (1640-1718), son of the painter and academician, Laurent de La Hire (a founder of the Académie Royale de Peinture et de Sculpture), was a scientist with an extraordinarily wide scope of interests. He was admitted to the Academy as an astronomer in 1678, taught mathematics both in the Collège Royal (appointed to Roberval's vacant chair in 1682) and in the Académie Royale d'Architecture (replacing Blondel in 1687), and published in fields as varied as physics, natural science, mechanics, meteorology, and art.[5]

La Hire also had interest in the nature and transmission of sound, expressed in essays presented in 1692[6] and 1716[7]—an especially fruitful period in examination of acoustical theory at the Academy. Initially building on the work of Huygens, Perrault, and Gallois,[8] and later on that of Sauveur and Carré, La Hire

---

[4] *Histoire*, 1700, p. 134.   [5] DSB, VII, 576-578.

[6] "Explication des différences des sons de la corde tendue sur la trompette marine," *Mémoires*, 1666-1699, IX, 330-350 (also issued in *Mémoires de mathématique et de physique* [Paris, 1694], pp. 213-232; and in *Oeuvres diverses* [Paris, 1730], pp. 500-529). An "Observation" for 1692, on an example of sympathetic vibrations, is noted in *Histoire*, 1686-1699, II, 87. Several acoustical presentations were made by La Hire in 1692, on 23 février, 8 mars, and 28 avril (Reg., T. 13, f. 81 and 85, T. 14, f. 13; see reference in Du Hamel, *Regiae*, p. 310).

[7] "Expériences sur le son," *Mémoires*, 1716, pp. 262-264, and "Continuation d'expériences sur le son," pp. 264-268. These are summarized in *Histoire*, 1716, pp. 66-68. Presentations were made on 22 août and 5 septembre 1716 (Reg., T. 35, f. 311v-312v and 321-323v).

[8] In his "Explication" (*Mémoires*, 1666-1699, IX, 342-343), La Hire refers to discussions on the nature of vibrating bodies that he held with l'Abbé Jean Gallois (1632-1707)—a man of wide interests, who was known at the Academy as a pub-

shows himself generally acquainted with current thought on problems of acoustics, even though he continued to maintain an earlier misconception (attributed to Perrault) that "sound is provoked not by vibration of the whole string but by molecular disturbance of its component parts."[9] Despite experiments that have been judged "haphazardly conceived and vaguely described,"[10] La Hire did make several contributions to the field that are noteworthy: he confirmed the role of partial vibrations (earlier called "ondulations" and later "frémissements") in determining the quality ("son") of the sound produced by a vibrating body, as distinct from its pitch ("ton"); he identified and compared acoustical differences of cylinders, solid bodies, and strings; and he examined the effect on a resultant sound of such factors as the elastic quality of a vibrating body, its relative moisture content, and the means by which it is set into motion.[11] Music unexpectedly finds its way into yet another *mémoire* presented by La Hire to the Academy, "Traité de la pratique de la peinture," where a device, called "une pâte," is described for ruling staff lines onto music manuscript paper.[12]

licist (he edited the *Journal des Sçavans*), a geometer, Hellenist, and confidant of Colbert. On 30 novembre 1692, Gallois presented a description, sent by François Quesnay (1665-1718; see René P. Tassin, *Histoire littéraire de la Congrégation de Saint-Maur* [Brussels and Paris: Humblot, 1770; repr., Ridgewood, N.J.: Gregg Press, 1965], p. 401), of an unusual echo at a house near Rouen (*Histoire*, 1686-1699, II, 87, and *Mémoires*, 1666-1699, X, 127-129; reported in Du Hamel, *Regiae*, p. 310). Three years later, on 30 juillet 1695 (Reg., T. 14bis, f. 158), he proposed "plusieurs problèmes touchant le son; il en donnera un mémoire." This last-named project, as with several he is known to have undertaken in other fields, was never realized. Further on Gallois, see Fontenelle's *éloge*, in *Histoire*, 1707, pp. 176-181; and DSB, V, 259.

Interest in reporting unusual echos persisted into the eighteenth century at the Academy. On 13 décembre 1710 (Reg., T. 29bis, f. 459v-460v), a description provided by Teinturier was read, describing a particularly reverberant echo between two towers near Verdun; and some sixty years later, on 13 janvier 1770 (Reg., T. 89, f. 5; letter in *pochette de séance*, summarized in *Histoire*, 1770, pp. 23-24), l'Abbé Guinet reported a singular echo at the Château de La Rochepot, near Châlons.

[9] Scherchen, *The Nature of Music*, p. 21.

[10] Truesdell, "The Rational Mechanics," p. 126.

[11] On La Hire's contributions to acoustics, see further, Truesdell, ibid., and Scherchen, *The Nature of Music*, pp. 26-27. See also, François-Joseph Fétis, *Biographie universelle des musiciens*, 2d ed. (Paris: Firmin-Didot, 1873-1875), V, 168.

[12] *Mémoires*, 1666-1699, IX, 438-439. The *Traité* is recorded as read to the assembly in 1709 (Reg., T. 28, f. 69 and passim). This device appears to be the very one

II. ACOUSTICS, PHONATION, AND AUDITION

The interest in music of Denis Dodart (1634-1707), a botanist and physiologist who was appointed to the Academy in 1673, was centered in phonation, his major contribution being the "Mémoire sur les causes de la voix de l'homme, et de ses différens tons," presented in 1700,[13] with "Suppléments" in 1706[14] and 1707.[15] The *mémoire*, which was intended to form the preliminary portion of a projected history of music that was never completed,[16] deals with the physical characteristics and formation of the human voice, and its quality of expression. M. D. Grmek credits Dodart with "pointing out the fundamental role of the vocal cords in phonation," as opposed "to the classic theory, which considered the larynx a type of flute. . . ."[17] For Dodart, "the glottis alone makes the voice and all the tones . . . ; no wind instrument can explain its functioning . . . ; the entire effect of the glottis on the tones depends on the tension of its lips and its various openings."[18]

Two additional musical references are associated with Dodart in the Academy's proceedings, both related to curiosities brought to his attention by others for communication to the assembly. The first (20 mai 1699)[19] describes a man who was capable of imitating the bass-viol so well, that his auditors were deceived ("on s'y trompoit"). The second (19 janvier 1707)[20] reports on the success of a musical concert used to help cure a musician ill with a delir-

referred to by d'Onsenbray, in his "Description et usage d'un métromètre" (*Mémoires*, 1732, p. 183), where he ascribes its invention to Etienne Loulié.

[13] Presentation: 13 novembre 1700 (*assemblée publique*, Reg., T. 19, f. 364-374v; printed in *Mémoires*, 1700, pp. 244-293, and published separately: Paris, 1703; summarized in *Histoire*, 1700, pp. 17-24, and in Du Hamel, *Regiae*, pp. 568-571). The *mémoire* was reread 6 and 20 juillet 1701 (Reg., T. 20, f. 234 and 257); "additions" were presented 23 mai 1703 (Reg., T. 22, f. 171).

[14] Presentation: 14 avril 1706 (*assemblée publique*, Reg., T. 25, f. 134-143v; printed in *Mémoires*, 1706, pp. 136-148 and 388-410; summarized in *Histoire*, 1706, pp. 15-21); reread 30 avril, 28 août, and 4 septembre (the last named by Geoffroy) 1706 (Reg., T. 25, f. 162, 332, and 338v).

[15] Presentation: 16 and 23 mars 1707 (Reg., T. 26, f. 89v-99v and 105; printed in *Mémoires*, 1707, pp. 66-81; summarized in *Histoire*, 1707, pp. 18-20).

[16] DSB, IV, 135. See also the reference in Fontenelle's *éloge* (*Histoire*, 1707), pp. 189-190; Dodart's musical training as a youth is mentioned on p. 182.

[17] DSB, IV, 135.

[18] Quoted ibid., pp. 135-136. These statements are drawn from 12 "vérités" of vocal production, summarized by Dodart in the *mémoire*, pp. 245-246.

[19] Noted in the *plumitif*, BN, MS fr.n.a. 5148, f. 4v.

[20] Reg., T. 26, f. 13v-14; printed in *Histoire*, 1707, pp. 7-8.

ium of fever;[21] it is referred to again the following year, in a similar report by M. de Mandajor, concerning a dancer with fever cured by familiar airs played on a violin.[22] The curative power of music is found in yet two other references at the Academy: in 1702, Etienne-François Geoffroy (1672-1731) described a musical cure for a tarantula bite observed while on a trip to Italy;[23] and in 1778, M. Bouvier read a "Mémoire sur les effets de la musique sur le corps humain." A committee was appointed to review it, but neither the *mémoire* nor the committee report survives.[24]

The celebrated philosopher and physicist, Nicolas Malebranche (1638-1715), read a paper on optics at the time of his appointment to the Academy in 1699, in which he forms an analogy between light and sound.[25] Somewhat conservative in his views, and building on the earlier work of others (principally Rohault, Huygens, and Ango),[26] Malebranche maintains that both light and sound are caused in nature by vibrations, which have two basic qualities— speed ("promptitude") and intensity ("force"). He argues that, in sound, these qualities determine the pitch and loudness, respectively, and in light, the color and brightness. Although he later revised details of his argument,[27] Malebranche's views on optics

[21] Mention should be made of a MS dealing with elements of musical composition, entitled "De la musique," in the hand and from the library of Dodart (BN, MS fr. 14,852), which proves to be a summary of the treatise by l'Abbé Droüyn, *Abrégé de musique* (BN, MS fr. 22,823, pt. 2; dated c. 1705).

[22] *Histoire*, 1708, pp. 22-23; noted in Reg., T. 27, f. 380.

[23] Presentation: 24 mars 1702 (Reg., T. 21, f. 131-136; summarized in *Histoire*, 1702, pp. 16-18). The use of music to accompany a whirling dance that legend held was a cure for "Tarantism" (a dancing mania supposedly resulting from the bite of a tarantula) has a long history, but was especially prevalent during the fifteenth-seventeenth centuries; the development of the dance type *tarantella* is related to this history. See further, Henry E. Sigerist, "The Story of Tarantism," in D. M. Schullian and M. Schoen (eds.), *Music and Medicine* (New York: H. Schuman, 1948), pp. 96-116; and Marius Schneider, "Tarantella," in MGG, XIII, cols. 117-119.

[24] Presentation: 20 juin 1778 (Reg., T. 97, f. 198); committee: Fouchy, Vandermonde, and Vicq d'Azyr.

[25] "Réflexions sur la lumière et les couleurs, et la génération du feu." Presentation: 4 avril 1699 (Reg., T. 18, f. 214-226; printed in *Mémoires*, 1699, pp. 22-36; summarized in *Histoire*, 1699, pp. 17-19; reported in Du Hamel, *Regiae*, p. 534).

[26] André Robinet, *Malebranche de l'Académie des Sciences, l'oeuvre scientifique, 1674-1715* (Paris: J. Vrin, 1970), pp. 275-276, which includes a thorough discussion of the derivation and development of Malebranche's theories on sound.

[27] See further, ibid., pp. 277-280; Pierre Costabel, "La participation de Male-

were largely made obsolete by those of his eminent contemporary, Isaac Newton.[28]

The mathematician and physicist Louis Carré (1663-1711) exhibited a special interest in music during his activity at the Academy, which was described by Fontenelle in his *éloge* in the following terms:[29]

> Il tourna ses principales vûës de ce côté-là, & embrassa tout ce qui appartenoit à la Musique, la Théorie du son, la description des différents Instruments, &c. Il negligeoit la Musique entant qu'elle est la source d'un des plus grands plaisirs des sens, & s'y attachoit entant qu'elle demande une infinité de recherches fort épineuses.

> [He turned his principal sights in this direction, & embraced all that pertained to Music, the Theory of sound, the description of different Instruments, &c. He ignored Music in so far as it is the source of one of the greatest pleasures of the senses, and applied himself, rather, to its demands for an infinity of thorny research.]

Almost all of Carré's investigations in music appear to have resulted from the assignment given to him by President Bignon in 1702, not long after his appointment to the Academy in 1699 (where he had been named a student member in 1697): "de décrire tous les instrumens de musique, dont on fait usage en France."[30] This was part of the *description des arts* undertaken by the group earlier in the seventeenth century (see Chapter III, *Les Arts et Métiers*). Although Carré was unable to complete the task before his death,[31] he nevertheless did present several papers on musical subjects to the Academy between the years 1702 and 1709. These were intended to serve as preliminary studies for the larger project and include the following:

---

branche au mouvement scientifique," in *Malebranche, l'homme et l'oeuvre, 1638-1715*, publ. Centre international de synthèse (Paris: J. Vrin, 1967). p. 88; DSB, IX, 51.

[28] See Maurice Daumas, "Les sciences physiques aux xvie et xviie siècles," in *Histoire de la science*, vol. 5 of *Encyclopédie de la Pléiade* (Paris: Gallimard, 1957), pp. 860-863.

[29] Found in *Histoire*, 1711, p. 105.

[30] Noted in *Histoire*, 1702, pp. 136-137: "to describe all the musical instruments used in France." See the references for 16 août 1702, in Reg., T. 21, f. 354, and in BN, MS fr.n.a. 5148, f. 53v.

[31] See his *éloge*; *Histoire*, 1711, pp. 105-106.

Date of Presentation	Topic
16 août 1702	"Mémoire sur le clavessin"[32]
12 décembre 1703	"Traité sur le son"[33]
15 novembre 1704	"Traité du monochorde"[34]
20 janvier 1706	"Traité mathématique des cordes par rapport aux instruments de musique"[35]
12 novembre 1707 (assemblée publique)	"Ecrit sur le son et sur les effets de la musique"[36]
16 février 1709	"Ecrit sur les sons des cilindres"[37]

Of these, only the last-mentioned has survived, but brief descriptions remain for some of the others; in one case ("Traité sur le son"), an extended summary exists.[38]

Carré's contributions to music lie in three principal areas of investigation: acoustics, mechanics, and musical systems. In acoustics, he inquired into the nature of vibrating strings and cylinders, tested the role of partial vibrations in determining the pitch and quality of sounds, and examined the functions of weight, density, and tension as they affected vibrating bodies.[39] In mechanics, he sought to describe in detail the nature and construction of a large quantity of musical instruments, and he built several different models of the monochord to serve both acoustical and performance purposes.[40] In musical systems, he examined the derivation

[32] BN, MS fr.n.a. 5148, f. 53v. Parts of this study were read throughout 1702; and on 16 décembre, Carré presented an "Ecrit sur la manière d'accorder le clavessin" (Reg., T. 21, f. 463).

[33] Reg., T. 22, f. 368 (reported in Histoire, 1704, pp. 88-89). Portions from this paper continued to be read before the Academy until 5 mars 1704.

[34] Reg., T. 23, f. 291. Earlier that year, on 7 mai 1704 (Reg., T. 23, f. 145), Carré had presented "un instrument qu'il a inventé pour accorder toutes sortes d'instruments de musique."

[35] Reg., T. 25, f. 23 (noted in Histoire, 1706, p. 124).

[36] Reg., T. 26bis, f. 384.

[37] Reg., T. 28, f. 47. The mémoire is included in Reg., T. 28, f. 49-60; printed in Mémoires, 1709, pp. 47-62; summarized in Histoire, 1709, pp. 93-96.

[38] In Journal des Sçavans, suppl. 1707, pp. 115-125.

[39] Truesdell, "The Rational Mechanics," pp. 125-126, notes that, in 1709, Carré confirmed Mersenne's law for vibrating rods, but that later, both Zendrini and Chladni pronounced his experiments faulty.

[40] Carré considered the monochord "la machine la plus simple" both for acoustical experiments and as an aid to tune musical instruments. While references are found to various types made by him, only one example is described in Machines, I, 101-102.

(23)

of musical pitches and intervals, described the structures of mode and scale, dealt (historically and acoustically) with the concepts of consonance and dissonance, and reviewed varied tuning systems (favoring one devised by Sauveur).

All in all, Carré proves to be an experimenter with intense interest in empirical evidence and demonstration, perhaps more than in novel ideas and mathematical proofs. His passion for detail, concern with mechanics, and knowledge of the literature and history of music theory[41] provided him with a strong base on which to build his work.

The Contributions of Joseph Sauveur

J'ai donc crû qu'il avoit une science supérieure à la Musique, que j'ai appellée *Acoustique*, qui a pour objet le Son en général, au lieu que la Musique a pour objet le Son en tant qu'il est agréable à l'ouïe.

[I believed, then, that there was a science superior to Music, which I called *Acoustics*, that has for its object Sound in general, whereas Music has for its object Sound in so far as it is agreeable to the ear.]

This statement by Joseph Sauveur (1653-1716), from the preface to his important *mémoire* of 1701, "Système général des intervalles des sons,"[42] signals a time at the Academy when both an increasing trend toward specialization and a general growth of interest in music are evident. Fontenelle describes the setting in the *Histoire* for 1700:[43]

La Science qui regarde le Sens de l'Ouïe, n'a peut-être pas moins d'étendue, que celle qui a la Vûe pour objet, mais elle a été jusqu'ici moins approfondie. Le besoin que les Philosophes ont eu des Télescopes & des Microscopes, les a obligés à étudier avec une extrême application les différens chemins & les différens accidens de la Lumière; mais comme ils n'ont pas eu le même besoin de connoître exactement tout ce qui appartient aux Sons,

---

[41] Among theorists referred to in his writings are Pythagoras, Boethius, Guido d'Arezzo, Glareanus, Zarlino, Folianus, Fabius Colonna, Kepler, Papius, and Huygens.

[42] *Mémoires*, 1701, p. 299.   [43] *Histoire*, 1700, p. 134.

& qu'ils ont le plus souvent traité la Musique comme une chose de goût, dont on ne devoit pas trop aller chercher les Règles dans le fond de la Philosophie, ils n'ont pas tant tourné leurs spéculations de ce côté-là.

[The Science that regards the Sense of Hearing is perhaps not any less developed than that which has Vision as its object, but until now it has been less thoroughly investigated. The need that Philosophers have had for Telescopes & for Microscopes have obliged them to study, with extreme diligence, the different qualities and varieties of Light; but as they have not had the same need to know precisely all that pertains to Sound, since they have most often treated Music as a matter of taste for the meaning of which one does not need to seek deeply into Philosophy, they have not turned their speculations in that direction.]

He adds, in the *Histoire* for 1701:[44]

M. Sauveur . . . propose un Système de Musique tout nouveau . . . qui changeroient entièrement la pratique ordinaire des Musiciens.

[M. Sauveur . . . is proposing an entirely new Musical System . . . which will completely change the common practice of Musicians.]

Indeed, when compared with Sauveur's work, contributions to the field by early investigators at the Academy appear tentative and incomplete—perhaps even haphazard and naive.[45] For Sauveur brought to the science of sound a new, disciplined spirit. His curiosity was intense and continuing, and he sought to satisfy it through a systematic and inclusive program of experimentation, the results of which were organized and presented in lucid, comprehensible language. R. Maxham[46] describes Sauveur's published papers as displaying "a single-mindedness, a tight organization, and absence of the speculative and the superfluous." While his researches appear largely original, many of his discoveries were not

---

[44] *Histoire*, 1701, p. 121.

[45] On this point, see Scherchen, *The Nature of Music*, pp. 27-28.

[46] Robert E. Maxham, *The Contributions of Joseph Sauveur (1653-1716) to Acoustics* (Ph.D. dissertation, Univ. of Rochester, 1976), I, 5.

new to the field. Yet his presentations do accurately summarize knowledge concerning vibrating strings and other acoustical phenomena at the turn of the eighteenth century, providing the basis for progress in the field for the century to follow.[47]

Sauveur began his studies of sound and music at the Academy shortly after his appointment as geometer in 1696. At the time, he was a well-known mathematician and teacher; he served as tutor at the Royal Court and, from 1686, occupied the chair in mathematics at the Collège Royal.[48] His activities at the Academy, however, predate his appointment by some fifteen years; from 1681 onward, his name appears in academic documents connected with problems in engineering and mechanics, as well as in mathematics.[49]

Although Sauveur's specific interest in music prior to his work at the Academy can be assumed, it is not documented.[50] He studied as a youth at the famous Jesuit school at La Flèche (where both Descartes and Mersenne had been students). In Paris, he attended the physics lectures of Jacques Rohault, whose popular textbook on the subject includes an enlightened and extensive chapter on the physics of sound.[51]

At all events, despite a serious speech defect which plagued Sauveur throughout his life (reportedly, he did not begin to speak until his seventh year), as well as a seemingly poor ear,[52] he em-

[47] See the assessment in Truesdell, "The Rational Mechanics," p. 121. Further on Sauveur's place in the history of acoustics, see Miller, *Anecdotal History*, p. 37; R. Bruce Lindsay, "The Story of Acoustics," in *Acoustics: Historical and Philosophical Development* (Stroudsburg, Pa.: Dowden, Hutchinson and Ross, 1972), p. 7; Scherchen, *The Nature of Music*, chap. I; Léon Auger, "Les apports de J. Sauveur (1653-1716) à la création de l'acoustique," *Revue d'histoire des sciences*, I (1947-1948), 323-336.

[48] Fontenelle's *éloge* (*Histoire*, 1716, pp. 79-87) is the principal source for information on Sauveur's life. See also, DSB, XII, 127-129; and Maxham, *The Contributions*, Introduction.

[49] See Scherchen, *The Nature of Music*, p. 26; and references, passim, in *Histoire*, 1666-1686, I, and in Du Hamel, *Regiae*.

[50] Fontenelle's *éloge* (*Histoire*, 1716, p. 85) informs: "Il entra dans l'Académie en 1696, déjà rempli d'un grand dessein qu'il méditoit, d'une Science presque toute nouvelle qu'il vouloit mettre au jour, de son Acoustique. . . ."

[51] Jacques Rohault, *Traité de physique* (Paris: veuve de Charles Savreux, 1671), pt. I, chap. XXVI: "Du Son"; the work had many editions. See further, Scherchen, *The Nature of Music*, p. 25.

[52] Fontenelle describes these defects in the *éloge* (*Histoire*, 1716, p. 85) as follows:

braced the subject of sound as his personal domain at the Academy, dominating work in that field for some twenty years. His experimental approach was one founded on observation and description, using musical experience as a basis. The results of his work were directed toward serving the practice of music rather than pure physics. Notwithstanding his own background in mathematics, the dynamical and mathematical explanations for many of his contributions had to wait for a later generation to supply.

Five papers printed among the Academy's *Mémoires*, together with the description of an early experiment found in the *Histoire* for 1700, comprise the corpus of printed material related to Sauveur's work in acoustics. These are supplemented by information on presentations by Sauveur before the Academy recorded in the *Registres*, which for the most part, describe versions of subject matter treated more systematically and thoroughly in the prints (see Appendix I).

One additional essay by Sauveur pertinent to his acoustical studies is the manuscript "Traité de la théorie de la musique," dated 1697. According to Sauveur's own testimony in 1701,[53] it was intended for his students at the Collège Royal. The essay already contains many of the ideas (some in embryonic form) that he was to develop in his later, mature papers.

In his work, Sauveur sought to establish a firm physical basis for the practice of music, through the development of a comprehensive and coordinated "système général de musique" contained in a projected "Traité complet d'Acoustique."[54] He early delineated what he considered to be the five stages in the comprehension of sound (a surprisingly modern conception): 1) its production, 2) its transmission, 3) its reception by the ear, 4) its interpretation by the brain, and 5) its psychological effect on the body ("l'âme").[55] While he addresses each of these in the *Traité* of 1697, he primarily

---

"Il n'avoit ni voix, ni oreille, & ne songeoit plus qu'à la Musique. Il étoit réduit à emprunter la voix ou l'oreille d'autrui, & il rendoit en échange des démonstrations inconnues aux musiciens." Maxham, *The Contributions*, p. 2, reviews interpretations of this passage by later writers. Sauveur occasionally had his papers read for him by colleagues at the Academy; specifically named (in the *plumitif*, BN, MS fr.n.a. 5148, f. 19v and 30v) are François Chevalier (his nephew) and Antoine Parent.

[53] *Mémoires*, 1701, p. 300.   [54] Ibid., p. 301.

[55] "Traité de la théorie de la musique par M. Sauveur, 1697" (BN, MS fr.n.a. 4674), p. 3.

concerns himself with the first and second in papers presented to the Academy.

Sauveur's principal contributions to the field he named acoustics are many.[56] He was the first to determine the absolute frequency of pitch ("son fixe") using the phenomenon of beats, and he later recommended adopting a power of 2—256 vps (middle c)—as a standard frequency in music. He developed a means of classifying temperaments and comparing pitches, through the logarithmic division of the octave into 43 equal parts (called *mérides*), each of which could be divided, in turn, into 7 units (*heptamérides*), and again into 10 (*décamérides*), deriving 3,010 combinable divisions (also a power of 2). He devised a practical scale (called *échomètre*), based on logarithmic division, for measuring the duration of sounds and the sizes of intervals.

Sauveur explained the presence and nature of partials as the aliquot vibration of strings, and devised a terminology to describe them that is still current: *son fondamentale* ("fundamental," the simple vibration of a whole string or vibrating body), *noeuds* ("nodes," points where no motion occurs), *ventres* ("loops" or "ventral segments," the active points between nodes), and *sons harmoniques* ("harmonics," vibrations of higher frequencies). Further, he stated explicitly, probably for the first time, that harmonics are components of all musical sounds and affect their quality; and he suggested that the relative consonance or dissonance of an interval, while largely a matter of the sensitivity and training of the listener's ear, may be partially explained by the nature and number of beats produced by that interval.

In addition, Sauveur attempted to fix the auditory limits of the human ear. He developed mathematical formulas to express the frequency of a vibrating string in precise terms of its length, tension and weight. Later, he derived the frequency of a vibrating string theoretically, treating it as a compound pendulum. He also

---

[56] Fontenelle (*Histoire*, 1716, p. 86) summarizes these as follows: "Une nouvelle langue de Musique, plus commode & plus étendue, un nouveau Système des sons, un Monocorde singulier, un Echomètre, le Son fixe, les Noeuds des Ondulations, ont été les fruits des recherches de M. Sauveur." For other summaries, see the references listed above in note 47. Specific contributions are also discussed, *inter alia*, in René Taton (ed.), *History of Science* (London: Thames and Hudson [1963-1966]), vol. 2, pt. 3, pp. 463 and 466; and Daumas, "Les sciences physiques," p. 864.

examined the phenomenon of tone decay and its relationship to the mass of a vibrating string.

Added to these contributions are those made by Sauveur directly to musical practice—such as a new system of solmization to suit that of the *mérides*, recommendations for the construction of organ pipes, and the design and building of different types of monochords to aid musicians in tuning their instruments. It thus becomes clear that, for Sauveur, *l'acoustique* was, indeed, a field superior to, but embracing and serving all of, music.

Later Developments in Acoustics

Following the work of Sauveur, little that was new was contributed to acoustical science at the Academy before the late eighteenth century; the main advance—the development of mathematical proofs for observed phenomena—took place largely outside of its domain.[57] During this entire period, activity at the Academy bearing on the production, propagation, and reception of sound for the most part refined and built onto earlier discoveries.

On 21 août 1726, the celebrated naturalist, mathematician, physicist, and chemist René-Antoine Ferchault de Réaumur (1683-1757) read a short *mémoire* entitled, "Sur le son que rend le plomb en quelques circonstances."[58] In it, he attempts to explain an observation made by his colleague Louis Lémery (1677-1743) that the metal—lead—poured into a certain shape ("culot"), produces a resonant sound when struck, whereas in any other shape and if forged, does not. His attraction to the problem seemingly derived from his extended work on metals and technology, rather than from special interest in the nature of vibrating bodies. Indeed, in his discussion he remarks, "nous n'en pourrions pourtant examiner les causes sans nous jetter bien avant dans la théorie des sons."[59]

A similar interest in a resonant substance was brought to the Academy's attention by the engineer and minerologist, Philippe-

---

[57] Acoustics dealt with in works principally devoted to developing musical systems will be covered in Chap. IV.

[58] Reg., T. 45, f. 261-265; printed in *Mémoires*, 1726, pp. 243-248; summarized in *Histoire*, pp. 1-3.

[59] *Mémoires*, 1726, p. 247: "we would not be able, however, to examine their causes without thrusting ourselves deeply into the theory of sound."

Frédéric, baron de Dietrich (1748-1793), over a half-century later. On 22 janvier 1785, he described a loadstone that had both magnetic and sonorous properties, owing to its unusual mineral composition.[60]

Interest in the propagation of sound had currency at the Academy during the second quarter of the century. Central to this interest was the work of the physicist Jean-Jacques Dortous de Mairan (1678-1771), who served in several administrative capacities for the Academy, but especially as *secrétaire perpétuel* from 1741 until 1743. Mairan's commitment to music is well documented, but nowhere is it better stated than in Fouchy's *éloge*:[61]

> Il étoit Musicien, & peut-être plus qu'aucun de ceux qui se sont occupés de cet objet. Il connoissoit cette partie des Mathématiques à fond, depuis la structure de l'organe de l'ouïe jusqu'à la pratique & au savant usage du clavier. . . .

> [He was a Musician, & perhaps more so than those who concerned themselves with this subject. He knew this part of Mathematics (i.e., music) in depth, from the structure of the organ of hearing, to the practice and learned application of the keyboard. . . .]

During his activity at the Academy, Mairan served on no less than thirty-eight committees assigned to review topics in music (see Appendix II, C); he is second only to Fouchy in frequency of such assignment. His own contributions to the field, however, are limited to examination of the propagation of sound and its relationship to light, expanding upon observations made by Newton on such a relationship.[62]

Mairan was fundamentally a Cartesian working at a time when Newton's theories were becoming known in France; some, he adapted to his own study, but many he rejected.[63] In acoustics, he

[60] Reg., T. 104, f. 13; Report (Sage and Berthollet): 23 février 1785 (Reg., T. 104, f. 42-42v, original in *pochette de séance*; notice in *Histoire*, 1785, p. 128).

[61] *Histoire*, 1771, p. 101.

[62] See *Observations de physique*: IV ("Sur les rapports entre les sept couleurs de prisme avec les sept notes de musique"), in *Histoire*, 1720, pp. 11-12. The idea of comparing light and sound, of course, was not new; it had currency in the seventeenth century and was presented to the Academy by Malebranche already in 1699 (see above, note 25).

[63] See the assessment in DSB, IX, 33.

took his point of departure from Newton's observation of the analogy between the seven colors of the light spectrum and the seven tones of the musical scale. Basic to his discussion was an understanding that sound is transmitted not by waves, but rather by particles in the air which, being different from one another, are responsible for the different sounds one hears.[64] This theory was not newly developed by Mairan; it already appears in rudimentary form in a paper on light presented by him in 1717 to the Academy in Bordeaux, with which he was associated before coming to Paris in 1718.[65]

Generally speaking, "Mairan's entire theory of acoustics hinges on the heterogeneous nature of air," notes A. R. Kleinbaum, adding that his discussions arising out of the eye-ear analogy are often metaphysical in nature and "of dubious significance."[66] Mairan's ideas on the propagation of sound were critically received by his contemporaries, and they appear to have had little relevance on the development of acoustical theory later in the century.[67]

The natural historian and physiologist, Georges-Louis Leclerc, comte de Buffon (1707-1788), unequivocally declared in his *mémoire*, "Dissertation sur les couleurs accidentelles" (read before an *assemblée publique* on 13 novembre 1743),[68] that the eye-ear relationship

[64] The most complete development of his ideas appears in the *mémoire*, "Discours sur la propagation du son dans les différents tons qui le modifient," presented 4 mai 1737 (Reg., T. 56, f. 81-89; printed with additions in *Mémoires*, 1737, pp. 1-60; summarized in *Histoire*, 1737, pp. 97-104), and added to on 21 août 1737 (Reg., T. 56, f. 180). The eye-ear analogy was further discussed on 17 décembre 1738 (Reg., T. 57, f. 196v) and continued 18 and 21 février 1739 (Reg., T. 58, f. 29 and 30v; printed in *Mémoires*, 1738, pp. 1-3). Indications of Mairan's communication of his ideas directly to Newton in 1720, and of additional experiments conducted on the transmission of sound in 1723, are contained in *Mémoires*, 1737, p. 3, and 1738, p. 1.

[65] See the summary in Barrière, *L'Académie de Bordeaux*, p. 176.

[66] Abby R. Kleinbaum, *Jean-Jacques Dortous de Mairan (1678-1771): A Study of an Enlightenment Scientist* (Ph.D. dissertation, Columbia Univ., 1970), pp. 181 and 184-185; see pp. 178-188 for a critical review of Mairan's contributions to acoustics.

[67] Concerning details of Mairan's controversies with leading figures on his acoustical theories (including J.-P. Rameau, D. Bernoulli, and L. Euler), see ibid., pp. 186-188.

[68] Reg., T. 62, p. 472; *mémoire* on pp. 501*-510*; printed in *Mémoires*, 1743, pp. 147-158. See further, Lesley Hanks, *Buffon avant l'"Histoire naturelle"* (Paris: Presses Universitaires de France, 1966), pp. 220-221 and 279. On Buffon's scientific attitude, see DSB, II, 581.

is groundless, and that the two senses cannot be submitted to common law: "ces deux phénomènes sont indépendans l'un de l'autre."[69] Three years later, on 16 novembre 1746, the body received an anonymous *mémoire*, entitled "Système physico-harmonique . . . envoyé de Padouë sur l'analogie entre les couleurs et les sons," which it rejected as being "très obscur, pour ne pas dire tout à fait inintelligible."[70] The eye-ear analogy was no longer considered a valid area for examination by midcentury, although it continued to have its champions outside the Academy.[71]

Of more pertinence was a renewed interest in the determination of the speed of sound, which occupied several investigators during the earlier part of the century. César-François Cassini de Thury (1714-1784), a member of a dynasty of scientists associated with the Academy (and a grandson of G. D. Cassini, who had led the Academy's effort in 1677 to measure the speed of sound; see Chapter I, The Founding Generation), undertook in 1738 to arrive at a more reliable measurement than was then available. He led a team that included Giovanni Domenico Maraldi (1709-1788) and l'Abbé Nicolas-Louis de La Caille (1713-1762) as well as others, which organized a set of carefully controlled outdoor experiments and arrived at a determination of 332m/s at 0°C., closely approximating modern measurements.[72]

[69] Reg., T. 62, p. 503*; *Mémoires*, 1743, p. 149: "these two phenomena are independent, one from the other."

[70] Reg., T. 65, p. 299: "very obscure, not to say altogether unintelligible." Report (Mairan and Fouchy): 22 juillet 1747 (Reg., T. 66, p. 340; original and extract in *pochette de séance*).

[71] Chief among them was Louis-Bertrand Castel, who developed an "ocular harpsichord" that had currency throughout the century. On this instrument, see Donald S. Schier, *Louis-Bertrand Castel, Anti-Newtonian Scientist* (Cedar Rapids, Iowa: Torch Press, 1941), pp. 135-196. For a historical review of the sound-color analogy, see Albert Wellek, "Farbenharmonie und Farbenklavier, Ihre Entstehungsgeschichte im 18. Jahrhundert," *Archiv für die gesamte Psychologie*, vol. 94 (1935), 347-375; and A. Wellek, "Das Doppelempfinden im 18. Jahrhundert," *Deutsche Vierteljahrsschrift für Literaturwissenschaft und Geistesgeschichte*, vol. 14 (1936), 76-79. Also, see Miller, *Anecdotal History*, pp. 25-27.

[72] Results of the experiments are contained in a *mémoire* by Cassini de Thury entitled, "Sur la propagation du son," initially presented on 15 mars 1738 (Reg., T. 57, f. 57), read at an *assemblée publique* on 16 avril 1738 (Reg., T. 57, f. 74v-84; printed in *Mémoires*, 1738, pp. 128-46; summarized in *Histoire*, 1738, pp. 1-5), and reread on 19 and 23 avril 1738 (Reg., T. 57, f. 85 and 87). The experiment is described in Hunt, *Origins in Acoustics*, p. 110. On Cassini de Thury, see DSB, III, 107-109.

It was only in 1740 that temperature was understood to influence the speed of sound. This was determined separately by Giovanni Lodovico Bianconi (1717-1781) in Bologna[73] and, afterward (1740-1744), by Charles-Marie de La Condamine (1701-1774) during the Academy's geodesic expedition to Peru.[74] Also on the expedition and having interest in the speed of sound was the astronomer, Louis Godin (1704-1760), who communicated his findings to the Academy by letter.[75]

Researchers in the latter part of the eighteenth century, however, were seemingly less interested in continuing experiments to gather information on acoustical events based on observation than they were in describing events already observed in mathematical terms. For with the invention of calculus by Newton and Leibniz early in the century, the tool for mathematical proofs of physical phenomena was in hand.[76] What evolved was an argument over a problem of mathematical physics—the dynamical solution of a vibrating string—which grew into a celebrated controversy that lasted almost a century and involved some of the most eminent mathematicians of the time. The leading protagonists were Leonhard Euler (1707-1783), Jean Le Rond d'Alembert (1717-1783), and Daniel Bernoulli (1700-1782), all affiliated with the Paris

[73] Bianconi's experiment was later published in the Academy's series, *Collection académique*, vol. 10 (Paris: Panckoucke, 1773), pp. 189-190.

[74] Reported in a *mémoire* entitled "Relation abrégée d'un voyage fait dans l'intérieur de l'Amérique méridionale . . . ," read at an *assemblée publique* on 28 avril 1745 (Reg., T. 64, p. 129), printed in *Mémoires*, 1745, pp. 391-492 (report on sound velocity on p. 488). See Hunt, *Origins in Acoustics*, p. 111. On La Condamine, see DSB, XV, 369-373.

[75] The earliest recorded correspondence is dated 14 août 1739, read at the Academy on 27 and 31 Janvier 1742 (Reg., T. 61, pp. 44-45), which refers to a "Mémoire sur la vitesse du son" that Godin was preparing. Godin was in communication with the chemist Charles-François de Cisternay Dufay (1698-1739) concerning the *mémoire*, and although Dufay is not known to have occupied himself with acoustics at the Academy, an autograph "Abrégé de physique" survives (*Dossier Dufay*, AdS), of which a portion is devoted to "de l'ouïe ou du son des corps" (f. 3-4v).

Dossier Godin (AdS) contains a copy of a letter dated 13 octobre 1740 from Godin to Pierre Bouguer (1698-1758), also on the mission to Peru, where reference is made to an acoustical experiment on which Bouguer had advised Godin. La Condamine is known to have made a report to the Academy of Godin's experiment on the speed of sound; see DSB, V, 435.

[76] See Miller, *Anecdotal History*, pp. 42-43; Lindsay, "The Story of Acoustics," p. 7; and Hunt, *Origins in Acoustics*, pp. 146-148.

Academy as well as with other leading academies in Europe; additional figures soon entered the fray, notably, Alexis-Claude Clairaut (1713-1765) and Joseph-Louis de Lagrange (1736-1813).[77]

The quarrel (which broadened to include fundamental questions of mathematical formalism) was fought largely outside the Paris Academy,[78] and except for one pertinent *mémoire*, there are only occasional references to it in the Academy's proceedings.[79] That *mémoire*, presented by Bernoulli in 1762, was entitled, "Recherches physiques, mécaniques et analytiques, sur le son et sur les tons des tuyaux d'orgues différemment construits."[80] It does not appreciably advance Bernoulli's prior harmonic theories, but it does provide him the opportunity to extend those theories to resonant bodies other than strings. H. Straub summarizes the contribution as follows:[81]

> [It] is a beautiful treatment of the oscillations inside organ pipes, using only elementary mathematics. It is assumed that the movement of the particles parallel to the axis, the velocities, and the pressure are equal at all points of the same cross section and that the compression at the open end of the pipes equals zero. Among other things, this work contains the first theory of conical pipes and an arrangement consisting of two coaxial pipes of different cross sections as well as a series of new experiments.[82]

[77] Concerning the controversy, see Truesdell, "The Rational Mechanics," pp. 237-295; Lindsay, "The Story of Acoustics," p. 8; Jerome R. Ravetz, "Vibrating Strings and Arbitrary Functions," in *The Logic of Personal Knowledge: Essays Presented to Michael Polanyi on his Seventieth Birthday* (London: Routledge and Kegan Paul, 1961), pp. 71-88; and Thomas L. Hankins, *Jean d'Alembert, Science and the Enlightenment* (Oxford: Clarendon Press, 1970), pp. 28-65.

[78] For the most part, the pertinent *mémoires* were published by the Berlin Academy. For bibliographical citations, see the sources referred to in note 77, above.

[79] Such as the report (by Le Monnier and Bézout) on vol. I. of d'Alembert's *Opuscules mathématiques*, presented to the Academy on 17 juin 1761 (Reg., T. 80, f. 111v-112; summarized in *Histoire*, 1761, pp. 86-91; original in *pochette de séance*).

[80] Presentation (by Fouchy): 4 décembre 1762 (Reg., T. 81, f. 297v-298; printed in *Mémoires*, 1762, pp. 431-485; summarized in *Histoire*, 1762, pp. 170-181). The paper was read during several sessions by Etienne Bézout, beginning 22 janvier and finishing 28 juin 1763 (Reg., T. 82, f. 19 and 253v).

[81] DSB, II, 41.

[82] One of these is singled out for treatment by Truesdell, "The Rational Mechanics," pp. 276-277, where he calls it "a beautiful experiment to demonstrate harmonic resonance."

At all events, the spate of arguments and counter-arguments in what Condorcet called "cette longue et glorieuse lutte,"[83] appears to have ebbed only at the death of the principal protagonists, and ended at the turn into the nineteenth century with the important contributions by Jean-Joseph Fourier (1768-1830) and Siméon-Denis Poisson (1781-1840).

Later Developments in Phonation and Audition

Dodart's earlier anatomical work on phonation was to form the basis for study by others in the century. Chief among them was the anatomist, Antoine Ferrein (1693-1769), who read a *mémoire* to the Academy in 1741, entitled "De la formation de la voix de l'homme,"[84] in which he modifies Dodart's theory. M. D. Grmek provides the following summary of his contribution:[85]

> According to Ferrein, the lips of the glottis form two true "vocal cords"; sounds arise solely from the vibration of these cords, which is produced by the stream of exhaled air. Thus the air performs the same function as a violin bow. In this hypothesis the larynx is considered to be a combination of wind and string instrument. Apart from Leonardo da Vinci's experiments, Ferrein was the first to study phonation experimentally by forcing air through the detached larynxes of various animals.

Shortly afterward, the physician Michel-Philippe Bouvard (1717-1787) took issue with Dodart's views on the function of the windpipe in the production of the voice. On 13 février 1743, he read a *mémoire* to the Academy, entitled "Sur la trachée-artère, par rapport à l'usage particulier qu'elle a dans la formation de la voix et des tons,"[86] in which he argues that the speed of air that passes through the windpipe, since it continually changes, is significant in determining the pitch produced by the voice. A committee was

[83] Bernoulli's *éloge* (*Histoire*, 1782), p. 89: "this long and glorious struggle."

[84] Presentation: 15 novembre 1741 (*assemblée publique*, Reg., T. 60, p. 454); reread 6, 9, and 16 décembre 1741 (Reg., T. 60, pp. 471, 472, and 475; *mémoire* on pp. 476-484; printed with additions in *Mémoires*, 1741, pp. 409-432; summarized in *Histoire*, 1741, pp. 51-56).

[85] DSB, IV, 590; see the summary in Fouchy's *éloge* (*Histoire*, 1769), pp. 156-157. See also the historical review in Harold M. Kaplan, *Anatomy and Physiology of Speech* (New York: McGraw-Hill, 1960), pp. 133-137.

[86] Reg., T. 62, p. 109.

appointed to examine the *mémoire*, comprising Ferrein, Jacques-Bénigne Winslow (1669-1760), and Joseph-Marie-François de Lassone (1717-1788). A month later, on 13 mars 1743, Ferrein resigned from the committee, indicating that he rejected the author's premise, and announcing that he intended to present his own views on the subject.[87] The report on Bouvard's work, given on 16 mars 1743 by the two remaining members of the committee, judged that his argument was not sustained, and that additional experiments were needed.[88]

Beginning on 3 avril and continuing through 11 mai 1743, Ferrein brought to the body "plusieurs éclaircissements . . . sur la formation des sons, et des tons de la voix humaine, et des différents animaux."[89] While these "éclaircissements" have not survived, it may well be that they were incorporated into the expansions found in the printed version of his *mémoire* of 1741 (published in 1744).

Part of the novelty of Ferrein's anatomical work concerns his investigation of sound produced not only by the human vocal mechanism, but also by that of different animals, reflecting general eighteenth-century advances in the developing biological sciences and in comparative anatomy.[90] Ferrein was not alone in this work, of course, and other researchers undertook to examine the vocal and aural organs of animals and fish, as well as the transmission of sound through media other than air.[91]

[87] Ibid., p. 163.

[88] Ibid., pp. 166-168; original *mémoire* in *Dossier Bouvard* (AdS), and *rapport* in *pochette de séance*.

[89] Presentations: 3, 6, and 27 avril, 4 and 11 mai 1743 (Reg., T. 62, pp. 201, 202, 208, 211, and 217): "Several clarifications . . . on the formation of sounds and tones of the human voice, and of different animals."

[90] For studies of these advances, see Jacques Roger, *Les sciences de la vie dans la pensée française du XVIIIᵉ siècle* (Paris: Armand Colin, 1963); and Maurice Caullery, "Les sciences biologiques du milieu du XVIIᵉ à la fin du XVIIIᵉ siècle," in *Histoire de la science*, pp. 1178-1203.

[91] See Daumas, "Les sciences physiques," in *Histoire de la science*, p. 865. Mention should be made of the contribution to knowledge of the structure of the ear by Ferrein's contemporary, the surgeon Claude-Nicolas Le Cat (1700-1768), a corresponding member of the Paris Academy. Le Cat's *Traité des sens* (Rouen, 1740), which includes a section devoted to "De l'ouÿe" (pp. 259-297), does not appear to have been presented to the Academy but rather to the Royal Society of London, of which he was a Fellow. See the review of the *Traité* in the *Philosophical Transactions* for 1742, vol. 42 (London: T. Woodward and C. Davis, 1744), 264-269. Le

Among them was l'Abbé Jean-Antoine Nollet (1700-1770), who studied the audition of fish and sound transmission through a liquid medium. These may appear to be unusual subjects for the author of the popular *Leçons de physique* (1743-1748), who was known at the time as the leading electrician among his countrymen. Yet, Nollet's general interests were as far-ranging as his contributions to physics were controversial.[92] His "Mémoire sur l'ouïe des poissons, et sur la transmission des sons dans l'eau" was read at the *assemblée publique* of 24 avril 1743.[93] In it, through controlled experiments (including his own total immersion in the river Seine), Nollet confirms that water transmits sound by means of vibrations, that the medium does not alter the pitch, and that fish are able to sense the transmitted vibrations. However, he can only conjecture as to the nature of those sensations, since his work on the audition of fish is based on inconclusive evidence produced earlier by others (especially, by Du Verney). His findings were repeated in vol. III of his *Leçons de physique* (1745),[94] and in Nicolas Desmarest's annotations to F. de Brémond's French translation of Francis Hauksbee's *Physico-Mechanical Experiments on Various Subjects* (London, 1709)[95]—a work that brought Hauksbee's experiments on the propagation of sound in compressed and rarefied air, as well as in water, to the general attention of the Academy (which formally endorsed the edition in 1754).[96] Subsequent anatomical studies on the audition of fish, by Geoffroy and Camper, are cited by Fouchy as sustaining Nollet's conjectures.[97]

Cat later presented a *Théorie de l'ouïe* to the Academy in Toulouse. Further on him, see DSB, VIII, 114-116.

[92] See DSB, X, 145-147.

[93] Reg., T. 62, p. 206; *mémoire* on pp. 236-257, printed in *Mémoires*, 1743, pp. 199-224, and summarized in *Histoire*, 1743, pp. 22-27; reread on 11, 15, 18, 22, 25, and 29 mai 1743 (Reg., T. 62, pp. 217, 219, 220, 226, 227, and 230).

[94] *Leçon XI*, pp. 416-420. A brief summary of this *leçon* appears in the *rapport* (Réaumur and Fouchy) on vol. III of Nollet's *Leçons*, read 6 mars 1745 (Reg., T. 64, pp. 61-62; original and extract in *pochette de séance*).

[95] *Expériences physico-méchaniques sur différens sujets*, 2 vols. (Paris: veuve Cavelier et fils, 1754); summary in *Histoire*, 1754, pp. 34-43 (information on acoustical experiments on pp. 40-41); Nollet's work is described on pp. 334-339. See DSB, VI, 175.

[96] Report (Le Monnier and Montigny): 19 juin 1754 (Reg., T. 73, p. 242; original and extract in *pochette de séance*).

[97] In Nollet's *éloge* (*Histoire*, 1770), pp. 126-127. Further on Nollet, see Jean Tor-

II. ACOUSTICS, PHONATION, AND AUDITION

Etienne-Louis Geoffroy, "fils" (1725-1810), one of a family of physicians associated with the Academy, became a member of the group only in 1798 but was active at its sessions well before then. His "Mémoire sur l'organe de l'ouïe des poissons" was received first in 1751,[98] and later in 1753[99] by the Academy, prior to its publication in 1778 as part of a study on the auditory organs of man, reptiles, and fish.[100] It was considered "an important work in comparative anatomy."[101] In the *mémoire*, Geoffroy describes the rudimentary hearing mechanism of fish.

The eminent Dutch anatomist Petrus Camper (1722-1789) also presented a paper on the audition of fish prior to his being named correspondent (1771) and later *associé étranger* (1785) at the Academy. A report on his "Mémoire sur l'organe de l'ouïe des poissons," made on 23 janvier 1768,[102] deemed the essay worthy of publication in the series of *Savants étrangers*.[103] In the *mémoire*, Camper attempts to show that sound is received by fish through a hearing mechanism which, although considerably less developed than that of man, is nevertheless complete. He further describes the central role played by the nervous system and brain in the process and is generally credited with discovery of the semicircular canals in the auditory organs of fish.[104]

Another comparative anatomist at the Academy who concerned himself with the processes of phonation was François-David Hérissant (1714-1773). In 1753, he presented a paper entitled "Re-

---

lais, *Un physicien au siècle des lumières, l'Abbé Nollet, 1700-1770* (Paris: Sipuco, 1954); and DSB, X, 145-148.

[98] Presentations: 1 and 4 décembre 1751 (Reg., T. 70, pp. 574 and 575); Report (Duhamel du Monceau and Morand): 18 décembre 1751 (Reg., T. 70, pp. 591-592; original in *pochette de séance*).

[99] Presentation: 23 mai 1753 (Reg., T. 72, p. 378); committee named: Jussieu, Ferrein, and Lassone. No report appears to have been issued.

[100] *Dissertation sur l'organe de l'ouïe de l'homme, des reptiles, et des poissons* (Amsterdam and Paris: Cavelier, 1778).

[101] DSB, V, 355. See also, Bayle and Thillaye, *Biographie médicale*, II, 495-496.

[102] Presentation: 17 and 20 juin 1767 (Reg., T. 86, f. 147 and 147v-148); Report (Macquer and Tenon) in Reg., T. 87, f. 8v-15 (original *rapport* in *pochette de séance*; see notice in *Histoire*, 1767, p. 188).

[103] *Mémoires de mathématique et de physique, présentés à l'Académie Royale des Sciences, par divers savans*, T. VI (Paris: Imprimerie Royale, 1774), 177-197. See the summary in the *éloge* by Condorcet, *Oeuvres*, III, 428.

[104] William A. Locy, *The Story of Biology* (New York: Garden City Publ. Co., 1925), p. 336.

cherches sur les organes de la voix des quadrupèdes, et de celle des oiseaux,"[105] in which the vocal organs of various animals and birds are described. Basing his work on that of Dodart and Ferrein, Hérissant classifies these organs according to their relative complexity when compared with the human vocal mechanism.

During the second half of the century, only minor contributions were made at the Academy to an understanding of audition and phonation in animals and humans,[106] except for the work of the renowned anatomist Félix Vicq d'Azyr (1748-1794), just prior to the revolution.[107] In addition to being a practicing physician and innovative educator, Vicq d'Azyr was a prolific researcher and writer, having special interest in comparative anatomy, neuroanatomy, and veterinary medicine. Among his many works, two concern mechanisms for the production and reception of sound in animals and humans: "De la structure de l'organe de l'ouïe des oiseaux comparé avec celui de l'homme, des quadrupèdes, des rep-

---

[105] Presentation: 2 mai 1753 (assemblée publique, Reg., T. 72, pp. 285-293; printed in Mémoires, 1753, pp. 279-295; summarized in Histoire, 1753, pp. 107-113, in Fouchy's éloge [Histoire, 1773], p. 127, and in Mercure de France, juin 1753, pp. 78-80). On Hérissant, see Jean C.-F. Hoefer (ed.), Nouvelle biographie générale, vol. 24 (Paris: Firmin-Didot, 1858), cols. 340-341.

[106] The Registres include the following references:

19 février 1752 (T. 71, pp. 91-94): "M. Morand a fait le rapport . . . du mémoire de M. [Charles] Le Roy, sur les organes de l'ouïe, et de la respiration de la tortuë" (original rapport in pochette de séance).

2 août 1769 (T. 88, f. 287): "M. Dufourni est entré et a lû un mémoire sur la différence du tems que les tons aiguës et les tons graves emploient pour parvenir à l'oreille; M. M. De Mairan et Le Roy ont été nommés pour l'examiner" (no report).

19 juillet 1783 (T. 102, f. 157v): "M. l'Abbé [Antoine] Mongez a lû un mémoire sur la réputation qu'a eue le cigne, de rendre de sons harmonieux; commissaires, M. M. Daubenton, Brisson et Vicq d'Azyr" (no report). The mémoire was also presented to the Académie des Inscriptions and subsequently published.

5 and 12 mai 1784 (T. 103, f. 107v and 126): "Mémoire de M. [André-Antoine] Touchy sur la voix des oiseaux, envoyé par la Société Royale de Montpellier . . . commissaires, M. M. Daubenton et Vicq d'Azyr" (no report). The mémoire was rejected; letters related to the review are in the pochette de séance du 5 mai 1784.

9 avril 1785 (T. 104, f. 57): "M. Rocquard est entré et a lû un mémoire sur l'organe de l'ouÿe et sur la partie molle du nerf auditif; commissaires M. M. Portal et Sabatier" (no report).

[107] On Vicq d'Azyr, see Bayle and Thillaye, Biographie médicale, II, 718-720; Léon-Noël Berthe, Dictionnaire des correspondants de l'Académie d'Arras (Arras: the author, 1969), p. 204; and especially DSB, XIV, 14-17, which includes an extended bibliography.

(39)

tiles et des poissons" (1778),[108] and "De la structure des organes qui servent à la formation de la voix, considérés dans l'homme et dans les différentes classes d'animaux, et comparés entr'eux" (1779).[109]

Both are studies in comparative anatomy, involving different classes of animals, in which Vicq d'Azyr seeks to arrive at general principles for the processes being examined for all the classes. As concerns the ear, while concentrating on the hearing of birds, he is able to identify anatomical parts of auditory organs that are common to most animals and therefore considered essential to the hearing process; he also describes those parts that are peculiar to mechanisms of different species. He approaches examination of the voice mechanism in much the same way, but begins his essay with an extended review of conclusions drawn by earlier investigators (especially Dodart, Ferrein, Camper, and Hérissant). After describing details of the vocal anatomy of humans and of varied species of animals, he arrives at a set of postulates, which conform closely to modern views: 1) that the glottis is not essential to phonation; 2) that the inferior membranes (vocal folds) of the larynx form the true organ of phonation, since they are the only parts capable of vibrating in voice mechanisms of most animals; and 3) that the vocal cavity and trachea serve but to intensify the sound produced, without affecting intonation. Vicq d'Azyr appears not to have completed the studies that he planned in order to prove these postulates.

[108] Presentations: 29 avril and 14 novembre 1778 (both *assemblées publiques*, Reg., T. 97, f. 135 and 313; printed in *Mémoires*, 1778, pp. 381-392; summarized in *Histoire*, 1778, pp. 5-6); repeated 22 janvier 1780 (Reg., T. 99, f. 14v).

[109] Presentation: 13 novembre 1779 (*assemblée publique*, Reg., T. 98, f. 290v; printed in *Mémoires*, 1779, pp. 178-206; summarized in *Histoire*, 1779, pp. 5-8); repeated and continued 3 mai and 9 août 1780 (Reg., T. 99, f. 122v and 200).

∽ III ∽

MACHINES ET INVENTIONS:
MUSIC AS CRAFT

Les Arts et Métiers

THE CLIMATE OF INQUIRY that stimulated experimentation at the Academy also provided a spur to its growing concern with the *arts et métiers*, since investigators quickly recognized the pressing need for the design and construction of ever-more precise and novel scientific instruments to facilitate their research.[1] As Daumas notes, once "science became experimental, its progress no longer depended solely on the exercise of intellectual faculties."[2] Indeed, its success relied increasingly upon collaboration of the professional craftsman with the scientist—and it was this collaboration that was largely responsible for the wide-ranging technological advances made by the scientific movement at the time.

Interest in the *arts et métiers* found expression, for yet another reason, early in the development of the Paris Academy. Initially devoted to consideration of questions related primarily to theoretical physics and mathematics, the Academy soon came to regard "la pratique"—that is, applied physics and mathematics—as a natural and desirable by-product of scientific investigation. Already in 1668, only two years after its founding, the Academy showed

---

[1] For the development of scientific instruments during the period of the Academy's activity, see Maurice Daumas, *Les instruments scientifiques aux xviie et xviiie siècles* (Paris: Presses Universitaires de France, 1953); English trans. by Mary Holbrook, *Scientific Instruments of the Seventeenth and Eighteenth Centuries* (New York: Praeger, 1972). The general setting for the evolution of technology in the eighteenth century is described in Abraham Wolf, *A History of Science, Technology, and Philosophy in the Eighteenth Century,* 2d ed. (London: G. Allen and Unwin, 1952), Intro. and pp. 498-501.

[2] Daumas, *Scientific Instruments,* p. 2; see also, Hahn, *The Anatomy,* pp. 68-69.

clear concern for the building and utility of machines (*les arts mécaniques*);[3] in 1672, the prime minister, Colbert, asked the group to consider establishing a "description des arts,"[4] and in 1675, to examine[5]

> les moyens de faire un traité de mécanique, avec une description exacte de toutes les machines utiles à tous les arts et métiers dont on se sert à présent en France et dans toute l'Europe.

> [the means of preparing a treatise on mechanics, containing an exact description of all the machines applicable to all the arts and crafts that are currently practiced in France and in all of Europe.]

As seen above (Chapter II, The Second Generation), the application of scientific investigation to utilitarian ends continued to be stressed after Colbert's death by the new prime minister, Louvois, who in 1686 instructed the Academy, in the interest of the state, to address itself increasingly to practical questions during the course of its work.[6]

That the academicians took the charge seriously is clear from the preliminary "description des Arts et Métiers" found appended to Tome 13 of the *Registres*, dated 1693—a project prepared principally by the mechanician Gilles Filleau Des Billettes and directed by President Bignon.[7] The growing importance of *mécaniciens* and of *machines et inventions* in the Academy's work is clearly reflected in the royal statutes issued to the group in 1699. The statutes assign to the Academy the responsibility of approving all machines submitted to the king for Royal Privilege. They further stipulate that, to be approved, a machine must be certified as novel and practical, and that a working model of each be deposited in the

---

[3] See Plantefol, "L'Académie des Sciences," p. 71.

[4] See Claire Salomon-Bayet, "Un préambule théorique à une Académie des Arts," *Revue d'histoire des sciences*, XXIII (1970), 230.

[5] Ibid., p. 234. See *Histoire*, 1666-1686, I, 131.

[6] Ornstein, *The Rôle of Scientific Societies*, p. 157; and Plantefol, "L'Académie des Sciences," p. 72. Concerning the development of interest in "useful arts" throughout Europe at this time, see Peter Mathias, "Who Unbound Prometheus? Science and Technical Change, 1600-1800," in A. E. Musson (ed.), *Science, Technology, and Economic Growth in the Eighteenth Century* (London: Methuen, 1972), pp. 80-81.

[7] Described in Salomon-Bayet, "Un préambule théorique," pp. 229-250.

permanent collection of the Academy.[8] Later, from 1703, signed plans were also required.[9]

The convergence of these two trends—the close collaboration between scientist and craftsman on the one hand, and the utilitarian ends of scientific investigation on the other—supported by the statutory reforms of 1699, created a climate for significant strides in the development of the *arts et métiers* throughout the eighteenth century. But these strides depended upon yet a third factor—amelioration of the restrictive nature of the system of trade guilds that had developed and become strongly established in France over a period of two centuries.

French guilds were exceedingly conservative organizations, based on economic monopoly and stringent control over its members. They jealously guarded their commercial prerogatives and techniques, and were quick to resort to litigation to preserve these.[10] However, certain freedoms from guild control were available to inventors, who could obtain special privileges bestowed on them by letters patent registered by Parliament. "These licences guaranteed them the exclusive right to exhibit their inventions for a fixed term and the liberty to construct [them] . . . without being bound by guild regulations."[11] Given its role as assessor of machines and inventions intended for Royal Privilege, the Academy naturally attracted the attention of craftsmen with novel ideas who preferred to express them outside the guild system. However, it was sometimes difficult to determine whether an idea was truly new, thereby deserving review by the Academy, or whether it was simply a refinement of an existing practice, in which case it fell under the jurisdiction of the guilds. The Academy was forced to intervene on several occasions to defend instrument makers from lawsuits filed against them by the guilds, which questioned the novelty of their inventions.[12]

Frank Hubbard notes that in eighteenth-century France "the liberal movement of opposition to the obfuscation and technical con-

[8] The statutes are reproduced in Maindron, *L'Académie des Sciences*, pp. 18-24.

[9] Reg., T. 22, f. 93-93v.

[10] See the discussion in Constant Pierre, *Les facteurs d'instruments de musique* (Paris: Ed. Sagot, 1893; repr., Geneva: Minkoff, 1971), Chaps. I-II.

[11] Daumas, *Scientific Instruments*, p. 99.

[12] Ibid., p. 98.

servatism of the guilds was sufficiently powerful to bring about the production of many volumes on the techniques of contemporary arts and trades." He adds that "those published by the Académie Royale des Sciences are particularly noteworthy."[13] Indeed, an important place was assigned to the *arts et métiers* in the Academy's yearly publication, the *Histoire et Mémoires*. Also, two special series were issued to describe details of advances made in technological design and construction: the *Machines et Inventions*, a series of seven volumes issued between 1735 and 1777;[14] and the *Description des Arts et Métiers*, a monumental set of eighty-four monographs in twenty-seven volumes published between 1761 and 1789.[15] The information contained in these publications was disseminated widely and had an important effect on the general development of the arts and trades both in and out of France.[16]

[13] Frank Hubbard, *Three Centuries of Harpsichord Making* (Cambridge: Harvard Univ. Press, 1965), p. 84.

[14] Publication of the *Machines et Inventions approuvées par l'Académie Royale des Sciences* was overseen by René-Antoine Ferchault de Réaumur and Jean-Jacques Dortous de Mairan, and edited by the engineer, Jean-Gaffon Gallon. That the publication of this series was prodded by plans for a similar enterprise announced by the shortlived Société des Arts is discussed by Hahn, *The Anatomy*, pp. 109-110 (for a broader context, see his "The Application of Science to Society: The Societies of Arts," in *Studies on Voltaire and the Eighteenth Century*, XXV [1963], 829-836). An "Album des dessins manuscrits," containing preliminary inked drawings of many of the plates (including several of musical instruments) that ultimately were used in the publication, is in the Bibliothèque du Conservatoire des Arts et Métiers in Paris, call number "Petit Folio B8"; most are signed, dated, and approved by Réaumur and Mairan, and some are provided with annotations. See the listing in *Histoire et prestige de l'Académie des Sciences*, publ. by Musée du Conservatoire National des Arts et Métiers (Paris, 1966), p. 94.

[15] Titles of monographs are listed in Maindron, *L'Académie des Sciences*, pp. 314-316. Plans for issuing a comprehensive *Description des Arts et Métiers*, while formed early in the work of the Academy, were realized only after (and probably as a consequence of) the appearance of the *Encyclopédie* after midcentury. Réaumur assumed charge of the project shortly after his election to the Academy, and at his death in 1757, Duhamel du Monceau became its principal director. Further on the *Description* and its publication, see *Histoire et prestige*, pp. 92-93, 95-96; and Salomon-Bayet, "Un préambule théorique," pp. 241-243.

[16] For the relationship of the *Description des Arts* to the *Encyclopédie* of Diderot and d'Alembert, see Salomon-Bayet, "Un préambule théorique," pp. 240-241. Bertrand Gille (in *Histoire des techniques*, vol. 41 of *Encyclopédie de la Pléiade* [Paris: Gallimard, 1978], pp. 685-687 and 1434-1436) argues that the *Description*, at least as conceived by Des Billettes, was concerned with the comprehensiveness and hierarchy of relationships among the "arts" (including both the liberal and mechan-

MUSIC AS CRAFT

Musical Instruments—General

Musical instruments appear in the original design for the "Description des Arts et Métiers" undertaken by the Academy.[17] Certainly, instruments had been brought before the group prior to this time. However, it is only after the turn into the eighteenth century that they increasingly became objects of the Academy's attention. It has already been mentioned that in 1702 President Bignon, wishing "to accelerate the general undertaking of the Description of the Arts," specifically directed the mathematician Louis Carré "to describe all the musical instruments used in France" (see above, Chapter II, The Second Generation).[18] This assignment served to identify the construction of musical instruments as an integral part of the *arts mécaniques*, at a time when there was generally an awakened interest at the Academy in the entire field of music.

Among the scientists early in the eighteenth century whose work expresses this interest is the mathematician-philosopher, Pierre-Louis Moreau de Maupertuis (1698-1759). In 1724, he presented a *mémoire* entitled "Sur la forme des instrumens de musique"[19] in which he reasons that since music is both a science and

---

ical arts) rather than with the development of technology itself (he describes the original conception of the *Description* as "un traité à double entrée logique et classificatoire" [p. 1435]). To him, the completed volumes that finally began to appear in 1761 are nothing but "une juxtaposition des descriptions." And so are those of Diderot and d'Alembert's *Encyclopédie*, which borrowed from work of the Academy, but was concerned not so much with encouraging progress, as with presenting and perfecting existing practices. For Gille, the true merit of the *Encyclopédie* to the evolving technology of the time "est d'avoir dressé un tableau d'ensemble des connaissances dans lequel la technique se trouvait être insérée" (p. 686). See further, Charles C. Gillispie, "The Natural History of Industry," in Musson (ed.), *Science, Technology, and Economic Growth*, p. 131.

[17] A classification of the *arts* intended for inclusion in the *Description* is found on a loose sheet labeled "Arts" in *Dossier Des Billettes* (AdS), where "Musique—Instruments" is listed among the "[Arts] Libéraux." Concerning the meaning of "arts" at this time, see Gille, *Histoire des techniques*, p. 1124.

[18] *Histoire*, 1702, p. 136. The entry indicates that there are more than sixty such instruments and names forty-eight of them, arranged in three categories: strings, winds, and percussion (a usual classification at the time). Carré is said to have begun his study "par le Clavecin, parce qu'il est d'un grand usage, & le plus parfait des instrumens à cordes" (p. 137).

[19] Presentation: 15 novembre 1724 (*assemblée publique*, Reg., T. 43, f. 315-322v; printed in *Mémoires*, 1724, pp. 215-226; summarized in *Histoire*, 1724, pp. 90-92); reread 25 novembre 1724 (Reg., T. 43, f. 351).

an art, the rules of theory derived from the one should lead naturally to the other. He further suggests that it would be far simpler to seek these rules directly from musical practice rather than from speculation, believing that music of his time had reached an advanced state of perfection and logic:[20]

> Les Musiciens nous ont trouvé les faits; c'est à nous à tâcher de les expliquer.

> [The musicians have provided us with the results; it remains for us to try to explain them.]

For Maupertuis, these rules extend equally to the structure of musical instruments, which he undertook to investigate in his *mémoire*. The study, limited to string instruments with wooden resonators, attempts to establish a relationship between the isochronous fibers of which resonating bodies are composed and the vibrations produced by the strings stretched across those bodies—a relationship which, although developed empirically over a long period of time, he believed to be verifiable through physical law.[21]

Maupertuis was not alone in his study. Instruments appear frequently in musical investigations at the Academy—in studies on acoustics, tuning systems, notation, time-measuring devices, harmony, and even music therapy. But it is in their capacity as *machines et inventions*—presented for academic approval and, thereby, Royal Privilege—that instruments served directly as subjects for investigation and are especially evident in surviving records. Of 121 proposals in music identified as having been submitted to the Academy for approbation between the years 1704 and 1792, 63 (or 52%) are classified as *machines et inventions*. Of these, 48 (or 40% of the whole) deal with musical instruments (see Appendix II).[22]

---

[20] *Mémoires*, 1724, pp. 215-216.

[21] See the critical review by Pierre Brunet, *Maupertuis*; T. II: *L'Oeuvre et sa place dans la pensée scientifique et philosophique du XVIIIe siècle* (Paris: A. Blanchard, 1929), pp. 280-288.

[22] Comparative statistics on other types and numbers of instruments presented to the Academy are lacking; see further, Salomon-Bayet, "Un préambule théorique," pp. 242-243, and Shelby T. McCloy, *French Inventions of the Eighteenth Century* (Lexington: Univ. of Kentucky Press, 1952), pp. 192-193. In Appendix II, it is worth noting that 61 different academicians served on committees to review 121 proposals in music, accepting 281 separate assignments. Among them, those who stand out as being especially active are Fouchy, Mairan, Vandermonde, and d'Alembert; indeed, one or more of them served on no less than 84 of the total

The process by which review took place, for any machine or invention, had crystallized by the early part of the century.[23] Normally, a formal request was presented by the builder or inventor to the entire assembly, either through the mediation of a sympathetic member of the Academy, or directly by the secretary; nonmembers were not permitted to attend meetings of the assembly or to address the group, except through invitation. The request was usually supported by a written description of the instrument or novelty proposed, and often by a working model as well. On occasion, the builder or designer would be invited to make his own presentation and, as applicable, arrange a demonstration. In music, this demonstration frequently included a performance.[24]

If the initial reaction of the group was favorable, a committee was appointed from among its members to study the proposal in detail, draft a report, and present its recommendations for consideration at a later meeting. This report, once acted upon by the entire body, was entered into the minutes of the session at which it was read and constituted an official document. As needed, an extract of the report was prepared by the secretary, in the form of a certificate, intended to serve purposes outside the Academy.

Depending on the nature and complexity of the initial proposal, the entire process could be completed within one week, although

committees appointed, and the sum of their assignments comprises over half the total nominations.

[23] Concerning development of the process, see Hahn, *The Anatomy*, pp. 22-24.

[24] While the minute-books often indicate that musical instruments were demonstrated before the Academy, and more often for the examining committee, they are usually silent on the nature of those demonstrations. Occasionally, identification is provided for performers brought in to participate in the presentation, such as "M. Landrieu," who played a model of Marius's *clavecin à maillets* for the assembly on 13 janvier 1717 (Reg., T. 36, f. 5); "M. Le Clerc," who performed L'Epine's *forté-piano organisé* in 1772, on separate occasions, for both the entire body and the committee (reported 14 août; Reg., T. 91, f. 287-291); and Joubert's young daughter, who played his *vielle organisée* for the group on 15 juin 1768 ("Extrait des Registres," in *pochette de séance*). Péronard's pedal-harpsichord was performed on 24 juillet 1779 (Reg., T. 98, f. 236v-237) by "M. Tapperet [= Jean-François Tapray], organiste de l'Ecole Royale Militaire, . . . après quoi, les trois enfants de M. Péronard ont exécuté un morceau dans lequel l'un jouoit du clavecin, le second de la harpe et l'autre du violon"; and the novel harp mechanism devised by Krumpholtz was demonstrated by his wife on 17 novembre 1787 (reported 21 novembre; Reg., T. 106, f. 382v-383), in a performance of several of his compositions, which he accompanied "à la fois avec le violon et avec son nouveau piano-forté contrebasse qui se touche avec le pied."

most took longer, occasionally as long as one year. Delays were often the result of clarifications or changes required by the examining committee in the invention or proposal before approval could be granted. Some were not resolved for several years, and still others were either never acted upon, or else withdrawn by their initiators. Comparatively few proposals are recorded as not approved; indeed, the minutes are silent on the final disposition of many of them. Such silence often indicated tacit disapproval of a proposal; but it was generally preferred to a formal rejection by the Academy, which could have very serious consequences on the future of both the project and its designer.

Musical instruments were proposed for academic review by 48 individuals, some of whom are relatively well known—such as Pascal Taskin, François-André Danican Philidor, Georges Cousineau, and Jean-Benjamin de Laborde—and others are unknown. By far their greatest number (29) were professional builders, approximately half of whom resided in Paris, one-quarter were from the provinces, and one-quarter were foreigners. Small groups of performer-teachers (8), musical amateurs (4), and engineers (3) were also represented, as were regular members of the Academy (4). Several of the builders did not restrict themselves to instruments of music and were also associated with discoveries or inventions in other fields (e.g., Marius, Pelletier, and Vaucanson).

The novelties proposed by these individuals were widely varied, and they generally reflected trends of the time. Instruments were redesigned to make them more efficient, to provide them with expanded performance capabilities, to reduce their costs of production, and to respond to the exigencies of travel, weather, or available space. Some builders were quick to take advantage of novel methods of construction and newly discovered materials or alloys in exercise of their craft; others responded directly to a growing public interest in novelty and to a changing aesthetic that demanded ever-new timbral, dynamic, and mechanical effects. Instruments were adapted to the requirements of experimental tuning systems; simple instruments were made more sophisticated, while complex ones were simplified; and widely differing types were combined, seemingly willy-nilly—both to demonstrate the technical prowess of the builder and to offer new qualities of sound to a receptive public.

All in all, the musical instruments proposed to the Academy

bespoke a growing market for such instruments in the eighteenth century, as well as an intensified competition among builders, and increased practical and technical concerns within the industry. The overriding interests of the great majority of builders or inventors who sought academic approbation were manifestly practical ones. For each of them, the value of a Royal Privilege was expressed in his enhanced reputation as a builder, in growing public recognition of his work, and ultimately, in sales of his product.

Musical Instruments—A Survey of Proposals

There are only a small number of references to musical instruments at the Academy before 1700. The earliest recorded one occurs in 1678, when J.-B. Cartois (described as a "Maître facteur de clavessins à Paris," but otherwise unknown) submitted a new type of harpsichord jack made with metal parts, of which the tongue was designed to return under its own weight.[25] Cartois returned eighteen years later, in 1696, to present a hurdy-gurdy ("un roüet à filer") capable of performing part-music.[26] Few details of either invention are given. The only other instruments recorded as proposed to the Academy during the seventeenth century are different forms of the monochord, designed by Louis Carré[27] and Etienne Loulié,[28] as aids in tuning the harpsichord.

Musical instruments are first given special attention at the Academy early in the eighteenth century, chiefly through the achieve-

[25] Presentation: 5 février 1678 (Reg., T. 7, f. 136): ". . . l'invention consiste principalement en ce que la languette, et la mortaise sont de métail, qu'au lieu de la plume il se sert d'un ressort d'acier, et qu'au lieu du ressort qui est ordinairement de soye de pourceau, il employe la pesanteur de la languette."

[26] Presentation: 16 mai 1696 (Reg., T. 15, f. 63): ". . . un roüet à filer chantant trois airs avec toutes les parties."

[27] Referred to above, in Chap. II, The Second Generation. The monochord by Carré described in Machines, I, 101-102, is designated as submitted "avant 1699," but is not recorded in the Registres.

[28] Presentation: 4 juillet 1699 (Reg., T. 18bis, f. 400); see Histoire, 1699, p. 121. Two varieties of Loulié's instrument, both called sonomètre, are described in Machines, I, 187-189. A more detailed description of both types was published by Loulié in Nouveau système de musique . . . avec la discription et l'usage du sonomètre (Paris: C. Ballard, 1698). Further on Loulié, see the author's "Etienne Loulié as a Music Theorist," Journal of the American Musicological Society, XVIII (1965), 70-72; and Richard T. Semmens, Etienne Loulié as Music Theorist: An Analysis of Items in Ms. Paris, fonds fr.n.a. 6355 (Ph.D. dissertation, Stanford Univ., 1980).

(49)

ments of Jean Marius (d. 1720),[29] who participated in its work over a period of two decades and was subsequently appointed adjunct mechanician in 1718. Marius had a degree in law and was skilled in mathematics, but it is as an inventor with a fertile imagination and a wide range of interests that he is best known. Outside of music, his inventions include a folding umbrella, a collapsible tent, a method for waterproofing cloth, a machine to sow seeds, a water pump, and an improvement to the pocket watch.

In music, Marius designed a portable organ,[30] experimented with construction of a bowed keyboard instrument,[31] sought to adapt pedals to the harpsichord for control of dynamics,[32] and contributed to the acoustical discoveries of Joseph Sauveur.[33] However, he is generally recognized for two principal novelties—the *clavecin brisé* (folding harpsichord), approved in 1700, and the *clavecin à maillets* (an early hammer-action keyboard instrument), approved in 1716. The first of these is a small harpsichord capable of being folded into several sections to make it portable. Marius maintained that, although portable and small in size, the instrument kept its tune well and required minimum maintenance. Particularly noteworthy in its design is the novel use of metal jacks, and of strings that are double-wound and of gold or silver. The *clavecin brisé* achieved a degree of popularity on the continent during most of the eighteenth century, and several examples survive.[34]

[29] Various documents relating to Marius, most in his personal hand, survive in *Dossier Marius* (AdS), from which the information below is principally derived. See further, Colombe Samoyault-Verlet, *Les facteurs de clavecins parisiens* (Paris: Heugel, 1966), pp. 58-59 and Document 17.

[30] Described in *Machines*, III, 91, and in *Dossier Marius*.

[31] Announced in *Histoire*, 1742, p. 147.

[32] Described in a letter to Sauveur, read to the Academy 21 février 1714 (*plumitif de 1714*, by Réaumur, AdS), and in *Dossier Marius*.

[33] Acknowledged by Sauveur in his *mémoire* "Rapport des sons . . . ," *Mémoires*, 1713, pp. 349-350.

[34] Described in *Machines*, I, 193-194; the illustration accompanying the description is reproduced in Geneviève Thibaut, Jean Jenkins, and Josiane Bran-Ricci, *Eighteenth Century Musical Instruments: France and Britain* (London: Eyre and Spottiswoode, 1973), pp. 8-9 (incorrectly dated 1715, for 1700).

Surviving instruments are listed in Samoyault-Verlet, *Les facteurs*, pp. 58-59, and Donald H. Boalch, *Makers of the Harpsichord and Clavichord, 1440-1840*, 2d ed. (Oxford: Clarendon Press, 1974), p. 110. For published descriptions and illustrations of these instruments, see Ghislaine Juramie, *Histoire du piano* (Paris: Editions

The *clavecin à maillets*, however, did not fare as well. Marius sub-mitted several different models of this innovation to the Academy. In all of them, the jack was replaced by a wooden block or peg which, by means of a simple mechanism, struck the string directly to sound it—either from above or below. One of the versions has the strings arranged vertically, at right angles to the keys (that is, a *clavicytherium*), and another combines both hammer- and pluck-ing-action in one instrument, either or both of which could be activated by means of a register.[35]

It has been suggested[36] that Marius may have been stimulated to experiment with the use of hammers in a harpsichord by François Cuisinié, who proposed a *clavecin-vielle* to the Academy in 1708. That instrument was intended to improve ("perfectionné") the hurdy-gurdy by making it self-standing and by providing it with a pedal to revolve the resined-wheel that sounds the strings, thereby freeing the player's hands. The keyboard action, however, was more similar to that of a clavichord than to that of either a harpsichord or a piano, since it used a tangent (called "maillet") at the end of the key, not to activate the string but rather to deter-mine its pitch and to control the quality of its sound.[37] In a later version of the *vielle*, reviewed in 1734, Cuisinié returned it to a more traditional size and action while extending its pitch range.[38]

Prisma, 1947), p. 63; Philip James, *Early Keyboard Instruments* (London: P. Davies, 1930; repr., London: Tabard Press, 1970), p. 126; Raymond Russell, *The Harpsi-chord and Clavichord*, 2d ed. (New York: W. W. Norton, 1973), illustration no. 45; and Franz Josef Hirt, *Stringed Keyboard Instruments, 1440-1880* (Boston: Boston Book and Art Shop, 1968), pp. 290-291. See also, Sibyl Marcuse, *A Survey of Musical Instruments* (New York: Harper & Row, 1975), p. 270.

[35] Described in *Machines*, III, 83-90; reproduction of illustrations accompanying the description are in Rosamond E. M. Harding, *The Piano-Forte* (Cambridge: Cambridge Univ. Press, 1933; repr., New York: Da Capo Press, 1973), pp. 12-15. No surviving instruments are known. See further, Boalch, *Makers*, pp. 110-111; Samoyault-Verlet, *Les facteurs*, pp. 58-59; and Marcuse, *A Survey*, p. 322.

[36] In Harding, *The Piano-Forte*, p. 11; and Russell, *The Harpsichord and Clavichord*, p. 57.

[37] Presentation: 14 janvier 1708 (Reg., T. 27, f. 7v); Report (La Hire and Des Billettes); 28 janvier 1708 (Reg., T. 27, f. 19v). Described in *Machines*, II, 155-156, and noted in *Histoire*, 1708, p. 142. See further, for Cuisinié, Boalch, *Makers*, p. 31, and for the instrument, Marcuse, *A Survey*, pp. 314 and 321.

[38] Presentation: 23 juillet 1729 (Reg., T. 48, f. 184); Report (Mairan and Maupertuis): 19 mai 1734 (Reg., T. 53, f. 141-141v; original and copy in *pochette de séance*, together with a sketch and brief description of the mechanism of the proposed instrument; condensed report in *Histoire*, 1734; p. 105).

III. *MACHINES ET INVENTIONS*

Whatever the source of Marius's interest in a hammer-action stringed keyboard instrument—and in spite of the advantages it offered of a simple mechanism, ease of repair, and control over dynamics—the novelty had no currency in France before the late 1760s and 1770s. The Academy had to wait almost a half-century for builders to begin to occupy themselves, once again, with the hammer action. During the interim, however, and until the final decade of the eighteenth century, the harpsichord continued to provide instrument makers with new design possibilities.[39]

In 1727, Thevenard, a builder from Bordeaux, proposed a novel harpsichord jack, in which the tongue and plectrum were of a single piece of molded copper or brass, capable of falling back by itself.[40] Several years afterward, in 1732, Louis-Charles Bellot, a harpsichord maker in Paris, proposed a new bridge[41] designed to give "the same speaking-length to each pair of unison strings," thereby securing "greater uniformity of tone."[42]

Later in the century, in 1766, the musician-inventor de Virbès (Virebez) presented a harpsichord (known as *clavecin acoustique* or *céleste*) whose main feature was its ability to imitate an unusually large variety of different instruments; he also equipped it with an expressive device—knee-levers (*genouillères*) to control dynamics.[43]

[39] See the "Abstracts of French Inventions," in Hubbard, *Three Centuries*, pp. 323-325, which is comprised principally of innovations to the harpsichord presented at the Academy.

[40] Presentation: 23 août 1727 (Reg., T. 46, f. 294v); Report (Mairan and Maupertuis): 30 août 1727 (Reg., T. 46, f. 296-296v; description of instrument in *pochette de séance*). The invention is noted in *Histoire*, 1727, p. 142, and included in *Machines*, V, 11-12. Contemporary reference in *Mercure de France*, novembre 1727 (pp. 2495-2496). See further, Marcuse, *A Survey*, p. 272.

[41] Report (Mairan and Maupertuis): 12 mars 1732 (Reg., T. 51, f. 116-116v). Noted in *Histoire*, 1732, pp. 118-119. For Bellot, see Boalch, *Makers*, p. 11, and Samoyault-Verlet, *Les facteurs*, p. 16.

[42] Boalch, *Makers*, p. 11.

[43] Presentation: 9 juillet 1766 (Reg., T. 85, f. 225v); Report (Mairan and Fouchy): 9 août 1766 (Reg., T. 85, f. 270v-273v; original in *pochette de séance*, condensed in *Histoire*, 1766, pp. 161-162). Contemporary references in *Mercure de France*, janvier 1768 (pp. 207-208), mai 1768 (pp. 177-178), mai 1771 (pp. 200-201), avril 1773 (pp. 194-197), juin 1776 (pp. 208-209); *Journal de Musique*, mars 1770 (pp. 43-45), avril 1770 (pp. 34-36); *Journal de Paris*, 26 août 1785 (p. 985); *L'Avantcoureur*, 25 août 1766 (p. 532), 2 avril 1770 (pp. 218-219), 11 mars 1771 (pp. 148-149); *Almanach Dauphin*, année 1777 (p. 46). See further, Rowland Wright, *Dictionnaire des instruments de musique* (London: Battley Bros., 1941), pp. 37-38 and 134; and Hubbard, *Three Centuries*, p. 325. On Virbès, see Boalch, *Makers*, p. 186; Samoyault-

And still later, in 1782, the well-known builder Jacques Germain (Goermans) produced a *clavecin* with divided keys, to allow for the different sizes of semitones in a tuning system devised by Jean-Benjamin de Laborde and argued by the theorist, Pierre-Joseph Roussier.[44] Reference should also be made to the *mémoire*, "Sur un clavier à double feuilles et sur un cilindre où l'on peut noter à volonté toutes sortes d'airs," read to the Academy in 1776 by Christophe II Chyquelier, the harpsichord builder and "garde des instruments du Roi." A committee was appointed to review the invention (undoubtedly an altered harpsichord), but no report was presented.[45]

Notwithstanding such innovations, it was in combination with other instruments (as an *instrument organisé*) that the harpsichord proved to be one of the principal means by which experimentation in the design of musical instruments took place at the Academy. Desirous of altering the instrument to suit the changing tastes of the time, particularly for sustained and expressive effects, builders were drawn to the bowed strings, the organ, and the forte-piano for sound qualities especially adaptable to the harpsichord.

The earliest of the bowed keyboard instruments proposed to the Academy was a singular *clavecin organisé* presented in 1742 by Jean

Verlet, *Les facteurs*, pp. 75-76; and Ernst Ludwig Gerber, *Historisch-biographisches Lexicon der Tonkünstler* (Leipzig: Breitkopf, 1790-1792), II, cols. 733-734. See also the description, by a present-day performer, of two eighteenth-century harpsichords fitted with knee-levers, in David Fuller (ed.), Armand-Louis Couperin, *Selected Works for the Keyboard, Part I: Music for Two Keyboard Instruments* (Madison: A-R Editions, 1975), pp. xvii-xviii.

[44] Presentation I (Laborde): 6 mars 1782 (Reg., T. 101, f. 33-33v); Presentation II (Roussier): 13 mars 1782 (Reg., T. 101, f. 38v); Report (Fouchy, d'Alembert, and Vandermonde): 8 mai 1782 (Reg., T. 101, f. 85v-86; original in *pochette de séance*). Roussier's *Mémoire sur le nouveau clavecin chromatique de M. de Laborde* (Paris: P.-D. Pierres, 1782; repr., Geneva: Minkoff, 1972), describes the tuning system which the new *clavecin* was built to accommodate, and only incidentally, the instrument; it includes a letter by Laborde, dated 9 janvier 1782 and addressed to the Academy, petitioning a hearing. The idea for such an instrument occurs earlier, in Laborde's *Essai sur la musique ancienne et moderne* (Paris: E. Onfroy, 1780; repr., New York: AMS Press, 1978), I, 343-345; concerning a reference by Laborde to still earlier Italian models, see Hubbard, *Three Centuries*, p. 36. The instrument is referred to in *Almanach musical*, 1782 (VII, 50). Further on Germain, see Boalch, *Makers*, p. 53, and Samoyault-Verlet, *Les facteurs*, p. 45.

[45] Presentation: 12 juin 1776 (Reg., T. 95, f. 183v-184; committee named: d'Alembert, Vandermonde, and Fouchy). For Chyquelier, see Boalch, *Makers*, p. 23, and Samoyault-Verlet, *Les facteurs*, p. 25.

III. *MACHINES ET INVENTIONS*

Le Voir, *valet de chambre* to the household of Jean-Jacques Amelot de Chaillou—an imposing personage who was controller-general of France and secretary of state for foreign affairs. It was through the intervention of Amelot de Chaillou that the Academy (of which he was also an honorary member) was enjoined to examine the unusual instrument of Le Voir, and it appeared particularly enthusiastic to do so.

Le Voir's instrument was in the shape of a harpsichord, the resonating box of which, however, contained a viola and a violoncello. By a complicated mechanism of movable bridges, of circular resonators (called "archets") propelled by a pedal device, and of pulleys activated by a keyboard, it was possible to approximate (according to the report) a group of string instruments playing together ("un concert de Symphonie").[46]

Twenty years later, Didier Le Gay, identified as a machinist in contemporary documents, submitted another type of bowed keyboard instrument that he called a *clavicordium*. Its resonating chamber was a hollow cylinder to which were fastened strings, set into motion by means of a resined wheel controlled by a pedal. A keyboard regulated the choice of strings to be sounded and (by pressure of touch) the dynamic level. A pedal-board was joined to the instrument, as was a second manual with its own set of gut strings activated by means of jacks furnished with hard-leather plectra. When plucked, the instrument was said to have sounded like a theorbo, mandolin, or guitar, and when bowed, like a viol.[47]

[46] Presentation I (a written petition from Amelot de Chaillou, read by Maupertuis): 11 mai 1742 (Reg., T. 61, p. 202); Presentation II (Le Voir): 14 juillet 1742 (Reg., T. 61, p. 316); Report (Mairan, Hellot, and Fouchy): 21 juillet 1742 (Reg., T. 61, pp. 345-348; original in *pochette de séance*, reprinted exactly in *Machines*, VII, 186-189, and in slightly altered form in *Histoire*, 1742, pp. 146-150). Description of instrument in *Machines*, VII, 183-186, largely reproduced in Curt Sachs, *Real-Lexicon der Musik-instrumente* (Berlin: J. Bard, 1913; new ed., New York: Dover, 1964), pp. 360-361. AN, FN[12] 993, contains documents related to Le Voir's instrument, and to formal solicitation for a Royal Privilege. Further on Le Voir, see Samoyault-Verlet, *Les facteurs*, p. 56; and on his instrument, see L. Dussieux and E. Soulié (eds.), *Mémoires du Duc de Luynes sur la cour de Louis XV (1735-1758)*, vol. 13 (Paris: Firmin-Didot, 1863), pp. 73-75.

[47] Presentation: 22 mai 1762 (Reg., T. 81, f. 209v); Report (Mairan and Fouchy): 16 juin 1762 (Reg., T. 81, f. 221-225v; original and extract in *pochette de séance*); condensed report in *Histoire*, 1762, pp. 191-192, reproduced in Sachs, *Real-Lexicon*, p. 361. Contemporary references in *Mercure de France*, août 1762 (pp. 155-156); *L'Avantcoureur*, 5 juillet and 30 août 1762 (pp. 425 and 554), 8 août 1763 (pp. 499-

Fifty years after the presentation of Le Voir's instrument, and reminiscent of its construction, was Anselme Montu's *violon harmonique* of 1792. Its case resembled that of a harpsichord, but it contained the resonating boxes of a treble- and a bass-violin, over which were placed sixteen bridges supporting fifty-eight strings. Sound was produced by a circular bow, set into motion by a pedal whose speed was controlled by a knee-lever. A keyboard mechanism selected the strings to be sounded.[48]

The *claviorganum* (a combination harpsichord-organ) is represented by several proposals at the Academy, the earliest being the *clavecin organisé* presented in 1765 by Joseph-Antoine Berger, a performer-builder from Grenoble. Berger's instrument combined a harpsichord with a small reed organ, each having its own manual—the two being capable of sounding together through coupling. Its most novel feature was the use of two knee-levers to control dynamics, for the design of which Berger was especially commended.[49]

A second such instrument was submitted in 1770 by another performer-builder, Obert, from Boulogne-sur-mer. His instrument, called *pneumacorde*, had its case set vertically, at right angles

---

501), 4 juin 1764 (p. 355), 27 mai 1765 (p. 322). See further, Marcuse, *A Survey*, p. 315 (except read "1762" for "1760").

[48] Presentation: 8 août 1792 (Reg., T. 109B, p. 239); Report (Lagrange, Vandermonde, and Haüy): 18 août 1792 (Reg., T. 109B, pp. 244-248; original in *pochette de séance*). Instrument is described in *Bulletin des sciences, par la Société philomathique de Paris*, ser. 1, 3 vols. (Paris, 1791-1805), I, 52. Montu, who identifies himself as a "membre de l'Académie des Philarmoniques de Bologne," participated in activities of the restructured Institut National des Sciences et des Arts after the Revolution, as both theorist and inventor; see the *Procès-verbaux des séances de l'Académie des Sciences*, I (1910), 441, 464, 571; II (1912), 476; III (1913), 159. For a review of instruments he subsequently designed, see Adolphe Le Doulcet de Pontécoulant, *Organographie, Essai sur la facture instrumentale* (Paris: Castel, 1861; repr., Amsterdam: Frits Knuf, 1972), II, 81-84.

[49] Presentation: 10 juillet 1765 (Reg., T. 84, f. 298); Report (Vaucanson, Le Roy, and Fouchy): 27 juillet 1765 (Reg., T. 84, f. 327v-329v; original and extract in *pochette de séance*; condensed in *Histoire*, 1765, pp. 138-139). Contemporary references in *L'Avantcoureur*, 12 décembre 1763 (pp. 790-791), 1 juillet 1764 (pp. 393-394); *Annonces, affiches et avis divers*, 23 octobre 1765 (p. 171); *Almanach Dauphin, année 1777* (pp. 45-46); *Art du faiseur d'instruments de musique et lutherie*, vol. IV, pt. 1. of *Arts et métiers mécaniques*, in *Encyclopédie méthodique* (Paris, 1785; repr., Geneva: Minkoff, 1972), pp. 11 and 13. See also, Pontécoulant, *Organographie*, I, 292; and references listed in Hubbard, *Three Centuries*, p. 324, and in Wright, *Dictionnaire*, p. 38. For Berger, see Boalch, *Makers*, p. 12.

to the keyboard. It was large, standing over eight feet in height, and was placed on rollers. Its one manual controlled several harpsichord and organ stops, which could be coupled. Regulation of dynamics was a prime feature of this instrument, apparently through use of a pedal.[50]

Examples of the harpsichord-piano, a chordophone whose strings are activated both by quill and by hammer, occur throughout the century at the Academy. The earliest presentation of such an instrument was that of Jean Marius in 1716, mentioned earlier. More significant, however, was the one submitted in 1759 by a builder named Weltman or Veltman (possibly Andries Veltman, a Dutch instrument maker), which had several novel features. In addition to jacks, it provided a set of hammers which could be used to strike the strings from beneath. There were knee-levers, enabling the performer to augment or diminish the volume of sound gradually, and a set of dampers was added. It also included a carillon struck by hammers and worked from the keyboard by means of a register. In its report, the committee identified a certain "M. Dumontier," in the service of the count of Clermont, as having originated the ideas of the hammer action and the knee-lever, both of which Veltman had adapted to a harpsichord owned by the count some two years earlier. Accordingly, approval for these two innovations was given to Veltman, not for their invention, but rather for their design and implementation.[51]

In 1779, the Parisian builder François-Balthazard Péronard presented a harpsichord to which he added a pedal using hammer action. The pedal-board of 2½ octaves sounded a set of gut strings

[50] Presentation: 7 juillet 1770 (Reg., T. 89, f. 194); Report (Vaucanson, Le Roy, and Fouchy): 18 juillet 1770 (Reg., T. 89, f. 211-212v; original in *pochette de séance*). Contemporary references in *Mercure de France*, avril 1768 (pp. 192-194); *L'Avantcoureur*, 25 juillet 1763 (pp. 473-474); *Journal de Musique*, juillet 1770 (pp. 42-44); *Annonces, affiches et avis divers*, 19 septembre 1770 (p. 151). On Obert, see Boalch, *Makers*, p. 117.

[51] Presentation I: 16 juin 1759 (Reg., T. 78, f. 474v-475); Presentation II: 20 juin 1759 (*plumitif de 1759*; letter of Dumontier, laying claim to Veltman's discovery, read to assembly); Report (Mairan and Fouchy): 14 août 1759 (Reg., T. 78bis, f. 669-672; extract in *pochette de séance*; condensed in *Histoire*, 1759, pp. 241-242, of which there is a partial English trans., in Edwin M. Ripin, "Expressive Devices Applied to the Eighteenth-Century Harpsichord," *The Organ Yearbook*, I [1970], 78-79). On Veltman, see Boalch, *Makers*, pp. 184, 189; and Alan Curtis, "Dutch Harpsichord Makers," *Tijdschrift van de Vereniging voor Nederlandse Muziekgeschiedenis*, XIX (1960-1961), 61-62. See also, Marcuse, *A Survey*, pp. 322 and 350.

in its own, separate case placed beneath the harpsichord; dynamics could be controlled by varying the foot pressure, and its sound was judged to resemble that of the bass strings of a harp. The report notes, as an advantage of the instrument, that it was capable of performing music originally intended for pedal organ.[52]

Interest in the development of the forte-piano as an independent instrument at the Academy was not as pronounced as that of the harpsichord, but is nevertheless of note and takes place only during the final quarter of the century. In 1776, the celebrated musician François-André Danican Philidor was invited by the Academy to demonstrate a forte-piano whose upper register consisted of steel strings that had been blued—that is, heat treated until they turned blue in color, a process that strengthened their surface. An experiment in England, based on research by Julien Le Roy (the royal watchmaker in France), determined that strings so treated had a richer sound than untreated ones. Philidor had learned of the experiment and had ordered a harpsichord from London supplied with such strings; it was this instrument that he demonstrated to the Academy. No committee was assigned to report on the instrument, but the secretary did enter into the minute-books that the sound of the instrument strung with blued strings "appeared noticeably sweeter and as well sustained" as one supplied with untreated strings.[53]

The most extensive report on a forte-piano at the Academy is that given to the innovations presented by Pascal Taskin in 1788. These include bi-chord lacing of unison strings; elimination of tuning pins in favor of screw-regulated wrest-pins; a means of securing the space between the soundboard and the wrest-plank; the use of a mechanism to regulate the key action; a special type of adjustable jack, called *clapette*, used to transfer the key motion to the hammer; a unique construction of the hammer, to which the damper is attached; as well as smaller details dealing with the

---

[52] Presentation: 24 juillet 1779 (Reg., T. 98, f. 236v-237); Report (Bochart de Saron, Vandermonde, and Laplace): 14 août 1779 (Reg., T. 98, f. 252-252v; original in *pochette de séance*). Contemporary references in *Almanach musical*, 1782 (VII, 49-50); *Encyclopédie méthodique: Musique*, I (Paris: Panckoucke, 1791; repr., New York: Da Capo Press, 1971), I, 287. On Péronard, see Boalch, *Makers*, p. 119; and Samoyault-Verlet, *Les facteurs*, p. 61. See also, Hubbard, *Three Centuries*, p. 112.

[53] Presentation: 20 juillet 1776 (Reg., T. 95, f. 233v). Contemporary description in *Almanach musical*, 1777 (III, 31-32).

nature of the peg screws, the method of constructing a lute stop, and determining for each string its most efficient point of hammer contact. All told, the examining committee commended "M. Pascal" for having simplified the forte-piano mechanism, while providing the performer with more control over the instrument, which was judged to have an excellent quality of sound.[54]

In 1791, a certain "M. Schmidt" recommended several minor changes in the novel bi-chord stringing technique proposed by Taskin,[55] who, himself, returned the following year with a new proposal adapting his own stringing technique to both the harpsichord and the square piano.[56] And in 1792, Langevin de Falaise proposed a lightweight forte-piano, which could be separated into two parts for ease of transportation. Its strings were contained in a triangular case arranged perpendicular to the keyboard. The hammer action was from above, and no dampers were used.[57] Finally, mention should be made of the "piano-forté" presented to

[54] Presentation: 22 novembre 1788 (Reg., T. 107, f. 267v); Report (Vandermonde, Haüy, and Dietrich): 13 décembre 1788 (Reg., T. 107, f. 280v-285; original in *pochette de séance*, largely reproduced in *Encyclopédie méthodique: Musique*, I, 288). Announced in *Journal de Paris*, 19 novembre 1788 (p. 1384). See the description and illustration of a forte-piano by Taskin, dated 1788, in Thibaut, Jenkins, and Bran-Ricci, *Eighteenth Century Musical Instruments*, no. 7. On Taskin's innovations, see further, Harding, *The Piano-Forte*, pp. 74-75.

[55] Presentation: 16 mars 1791 (Reg., T. 109, p. 300); Report (Vandermonde and Haüy): read 20 juillet 1791 (Reg., T. 109, p. 381), transcribed in minutes of 23 juillet 1791 (Reg., T. 109, pp. 388-390). Identification of builder is complicated by the various spellings of his name in the *Registres*: Schmidt, Schmitz, Smith—all related to the same invention. In addition, he is confused with a "Schmidt" who designed a hydraulic water pump during that same period. Nevertheless, his invention is attributed to "Le Sr. Schmidt, facteur de clavecin & de forté-piano, rue St.-André-des-Arts, passage du Commerce," in *Journal de Paris*, 10 février 1789 (pp. 179-180). On 2 décembre 1789 (Reg., T. 108, f. 229), a "M. Schmitz" presented "un clavecin organisé," to examine which a committee was appointed (Vandermonde and Sabatier), but no report survives.

[56] Presentation: 4 août 1792 (Reg., T. 109B, p. 237); Report (Vandermonde and Pingré): 5 septembre 1792 (Reg., T. 109B, pp. 283-284; original and extract in *pochette de séance*, which also contains a letter of petition by Taskin, dated 8 août 1792).

[57] Presentation I (an inquiry): 22 janvier 1791 (Reg., T. 109, p. 279); Presentation II: 16 mai 1792 (Reg., T. 109B, p. 151); Report (Pingré and Haüy): 23 mai 1792 (Reg., T. 109B, p. 158; original in *pochette de séance*). Langevin brought a "seconde édition de son harpo-piano pyramidal" to the Institut National after the Revolution, in 1800-1801, but a report is lacking; see *Procès-verbaux des séances de l'Académie des Sciences*, II, 274, 278, 357, 374.

the Academy in 1784 by a builder named Bosch. While a committee was named to review the proposal, no report was given, nor are any details of the instrument available.[58]

There is one example of an *instrument organisé*, that combined forte-piano with organ, brought to the Academy. It was proposed in 1772 by Adrien de l'Epine, the Parisian builder, and joined together a hammer-action chordophone with a small flute organ, each having its own manual. The instrument was supplied with a pedal-board and was entirely enclosed in a case resembling a piece of furniture. Like other new keyboard instruments of the time, it, too, featured a means of controlling dynamics, through use of a pedal device.[59]

L'Epine's instrument is described in detail, in volume IV of Dom François Bedos de Celle's *L'Art du facteur d'orgues*,[60] the one musical work published by the Academy in its series, *Description des Arts et Métiers*, mentioned earlier.[61] Dom Bedos deals also with

[58] Presentation: 20 novembre 1784 (Reg., T. 103, f. 243; committee named: Pingré, Vandermonde, Sabatier, and Condorcet). For Bosch, see Pierre, *Les facteurs*, p. 141.

[59] Presentation: 22 juillet 1772 (Reg., T. 91, f. 260; in the *pochette* are a petition by the author and a description of the proposed instrument); Report (Duhamel du Monceau, Montalembert, and Fouchy): 14 août 1772 (Reg., T. 91, f. 287-291; original in *pochette de séance*, condensed in *Histoire*, 1772, I, 109). A descriptive entry for the *instrument organisé* is found in the *plumitif de 1772* (22 juillet) by Lavoisier (AdS); see also, Marcuse, *A Survey*, p. 306. Concerning l'Epine, see Félix Raugel, *Recherches sur quelques maîtres de l'ancienne facture d'orgues française* (Paris: H. Hérelle, Fortemps, [1925?]), p. 15; and Norbert Dufourcq, *Le livre de l'orgue français, 1589-1789*, I (Paris: A. and J. Picard, 1971), passim.

A presentation on 23 août 1721 (Reg., T. 40, f. 239) by "Mr. de L'Epine . . . un nouvel instrument à clavier," for which there is no report (although a committee was appointed: Reneaume, Mairan, and Vaillant), may refer to Adrien de l'Epine's uncle, Adrian, for whom, see Dufourcq, *Le livre de l'orgue*, item no. 463.

[60] François Bedos de Celles, *L'Art du facteur d'orgues*, 4 vols, (Paris: L. F. Delatour, 1766-1778); repr., Kassel: Baerenreiter, 1963-1966; English trans. by C. Ferguson, 2 vols. (Raleigh, N.C.: Sunbury Press, 1977). L'Epine's *piano-forté organisé* is described in vol. IV, 634-640, and plates 130-133.

[61] Bedos de Celles (1709-1779) was charged by the Academy as early as 1760 with writing his organ treatise; a letter dated 7 décembre 1760 (in *Dossier Bedos de Celles*, AdS) deals with early thoughts on the contents of the work. On 27 juillet 1763 (Reg., T. 82, f. 261v), the treatise was announced to the assembly; on 23 décembre 1766 (Reg., T. 85, f. 350), the group approved a motion to insert an *Avertissement* at the beginning of part one, noting the Academy's appreciation to the author, a draft of which was read on 10 janvier 1767 (Reg., T. 86, f. 5-5v); and on 18 février 1767 (Reg., T. 86, f. 34v), the first published part was distributed (a

two other types of *instruments organisés* involving the organ: the *clavecin organisé* and the *vielle-organisée*. For each of these types, he includes plans and a description; so far as can be determined, they appear to be of his own design.[62]

The organ is represented in yet other examples of *instruments organisés* at the Academy. In 1748, Jean-Baptiste Micault (Micot), a builder from Lyon, proposed a small flute organ in which a violin was placed horizontally, each instrument being played by its own keyboard. Four circular bows ("archets") of sheep's skin, one for each string, were stretched over the violin on movable pulleys and set in motion by a pedal. Frets, placed above the strings, were lowered by pressing the keys of the manual, which also set the bow in motion, thereby producing the desired sound. While the committee found the mechanism ingenious, it suggested that changes be made in the instrument to secure a more pleasant violin sound, since its sound was judged to be hard, dry, shrill, often weak, and uneven.[63]

An instrument combining a small flute organ and a *vielle* was presented in 1768 by Henri Joubert, a *maître luthier*, in which one keyboard controlled both instruments, either by themselves or coupled. The hand crank which turned the wheel to sound the *vielle* also pumped the bellows supplying air to the organ.[64]

list of those who received copies of this part is found in the *pochette de séance*). A review of part one appears in *Histoire*, 1767, pp. 180-181, of parts two and three in *Histoire*, 1770, pp. 110-111, and of part four in *Histoire*, 1778, p. 48. A report (Duhamel du Monceau and Fouchy) read on 20 décembre 1775 (Reg., T. 94, f. 287v-290v; original in *pochette de séance*), on the fourth and final part of the large work, comments specifically on that part, and generally on the entire treatise.

Bedos de Celles was named a corresponding member of the Paris Academy on 25 novembre 1767. Earlier, on 3 avril 1759, he was named an associate member of the Bordeaux Academy, to which he sent copies of his treatise as parts were published (see Bordeaux, Bibliothèque Municipale, MSS 828[21], letter No. 1, and 1696[28], letter No. 65). Further on Bedos de Celles, see the *Begleitwort* by C. Mahrenholz to the facsimile ed. of the treatise (which includes a bibliography); the "Translator's Preface" to the English ed. by C. Ferguson (I, xix-xxii); Barrière, *L'Académie de Bordeaux*, p. 44; Dufourcq, *Le livre de l'orgue*, passim; and Jean Martinod, *Répertoire des travaux des facteurs d'orgues* (Paris: Fischbacher, 1970), no. 87.

[62] The two instruments are described in vol. IV, 641-646, and plates 134-136. For a discussion of the *clavecin organisé*, see Hubbard, *Three Centuries*, pp. 131-132.

[63] Presentation: 27 mars 1748 (Reg., T. 67, p. 127); Report (Mairan, Vaucanson, and Fouchy): 11 mai 1748 (Reg., T. 67, pp. 251-252). For Micault, see Dufourcq, *Le livre de l'orgue*, passim: and Martinod, *Répertoire*, no. 996a.

[64] Presentation: 18 mai 1768 (Reg., T. 87, f. 90); Report (Mairan and Fouchy):

As a separate instrument—and aside from Dom Bedos's *L'Art du facteur d'orgues*—the organ was likewise treated as an object for innovative thought at the Academy. A travelling organ, which folded for portability, was proposed in 1756 by a builder from Bar-le-duc named Joinville;[65] an automatic water organ was presented in 1759 by Puisieux, a Parisian inventor;[66] and an Italian organist, Frederic (Federigo) Rigi, suggested a new means for determining the diameters of organ pipes in 1775.[67]

The *vielle*, too, had its champions. In 1773, the Parisian builder Jean Delaine adapted the mechanism of a *vielle* to the *pardessus de viole*, providing the instrument with twelve sympathetic strings, one for each degree of the chromatic scale.[68] Six years later, he

---

15 juin 1768 (Reg., T. 87, f. 130v-132v; original and extract in *pochette de séance*; condensed in *Histoire*, 1768, p. 130). Contemporary references in *Annonces, affiches et avis divers*, 22 décembre 1766 (p. 987); *Mercure de France*, mars 1769 (pp. 199-200); *L'Avantcoureur*, 20 février 1769 (p. 117); *Almanach Dauphin, année 1777* (among "Luthiers"). On Joubert, see Pierre, *Les facteurs*, p. 120.

[65] Presentation: 7 janvier 1756 (Reg., T. 75, p. 1); Report (Mairan and Fouchy): 12 mai 1756 (Reg., T. 75, pp. 245-248; original and extract in *pochette de séance*). A later reference to a *clavecin organisé* by Joinville appears in *Almanach musical*, 1777 (III, 33).

[66] Presentation: 17 janvier 1759 (Reg., T. 78, pp. 28-29); Committee named (Camus, Pingré, and Deparcieux): 20 janvier 1759 (Reg., T. 78, p. 62). The organ was but one "de plusieurs machines inventées par M. Puisieux," who is identified as "un des trente architectes expert jurés du Roy et Controlleur du bâtiment de l'Eglise de Sainte-Geneviève." The inventor may be the architect Jean-Baptiste de Puisieux, who published a treatise on geometry in 1765; see further, Hoefer (ed.), *Nouvelle biographie générale*, XLI, 187.

[67] Presentation: 14 janvier 1775 (Reg., T. 94, f. 11v; original letter, written in Italian and dated "Città S. Sepolcro, 12 9bre 1774," in *pochette de séance*); Report (Lalande and Vandermonde): 29 mars 1775 (Reg., T. 94, f. 89-89v; original in BN, MS fr.n.a. 3258, f. 117-117v).

On 17 décembre 1760 (Reg., T. 79, f. 483v), the Academy considered a letter and "un manuscrit sur l'art de la facture d'orgue" from a "religieux et organiste de Clairvaux" named Thierri. It is not known if he was a member of the family of organ builders having this name (see Dufourcq, *Le livre de l'orgue*, I, 254). In any event, no committee was assigned to review the MS, but the secretary does note in the minutes, "l'Académie m'a chargé de le remercier."

[68] Presentation: 27 novembre 1773 (Reg., T. 92, f. 209-209v); Report (Vandermonde and Fouchy): 11 décembre 1773 (Reg., T. 92, f. 238-239; original in *pochette de séance*). Contemporary references in *Journal de Musique*, 1773 (pp. 77-78); *Mercure de France*, janvier 1774 (pp. 181-183), where the *rapport* is reproduced; *Almanach musical*, 1775 (I, 35).

Another *violon-vielle* is noted as brought before the Academy on 4 décembre 1776 (Reg., T. 95, f. 304v), but there is no report and no indication on the nature

made additional changes to the model, enlarging its range and devising a more efficient keyboard mechanism for it.[69]

A provincial amateur performer, Philippe Musset, submitted a proposal in 1774, in which he adapted the sounding mechanism of a *vielle* to a violin. The instrument was "fingered" by a set of rods set into jacks and activated by keys. As in Delaine's model, Musset's supplied sympathetic strings for the twelve chromatic notes.[70]

Outside of the *vielle* and *instruments organisés*, relatively little interest was paid to innovations in string instruments at the Academy. Louis Lagette (Lagetto), an Italian builder established in Paris, proposed novelties to the construction of the violin both in 1756 and in 1759.[71] However, no reports were made on these proposals.

Also in 1756, a lawyer named Jean-Baptiste Domenjoud proposed two novelties for the peg box of the violin: screw mechanisms to replace the pegs and facilitate tuning of the individual strings, and a redesigned box making possible the tuning of all four strings at once. The committee saw value in the first of these but not in the second. This notwithstanding, the following year Domenjoud published the original proposal, virtually unchanged, together with the Academy's judgment.[72]

---

of the instrument (committee named: Fouchy and Vandermonde). The *Almanach musical* for 1777 (III, 34) describes an innovative instrument by Delaine, which may well be the one presented to the Academy, as follows: "La roue de la vielle déplaît à beaucoup de gens. M. D'Laine a imaginé d'adapter ses touches sur un gros violon qu'on joueroit avec l'archet. La position où il faut tenir cet instrument pour se servir des touches, n'est peut être pas la plus favorable pour se servir de l'archet, mais c'est au tems & à l'expérience à fixer le degré de mérite de cette invention."

[69] Presentation: 23 juin 1779 (Reg., T. 98, f. 201v); Report (Sabatier, Vandermonde, and Fouchy): 10 juillet 1779 (Reg., T. 98, f. 222-223; original in *pochette de séance*). Contemporary description in *Almanach musical*, 1781 (VI, 61-62). Delaine is also known as an innovative builder of harpsichords, being credited chiefly with adding a mechanism to the instrument to permit control of dynamics by means of pedals, and with using leather plectra for jacks; see further, Boalch, *Makers*, p. 98; and Samoyault-Verlet, *Les facteurs*, p. 27.

[70] Presentation: 1 février 1774 (Reg., T. 93, f. 35v-36); Report (Vandermonde and Fouchy): 9 février 1774 (Reg., T. 93, f. 44-44v; original in *pochette de séance*, together with an extract from the *Registres* of the Academy of Toulouse, dated 29 avril 1773, which describes the instrument and approves it).

[71] Presentation: 27 novembre 1756 (Reg., T. 75, p. 561; committee named: Mairan, Lassone, and Fouchy); and 20 juin 1759 (Reg., T. 78, f. 476; committee named: Brancas de Lauraguais and Fouchy). On Lagette, see Albert Jacquot, *La lutherie lorraine et française* (Paris: Fischbacher, 1912), p. 159.

[72] Presentation: 11 août 1756 (Reg., T. 75, p. 466; original *mémoire* in *pochette de*

In 1769, Nicolas Gosset, the builder from Reims, recommended replacement of the gut frets, normally found on guitars and other plucked and bowed string instruments, with short bars glued onto the fingerboard under each string; this made it possible to precisely locate the major and minor semi-tones on that string for the player.[73]

The harp was subject to improvements at the Academy late in the eighteenth century. By far the most significant were proposed in 1782 by Georges Cousineau, the celebrated Parisian builder and *luthier de la Reine*. Cousineau designed a new mechanism consisting of movable bridges with multiple hooks or crutches ("système à béquilles"), supplied with dampers, which permitted more precise tuning of the instrument and allowed for the addition of a third row of pedals. He further recommended tuning the harp by fifths instead of scalewise, a system described by Pierre-Joseph Roussier in his "Mémoire sur la nouvelle harpe de M. Cousineau," issued that same year.[74]

---

séance); Report (Le Roy and Fouchy): 1 décembre 1756 (Reg., T. 75, pp. 562-564; extract in *pochette de séance*; condensed in *Histoire*, 1756, pp. 130-131). The invention is described in *Mémoires pour l'histoire des sciences et beaux-arts* (= *Journal de Trévoux*), juillet 1757 (pp. 1903-1905); and in *Almanach Dauphin, année 1777* (suppl., p. 51). The *mémoire* was published as *De la préférence des vis aux chevilles, pour les instrumens de musique* (Paris: Thiboust, 1757; repr., Geneva: Minkoff, 1972); the "Extrait des Registres" appears on pp. 19-20.

[73] Presentation: 29 novembre 1769 (Reg., T. 88, f. 372v); Report (Mairan and Fouchy): 16 décembre 1769 (Reg., T. 88, f. 396v-398v; original in *pochette de séance*; condensed in *Histoire*, 1769, pp. 131-132). Contemporary descriptions in *L'Avantcoureur*, 13 novembre 1769 (pp. 724-727); *Mercure de France*, décembre 1770 (pp. 178-180). See further, Jacquot, *La lutherie*, p. 119. Gosset was also a builder of harpsichords, referred to in *Mercure de France*, septembre 1776 (pp. 187-188); see also, Boalch, *Makers*, p. 54.

[74] Presentation: 19 janvier 1782 (Reg., T. 101, f. 7v; *pochette de séance* includes a MS, "Extrait d'un Mémoire de M. l'Abbé Roussier sur la harpe perfectionnée par M. Cousineau, Luthier de La Reine," quoted entirely in *Art du faiseur d'instruments*, pp. 41-42, and published in enlarged form by Roussier [Paris: Lamy, 1782; repr., Geneva: Minkoff, 1972]; *pochette de séance* also contains an inked drawing of the harp mechanism proposed); Report (Bochart de Saron, Berthollet, and Vandermonde): 6 février 1782 (in *plumitif de 1782* [AdS], but missing from the *Registres*; original in *pochette de séance*; large portion quoted in *Art du faiseur d'instruments*, pp. 38-41). Contemporary description in *Almanach musical*, 1782 (VII, 47-49). On Cousineau, see Jacquot, *La lutherie*, pp. 68-69; and Sylvette Milliot, *Documents inédits sur les luthiers parisiens du XVIIIe siècle* (Paris: Heugel, 1970), pp. 73-77. Roslyn Rensch, *The Harp* (New York: Praeger, 1969), p. 101, denigrates the instrument because of its complex mechanism and large number of pedals (14), at least when compared to the later model by Erard. See further, Marcuse, *A Survey*, p. 395.

III. *MACHINES ET INVENTIONS*

The performer-composer Johann-Baptiste Krumpholtz designed a new, expressive harp, built by the *maître luthier* Jean-Henry Naderman and presented to the Academy in 1787. It featured two special pedals: one controlled shutters to reinforce the sound and regulate the dynamics; and the other actuated leather dampers to soften the sound.[75]

A curious *instrument organisé*, comprising a forte-piano and a harp, was proposed to the Academy in 1788 by a Parisian builder named Lami. The harp was placed horizontally into the case of a large forte-piano, so that the strings of one corresponded in position and pitch to those of the other. Through jacks attached to the key ends, the harp could be played much in the manner of a harpsichord, or it could be coupled with the forte-piano, which also was capable of being played alone—all at one keyboard. The committee's report noted that the coupled sound, being more forceful than that of a forte-piano played by itself, was especially well suited to orchestral use.[76]

[75] Presentation: 17 novembre 1787 (Reg., T. 106, f. 380); Report (Haüy and Vandermonde): 21 novembre 1787 (Reg., T. 106, f. 382v-383; original in *pochette de séance*; extract published in *Journal de Paris*, 27 novembre 1787 [p. 1431], and *Almanach musical*, 1789 [X, 8-9]).

A detailed description of the harp mechanism appears in Krumpholtz's publication *Les deux dernières sonates de la collection de pièces de différents genres*, Op. 14 (Paris: the author and H. Naderman, n.d.), pp. 10-12. In this collection, Krumpholtz devises a set of signs (p. 12) which he applies to the music to designate use of the expressive devices of his new harp. Also described, in both Opp. 13 and 14 (although only briefly), is a "Contre-basse ou clavicorde à marteau" in the form of a pedal-board, on which the harp is intended to be placed, to provide the harpist with a means of accompanying himself while playing. No construction details of the *contre-basse* are given, but in the *Journal de Paris* of 8 février 1786 (p. 157), the pedal-board is described as capable of matching the swelling of the new harp, confirming its hammer action and control of dynamics by the player. While the *contre-basse* did not form part of Krumpholtz's proposal to the Academy, it is referred to in the *rapport* (as a "piano-forté contrebasse"), in a description of a performance given before the group to demonstrate the novel harp (see above, note 24). Krumpholtz reproduces the *rapport* (with some additions) in both his Opp. 13 and 14.

Further on Krumpholtz, see Rensch, *The Harp*, p. 109; Fétis, *Biographie universelle*, V, 122; and Gerber, *Historisch-biographisches Lexicon*, I, cols. 760-761. On Naderman, see Jacquot, *La lutherie*, pp. 215-216; and Milliot, *Documents*, pp. 80-87. The *Almanach musical*, 1788 (IX, 11-12), mentions that the house of Cousineau was producing harps equipped with Krumpholtz's new mechanism.

[76] Presentation: 26 juillet 1788 (Reg., T. 107, f. 197; *pochette de séance* includes a *mémoir[e]* signed by Lami, in which the author identifies himself as a "facteur de

The impact of Benjamin Franklin's glass harmonica on the Academy's work should be noted, especially since Franklin was elected an associate member of the group in 1772, and actively participated in its deliberations later, while a statesman in Paris. The writings of Franklin were made available to members of the Academy through a new French translation of his works by Barbeu Du Bourg, published in 1773 and formally presented to the group by the translator that same year. The work includes a description of the *armonica*.[77]

An alderman from the city of Malines, A.C.G. Deudon, sought to rectify what he considered were faults with the design of Franklin's new instrument, through modifications recommended to the Academy in 1788. According to Deudon, these faults were of two basic types: owing to many variables, the friction of the finger against the edge of the vibrating glass was not an ideal sounding agent, since by this means, the performer could not be assured of producing the desired quality of sound at a precise moment; and because the rotating glasses were of different sizes on Franklin's instrument, they turned at different speeds, making control of dynamics difficult. Deudon sought to remedy the first of these problems by placing a thin piece of specially treated cloth between the glass and the finger to act as the vibrating agent, and the second, by constructing an elliptical axle to compensate for the graduated changes in size of glasses. In addition, the instrument was equipped with a device to increase or diminish the speed of rotation, which helped control dynamics, and the glasses were tuned to equal temperament.[78] These revisions attracted the attention of the master

piano-forté . . . Abbaye St. Germain, cour des religieux"); Report (Dietrich, Vandermonde, and Haüy): 3 septembre 1788 (Reg., T. 107, f. 245v-249; original in *Dossier Dietrich* [AdS]; *pochette de séance* contains a drawing of the mechanism of Lami's instrument, together with an original and a copy of its description).

[77] *Oeuvres de M. Franklin, . . . traduites de l'anglois sur la quatrième édition, par M. Barbeu Du Bourg*, 2 vols. (Paris: Quillau, Esprit, and the author, 1773). The work was presented to the Academy on 21 août 1773 (Reg., T. 92, f. 178) and reviewed in *Histoire*, 1773, pp. 77-83, in which notice on the *armonica* appears on p. 81.

[78] Presentation: 20 février 1788 (Reg., T. 107, f. 37); Report (Vandermonde and Haüy): 5 mars 1788 (Reg., T. 107, f. 58-60v; original and *mémoire* in *pochette de séance*). Contemporary descriptions in *Journal de Paris*, 24 mars 1788 (pp. 365-366); and *Almanach musical*, 1789 (X, 4-7). A large portion of the *mémoire*, in revised form, appears in *Journal encyclopédique*, 15 mai 1789 (IV, i, 135-147). Among later inventions proposed by Deudon to the Academy ("paquets cachetés," 17 août 1791

builder Cousineau, who is known to have constructed examples of Deudon's model in 1789 for sale to the public.[79]

Shortly before, a builder in Paris, Beyer, sought to combine glass vibrators with a forte-piano action in an instrument called *glass-cord*, which he brought to the Academy in 1785. Visually, it resembled a forte-piano, but instead of metal strings, it had thin glass plates stretched over two bridges; these were set into motion by hammer-heads, covered with wool and provided with unusually thin stems to better regulate the strength of the hammer blow and prevent the glass from breaking. Although its lowest notes were judged less agreeable than its middle and upper ones, the sound of the instrument was generally considered pleasant and especially well suited to the voice.[80] In 1790, Beyer returned to the Academy with a glass harmonica played with a bow. However, since a committee report was not made, no information is available on this instrument.[81]

One final keyboard stringed instrument should be mentioned, the *anémocorde*, invented by the builders Schnell and Tschirszcki, and proposed to the Academy in 1790. Its strings were set into motion by wind pressure controlled at a keyboard, and its sound was said to approach the quality of the human voice, although the committee found its mechanism noisy and not especially novel.[82]

and 4 juillet 1796), only one relates directly to music—a transposing keyboard, called "transporteur musical," adaptable to piano, harpsichord, and organ (see *Procès-verbaux de l'Académie des Sciences*, I, 67).

[79] Milliot, *Documents*, pp. 74-75; *Almanach musical*, 1789 (X, 7); and *Journal encyclopédique*, 15 mai 1789 (IV, i, 144-145).

[80] Presentation: 19 janvier 1785 (Reg., T. 104, f. 11v); Report (Bochart de Saron, Vandermonde, Fouchy, and Haüy): 18 mars 1785 (Reg., T. 104, f. 52v-53v; original in *pochette de séance*).

A notice in the *Journal de Paris* for 24 août 1785 (p. 977) informs the reader that "Le premier instrument que le Sr. Beyer ait exécuté, a été emporté en Amérique par M. Francklin [*sic*], qui l'a nommé *glass-cord*, . . . qui désigne un instrument à cordes de verre." The instrument is referred to again in the issue of 18 novembre 1785 (pp. 1326-1327), where there is also a description of a non-musical invention of Beyer ("un porte-feuille avec lequel on peut écrire sans voir") and his address in Paris ("rue Montmartre, vis-à-vis celle Grange-Batelière à la Boule rouge"). On the instrument, see Marcuse, *A Survey*, p. 29; Wright, *Dictionnaire*, p. 74. On Beyer, see Gerber, *Historisch-biographisches Lexicon*, I, col. 158; Fétis, *Biographie universelle*, I, 401.

[81] Presentation: 24 avril 1790 (Reg., T. 109, p. 97; committee named: Vandermonde and Haüy).

[82] Presentation: 13 janvier 1790 (Reg., T. 109, p. 2); Report (Vandermonde, Le Roy, Haüy, and Sabatier): 27 février 1790 (Reg., T. 109, p. 66; does not include

A strongly worded letter to the Academy from the inventors contests the critical nature of the report. A larger committee was subsequently formed to either correct the first report or to issue a new one, which it did in a statement that is considerably more flattering to the builders than the earlier one.[83]

Wind instruments, other than the organ, are least apparent at the Academy as subjects for invention. In 1738, the mechanician Jacques de Vaucanson (1709-1782) submitted a "flûteur automate"—a clockwork mechanism which simulated a performance of music by a flutist and had enormous influence on the production of such machines throughout the century.[84] Some fifty years later, the engineer-machinist François Pelletier presented a similar

rapport, but an extract is in *pochette de séance*). Description in *Journal de Paris, Supplément*, 30 janvier 1790 (p. iii).

[83] The letter was read before the assembly on 20 mars 1790 (Reg., T. 109, p. 80; it is filed in the *pochette* of 27 février 1790). The new report (by Le Roy, Laplace, Vandermonde, Sabatier, and Haüy) was presented on 24 avril 1790 (Reg., T. 109, pp. 94-97; original in *pochette de séance*). Contemporary description of the instrument in *Almanach musical*, 1782 (VII, 46-47). See further, Pontécoulant, *Organographie*, I, 285, and II, 77-78; Sachs, *Real-Lexicon*, p. 12; Sibyl Marcuse, *Musical Instruments, A Comprehensive Dictionary*, corrected ed. (New York: Norton, 1975), p. 16. On Schnell, see Boalch, *Makers*, p. 153; Samoyault-Verlet, *Les facteurs*, p. 66; Harding, *The Piano-Forte*, p. 92.

[84] Presentation: 26 avril 1738 (Reg., T. 57, f. 88; the *pochette* contains the MS *mémoire*, "Concernant le flûteur automate," publ. as *Le mécanisme du flûteur automate* [Paris: Guérin, 1738; repr., Amsterdam: Frits Knuf, 1979], which includes a copy of the Academy's report, pp. 19-20); Report (Dufay and Cassini de Thury): 30 avril 1738 (Reg., T. 57, f. 89-89v; original in *pochette de séance*). On Vaucanson and his contributions to the Academy, see André Doyon and Lucien Liaigre, *Jacques Vaucanson, mécanicien de génie* (Paris: Presses Universitaires de France, 1966); see also, *éloge*, in Condorcet, *Oeuvres*, II, 643-660. Further on *le flûteur automate*, see Alfred Chapuis, *Histoire de la boîte à musique et de la musique mécanique* (Lausanne: Scriptar, 1955), Chap. IV; Albert Protz, *Mechanische Musikinstrumente* (Kassel: Bärenreiter, 1940), pp. 84-85; Arthur W.J.G. Ord-Hume, *Clockwork Music* (New York: Crown, 1973), pp. 25-38, which contains a facsimile of the English trans. of Vaucanson's treatise by John T. Desaguliers, *An Account of the Mechanism of an Automaton* (London: T. Parker, 1742); *Histoire et prestige*, pp. 134-136; and McCloy, *French Inventions*, pp. 103-105.

A German-made mechanical musical instrument ("Joueuse de tympanon") was offered to the Academy by the Queen, Marie-Antoinette, on 3 mars 1785 (Reg., T. 104, f. 46; letter by Lassone relating to the offer in *pochette de séance*). On the following 16 mars (recorded in *plumitif* for 1785), the examining committee (Brisson, Desmarest, Rochon, and Le Gendre) recommended that it be accepted by the Academy for its collection. The instrument survives in the museum of the Conservatoire National des Arts et Métiers (Inv. 7,501); see the description in *Catalogue du Musée, Section Z: Automates et mécanismes à musique* (Paris, 1973), pp. 31-34.

musical mechanism to the Academy,[85] and still later, in 1792, he read a *mémoire* on "une nouvelle méthode de perfectionner les instruments à vent." However, no report of this latter study survives, even though a committee was assigned to review it.[86]

Other Musical Inventions

Instruments were not the only tools of musical practice subject to innovation at the Academy. So, too, were time-measuring devices, musical notation, printing and writing methods, and—by extension—even dance procedures.

Certainly, the measurement of time by mechanical means had made great strides by the seventeenth and eighteenth centuries, chiefly through progress in chronometry, which in many ways was responsible for the "precision mechanics"[87] that characterized so much of instrument making at the time. The need for a time-measuring device specifically suited to the requirements of musical performance, while not a new problem,[88] was nevertheless given renewed attention at this time. Among the many devices developed for the purpose, several were directed to the Academy's attention.

The earliest of these was by Joseph Sauveur, who sought to design a time-measuring device that was both practical and calibrated in accordance with the laws of physics. His point of reference and model for this work was the *chronomètre*, a pendulum mechanism invented by Etienne Loulié and described in his *Eléments ou principes de musique* of 1696.[89] Sauveur considered the

---

[85] Presentation: 23 février 1788 (Reg., T. 107, f. 39v; committee named: Brisson and Vandermonde). Pelletier returned with his *flûteur* to the Academy after the Revolution; see *Procès-verbaux des séances de l'Académie des Sciences*, II, 413, 420. His various inventions, including the *flûteur* and others in music, are described in his *Hommage aux amateurs des arts* (Saint Germain-en-Laye: the author, and Paris: veuve Thiboust and l'Abbé Lesueur, 1782), pp. 38-41. Further on Pelletier, see AN, F[12] 1138, dossier 6, which contains documents related to his petition for state support in 1793.

[86] Presentation: 25 avril 1792 (T. 109B, p. 131; committee named: Pingré, Vandermonde, and Delambre).

[87] Daumas, *Scientific Instruments*, p. 116.

[88] See the survey in Rosamond E. M. Harding, *Origins of Musical Time and Expression* (Oxford: Oxford Univ. Press, 1938), pp. 9-19.

[89] See the author's English ed., *Elements or Principles of Music* (Brooklyn, N.Y.: Institute of Medieval Music, 1965), pp. x, 88-89.

instrument faulty, since it was measured in inches and did not conform with "any known relation to the duration of a second."[90] He attempted to repair its limitations by recommending that it be marked according to the scale of his *échomètre*, measured in *méridiens*.[91]

In 1732, Louis-Léon Pajot, comte d'Onsenbray (1678-1754), the *Intendant général des postes et relais de France* and an honorary member of the Academy, presented a *mémoire* to the group entitled, "Description et usage d'un métromètre, ou machine pour battre les mesures et les temps de toutes sortes d'airs."[92] Much as did Sauveur earlier, so does d'Onsenbray take as his point of departure the *chronomètre* of Loulié, seeking to correct its principal faults. He identifies these as three in number: it is not measured in accordance with the duration of a second (Sauveur's main objection); the beginning and end of each of its pendulum swings, which should be precisely marked, are difficult to determine by sight alone; and moreover, in order to use the device the musician needs to memorize his music, "puisqu'il est obligé d'avoir les yeux continuellement sur la Machine."[93] D'Onsenbray's *métromètre* rectifies these errors: it is measured in parts of a second, and it identifies the beginning and end of each pendulum swing by means of an aural signal. In addition, it provides a dial on which the measure can be clearly indicated by a pointer. The *métromètre* may have gained favor among musicians, were it not for its cumbersome size and complicated pendulum mechanism. As it was, smaller, simpler, and more practical time-measuring musical devices continued to be developed later in the century.[94]

[90] Maxham, *The Contrubutions*, p. 30; Chap. I, "The Measurement of Time," pp. 25-41, is devoted to a comprehensive analysis of Sauveur's device.

[91] The recommendation is made by Sauveur in his "Système général" of 1701, of which Plate II compares Loulié's chronometer directly with his own (reproduced in Harding, *Origins*, as plate 9). An example of the *échomètre*, made by Chapotot, survives at the Conservatoire des Arts et Métiers in Paris; see the listing in *Histoire et prestige*, p. 84.

[92] Presentation: 23 avril 1732 (*assemblée publique*, Reg., T. 51, f. 163v; printed in *Mémoires*, 1732, pp. 182-196; summarized in *Mercure de France*, juin 1732 [pp. 1151-1154]); reread 3 mai 1732 (Reg., T. 51, f. 168). Harding, *Origins*, pp. 12-17, quotes large sections from the *mémoire*.

[93] *Mémoires*, 1732, p. 184: "since he is forced to keep his eyes continually on the machine."

[94] A model of d'Onsenbray's *métromètre* survives at the Conservatoire des Arts et Métiers in Paris (Inv. 1396); see the listing in *Histoire et prestige*, p. 84. The device is mentioned in Fouchy's *éloge* of d'Onsenbray (*Histoire*, 1754), p. 148.

Such a device was presented to the Academy some fifty years afterward, in 1786, by a clock-maker named Dubos.[95] The group devoted several sessions to review of the committee report; and while that report does not survive, an inscription on the title page of the MS *mémoire* makes it clear that there was a difference of opinion among the academicians as to the value of the invention: "La conclusion [du rapport] n'a pas été acceptée de la compagnie."[96] The *mémoire*, entitled, "Chronomètre ou machine pour battre la mesure," describes a variable-speed clock mechanism that produces a pulsating sound. Its speed is regulated by means of a needle moved along a graduated, semicircular dial, which is marked in accordance with differing time signatures and tempi ("Largo" and "Presto" are noted as extremes). The device—also called *rithmomètre* (or *rhythmomètre*)—is found advertised later in the century, but there is no indication that it ever received formal academic approval.[97]

Reform in musical notation also occupied the Academy, and once again, it was Joseph Sauveur who presented the earliest recommendations for such reform to the group. For Sauveur, changes in the notational system were required by the comprehensive musical system he proposed. This system, based on the *mérides*, was not capable of being expressed through conventional symbols. He recommended simplifying existing notation by the reduction or elimination of staff lines and clefs, and by the standardization of time values, signatures, and meters. He also suggested new symbols for notes, which—when appended with varied stems, hooks, dots, dashes, slashes, and numbers—were capable of expressing all pitches in his new system, as well as most rhythms. He further recommended abandoning the traditional solmization syllables for others that could be more easily adapted to his system of *mérides*.[98]

---

[95] Presentation: 16 décembre 1786 (Reg., T. 105, f. 363); Report (Le Roy, Vandermonde, and Haüy): 14, 21, and 30 mars 1787 (Reg., T. 106, f. 89, 124v and 139).

[96] The *mémoire* survives in *pochette de séance du 30 mars 1787*: "The conclusion [of the report] was not accepted by the company."

[97] The invention is referred to in the *Journal de Paris*, 7 juin 1787 (pp. 692-693); *Almanach musical*, 1788 (X, 7-8); AN, F¹² 1138, Dossier 18; and Pontécoulant, *Organographie*, I, 299. See further, Wright, *Dictionnaire*, p. 147.

[98] Sauveur's notational proposals first appear in his "Traité de la théorie de la musique" of 1697, and are given a more developed presentation in his "Système général" of 1701 (see especially the Tables appended to the latter study). His later

Although comprehensive and systematic, Sauveur's proposals for changes in musical notation were for the most part impractical, as was the system of *mérides* on which they were largely dependant. It would be of interest to learn if his "nouvelle manière d'écrire la musique . . . musique colorée"—which was described to the Academy in 1706 (see Appendix I), but which has not survived—was also related to that system.

Perhaps a more practical notational system was the one presented in 1726 by Jean-François Demoz, a French priest from the diocese of Geneva. In a *mémoire* entitled "Nouvelle méthode de plein-chant," he proposes a simplified musical notation, intended to facilitate the teaching of chant and to lower the cost of printing chant books.[99] Demoz recommends the elimination of staff lines from traditional notation, while retaining its metrical and rhythmic conventions. In his system, the direction of stem-line determines the pitch for each note; and the shape of the note-head, its octave-species. Shortly afterward, and despite criticism,[100] Demoz published his method as well as a collection of music adapted to the novel notation.[101] Twenty-two years later, in 1748, he returned to the Academy to propose "quelques changemens" to the method.[102] Although the committee appointed to review these changes saw

---

papers refer only to aspects of these proposals, adding little. On his solmization system, see Georg Lange, "Zur Geschichte der Solmisation," *Sammelbände der Internationalen Musikgesellschaft*, I (1899-1900), 597.

[99] Presentation: 1 juin 1726 (Reg., T. 45, f. 183); Report (Mairan and Maupertuis): 5 juin 1726 (Reg., T. 45, f. 185-186; summarized in *Histoire*, 1726, p. 73). The presentation is also reviewed in *Mercure de France*, juin 1726 (II, 1421-1423). The notational system is described in *Machines*, IV, 217-219.

[100] Sébastien de Brossard was especially critical of Demoz's system; see the discussion in Fétis, *Biographie universelle*, II, 466.

[101] *Méthode de musique selon un nouveau système* (Paris: P. Simon, 1728); and *Méthode de plein-chant selon un nouveau système* (Paris: G.-F. Quillau fils, 1728). The latter work is described in *Mercure de France*, mars 1728 (pp. 518-519). Concerning Demoz's publications, see further, Michel Brenet, "La librairie musicale en France de 1653 à 1790," *Sammelbände der Internationalen Musikgesellschaft*, VIII (1906-1907), 430-431.

[102] Presentation: 12 juin 1748 (Reg., T. 67, p. 264); Report (Mairan and Fouchy): 15 juin 1748 (Reg., T. 67, p. 266; original in *pochette de séance*; summarized in *Histoire*, 1748, p. 121). Demoz was granted a Royal Privilege in 1748 for additional publications using his new system (see Brenet, "La librairie musicale," p. 447); Fétis (*Biographie universelle*, II, 466) believes that his death prevented completion of this work.

little new in Demoz's proposal, it did reaffirm the Academy's earlier approbation of his notation system.[103]

Jean-Jacques Rousseau, the celebrated philosopher and writer from Geneva, was also interested in notational reform. In 1742, he brought his "Projet concernant de nouveaux signes pour la musique" to the Academy. The young Rousseau had designed a novel system of notation that he believed to be superior to the traditional one, since it was capable of representing all sorts of music with precision, but in a simplified way. He had developed his system over a period of several years, but by 1741, while at Chambéry, he became convinced of its special value and was determined to present it to the Paris Academy for its approbation. He writes in his *Confessions*:[104]

> Dès ce moment je crus ma fortune faite, et . . . je ne songeai qu'à partir pour Paris, ne doutant pas qu'en présentant mon projet à l'Académie je ne fisse une révolution.
>
> [From that moment I thought of my fortune as made; and . . . I thought only of going to Paris. For I did not doubt that when I put my scheme before the Academy it would cause a revolution.]

Rousseau arrived in Paris in late 1741 or 1742.[105] Through the mediation of a friend, he met Réaumur, who agreed to sponsor his presentation before the Academy;[106] this event took place on 22 août 1742.[107] He was courteously received by the group, but was disturbed by the committee assigned to judge his work—Hel-

[103] An additional *mémoire* by Demoz, "Le projet d'alphabet," was presented 21 juin 1748 (Reg., T. 67, p. 267); Mairan and Fouchy were appointed to review the proposal. But on 26 juin 1748 (Reg., T. 67, p. 281), Demoz is noted as having withdrawn the work, owing to "quelques difficultés" arising from the project. It is not known if this new proposal related in any way to the others, or to music.

[104] Jean-Jacques Rousseau, *Oeuvres complètes*, ed. Michel Launay, I (Paris: Editions du Seuil, 1967), 225. English trans. from John M. Cohen, *The Confessions of Jean-Jacques Rousseau* (London: Penguin, 1953), p. 257.

[105] Concerning the question of an unclear date, see J.-J. Rousseau, *Les Confessions*, ed. Jacques Voisine (Paris: Garnier frères, 1964), p. 328.

[106] Rousseau, *Oeuvres*, I, 229.

[107] Reg., T. 61, p. 376. The citation is quoted in R. A. Leigh (ed.), *Correspondance complète de Jean Jacques Rousseau*, I (Geneva: Institut et Musée Voltaire, 1965), 317; and in Théophile Dufour (ed.), *Correspondance générale de J.-J. Rousseau*, I (Paris: Armand Colin, 1924), 379. The *mémoire* survives in *Dossier Rousseau* (AdS).

lot, Fouchy, and Mairan—of whom he wrote: "pas un ne savait la musique, assez du moins pour être en état de juger de mon projet."[108] The committee report was, indeed, critical of his new notation.

Rousseau's system replaced the common solmization syllables, *ut, re, mi, fa, sol, la, si,* with the numbers, 1, 2, 3, 4, 5, 6, 7. The final ("son fondamental") of the major mode or key was always represented by 1, and the minor by 6. When a modulation to a new tonal center occurred within a piece, the new final assumed the designation 1 or 6, and the other numbers were adjusted to suit the change of key (that is, the numbers functioned as a "movable do" system). The sequence of numbers representing pitches was placed along a straight line, eliminating the need for a staff. Dots placed above or below the numbers indicated octave-species, and slashes through them, accidentals. Rousseau reduced all meters to either duple or triple. Bar-lines were retained to mark off each of the metrical units, commas to separate the beats, and dashes to indicate rhythmic configurations within the beat. A held note was designated by a dot following a number; rests were shown by the one common symbol, 0. According to Rousseau, the principal advantages of the system were its convenience and relative simplicity, making it easy to learn.

The Academy's lengthy report, read on 5 septembre 1742,[109] is divisible into three sections: the first summarizes the main features of Rousseau's system, the second provides a brief history of the development of notational innovations related to that system, and the third judges the novelty and utility of the proposal. Citing historical evidence (commencing with writers in ancient Greece and leading to the methods proposed, among others, by J. Burmeister, J.-J. Souhaitty, Sauveur, Brossard, and Demoz), the examining committee did not find the substitution of numbers for notes on a staff to be innovative on Rousseau's part, although it acknowledged the thoroughness with which his presentation was made. It further conceded the value of such a system to vocal music, but expressed reservations regarding its applicability to in-

[108] Rousseau, *Oeuvres,* I, 229: "not one of them knew about music, at least enough to be capable of judging my project."

[109] Reg., T. 61, pp. 391*-396. The report is reproduced in Leigh (ed.), *Correspondance complète,* I, 317-322; and in Dufour (ed.), *Correspondance générale,* I, 380-384.

struments. It commended Rousseau for the clarity of his expression and urged him to continue his research, in the interest of musical practice ("pour la facilité de la pratique de la musique").

Rousseau responded angrily, if not bitterly, to the Academy's report,[110] partly because of criticisms he believed to be unjust, and partly because his hopes—"[de] faire une révolution dans cet art, et parvenir de la sorte à une célébrité"—had been dashed.[111] In his *Confessions*, he described working arduously for two or three months after the decision to ready the "projet" for publication.[112] Rousseau continued to argue the merits of his system in later writings,[113] but it was only after his death that a revised form of the "projet" saw print.[114]

Of less moment were the additional innovations in musical notation proposed to the Academy later in the century. In 1766, Laurent "de Valenciennes" proposed "une nouvelle manière d'écrire la musique";[115] in 1782, Delaunay read a "Mémoire sur un nouveau caractère pour écrire la musique";[116] and at that same session in 1782, "M. Charles" presented a "Mémoire sur l'accompagnement, ou nouvelle méthode de le chiffrer."[117] In none of these cases is

[110] His written response ("Eclaircissement") survives in *Dossier Rousseau* (AdS), together with the "Projet." It is reproduced in Leigh (ed.), *Correspondance complète*, I, 161-167, which has a review of the arguments presented, pp. 167-169. See also, Joseph-L.-F. Bertrand, "Quelques pages inédites de Jean-Jacques Rousseau," *Journal des Savants*, avril 1880, pp. 222-231.

[111] Rousseau, *Oeuvres*, I, 230: "[of] causing a revolution in this art, and thereby to attain a celebrity."

[112] Ibid.

[113] See his *Dissertation sur la musique moderne* (Paris: G.-F. Quillau, 1743); *Dictionnaire de musique* (Paris: veuve Duchesne, 1768; repr., Hildesheim: G. Olms, 1969), article "Notes"; and letters in Leigh (ed.), *Correspondance complète*, I, 169-181. Contemporary views of the system are essentially a reaction to these later writings; see, for example, the favorable review in *Journal de Trévoux*, avril 1743 (pp. 615-640).

[114] For an extended discussion of Rousseau's notational system, see Albert Jansen, *Jean-Jacques Rousseau als Musiker* (Berlin: G. Reimer, 1884), pp. 44-65. See also the review in Arthur Pougin, *Jean-Jacques Rousseau, musicien* (Paris: Fischbacher, 1901), pp. 23-28.

[115] Presentation: 22 mars 1766 (Reg., T. 85, f. 105; committee named: Mairan and Fouchy). The inventor is presumably the "M. Laurent, ancien Directeur de la Poste à Valenciennes" who presented a *mémoire*, "sur le sistème du monde" on 24 mars 1764 (Reg., T. 83, f. 65v).

[116] Presentation: 27 juillet 1782 (Reg., T. 101, f. 139v; committee named: Fouchy and Vandermonde). The author is identified simply as "avocat."

[117] Presentation I (Charles): 27 juillet 1782 (Reg., T. 101, f. 139v); Presentation

additional information available; committees were appointed to review all three, but no reports were made.

Also related to notation was the proposal presented in 1766 by a correspondent of the Academy, Alexandre-Henry-Guillaume Le Rohbergherr de Vausenville (1722-after 1797), entitled "Une méthode variable pour rayer par une voie plus prompte et plus expéditive que l'impression même, toutes sortes de papiers destinés à la musique, au plain-chant, à la fabrication des registres, états, etc."[118] Vausenville who is described in a later document as an "astronome-mathématicien-géomètre . . . auparavant caissier des troupes de France dans l'isle de Corse,"[119] proposed an instrument to facilitate the ruling of staff lines on paper. It is composed of two parts: a table, called "métier," on which the paper is held by means of a clamping device; and an inking mechanism, termed "rayeur," that regulates the lines, spaces, and margins on the paper. Vausenville's invention (later given the name "L'art gammographique") was said to have made it possible for one person to prepare as many sheets of ruled paper in the same time as two men operating a printing press.[120]

A famous polemical battle[121] in the field of music printing was brought before the Academy during the second half of the eighteenth century. The principal protagonists were the typefounder Pierre-Simon Fournier le jeune and the printers Nicolas and Pierre-François Gando, father and son. Others joined the fray outside the

II (Condorcet): 7 août 1782 (Reg., T. 101, f. 149; committee named: Vandermonde and Condorcet).

[118] Presentation: 12 juillet 1766 (Reg., T. 85, f. 229); Report (Mairan and Fouchy): 3 septembre 1766 (Reg., T. 85, f. 298v-301v; original in *pochette de séance*; summarized in *Histoire*, 1766, p. 162).

[119] AN, F¹² 2270: "astronomer-mathematician-geometer . . . formerly treasurer for the French troops on the isle of Corsica."

[120] Documents bearing on this invention are found in AN, ibid., and F¹² 994; BN, MS fr. 22,082 (Collection Anisson-Duperron), no. 83; Bordeaux, Bibliothèque Municipale, MS 1696 (29), no. 27. It is reviewed in *Journal de Trévoux*, décembre 1767 (p. 556). An earlier device, intended to facilitate the drawing of staff lines onto paper, was described by La Hire; see above, Chap. II, note 12.

[121] Concerning the quarrel, see Harry Carter (ed.), *Fournier on Typefounding. The Text of the Manuel Typographique (1764-1766) translated into English* (London: Soncino Press, 1930), pp. xxi-xxxi; Marius Audin, *Les livrets typographiques des fonderies françaises créées avant 1800* (Amsterdam: G. T. van Heusden, 1964), pp. 97-98; Allen Hutt, *Fournier, The Compleat Typographer* (Totowa, N.J.: Rowan and Littlefield, 1972), pp. 38-41; and MGG, IV, cols. 608-610.

Academy, essentially in the law courts of Parlement and through articles appearing in contemporary journals.

At issue were the restrictive nature of membership in the printers' guild (Communauté des Imprimeurs) and the monopoly for the printing of music (held for some two hundred years in France by the Ballard family). Fournier concerned himself with both issues shortly after midcentury. He had been experimenting with new type-fonts that would make the printing of music more efficient and less costly than those used by the Ballards. Sparked, especially, by the technical innovations brought to music printing by Breitkopf in Germany,[122] Fournier developed a novel musical type, which he submitted to the guild in 1762, petitioning for entry as a printer. This was denied, and Fournier took the matter to the courts at Parlement;[123] shortly afterward, he presented his new characters of type to the Academy for approval.[124] In granting him a certificate, the examining committee cited the precision of his work, and the reduction in the cost of printing music made possible by his method.

Two years later, in 1764, Parlement decided the case in Fournier's favor, making it possible for all typographers in France to print music, but reserving for the Ballard family the designation of sole music printers for the king.[125] Accordingly, early in 1765, Pierre Gando submitted an example of his work ("un essay de musique imprimée de sa façon") to the Academy for its approbation. This was given, with the indication that the double-impression method proposed, while difficult to apply and not entirely new, was nevertheless capable of yielding excellent results using movable type.[126]

[122] Described in H. Edmund Poole, "New Music Types: Invention in the Eighteenth Century, I," *Journal of the Printing Historical Society*, I (1965), 21 and 36.

[123] Original documents related to the case are found in BN, MS fr. 22,117 (Collection Anisson-Duperron), passim.

[124] Presentation: 11 août 1762 (Reg., T. 81, f. 255-255v; original *mémoire* in *pochette de séance*; Report (Montigny, Vaucanson, and Fouchy): 18 août 1762 (Reg., T. 81, f. 260v-261; original and extract in *pochette de séance*; summarized in *Histoire*, 1762, pp. 192-193).

[125] See Carter, *Fournier on Typefounding*, p. xxx.

[126] Presentation: 16 janvier 1765 (Reg., T. 84, f. 4v); Report (Duhamel du Monceau, Le Roy, and Fouchy): 30 avril 1765 (Reg., T. 84, f. 194v-198; original in *pochette de séance*; summarized in *Histoire*, 1765, pp. 134-135).

1. "Nouveau système de musique" by Joseph Sauveur, *Traité de la théorie de la musique*, 1697

2. Certificate (1699) signed by musicians of the King's Chapel, endorsing the *clavecin brisé* by Jean Marius

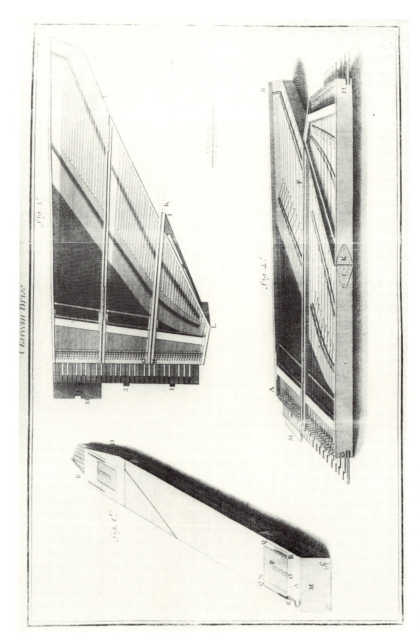

3. Engraving of *clavecin brisé* (1700) by Jean Marius

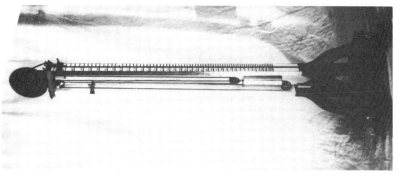

6. Surviving model of d'Onsenbray's *Métromètre*

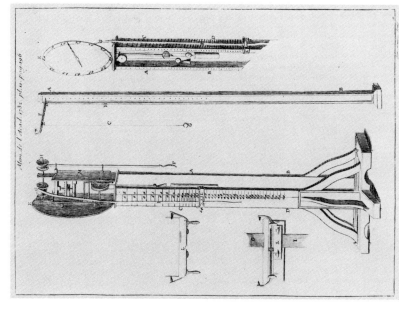

5. Engraving of *Métromètre* (1732) by Louis-Léon Pajot, comte d'Onsenbray

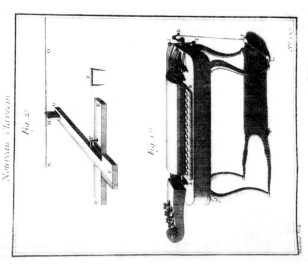

4. Engraving of the *clavecin-vielle* (1708) by François Cuisinié

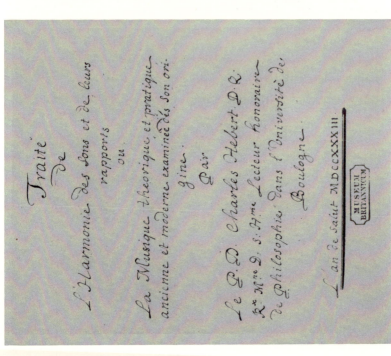

Traité
De
L'Harmonie des Sons et de leurs
rapports
ou

La Musique theorique et pratique
ancienne et moderne examinée dés Son origine.
Par

Le P.D. Charles Hebert D.R.
Bx Mre D. S. Hme Lecteur honoraire
De Philosophie dans l'Université de
Boulogne.

L'an De Salut MDCCXXXIII.

MUSEUM
BRITANNICUM

7. Title page of the *Traité de l'harmonie* (1733)
   by Charles Hébert

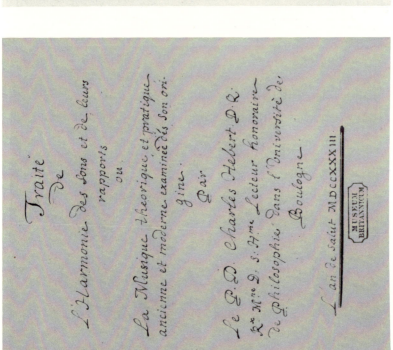

8. Frontispiece from *Le flûteur automate* (1738) by
   Jacques de Vaucanson

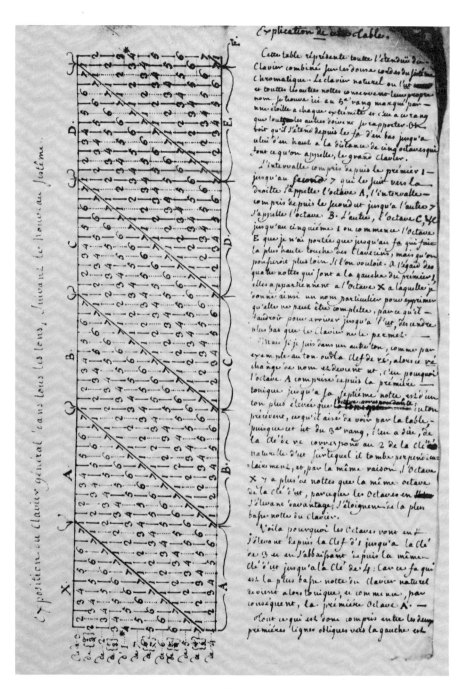

9. Table of the new notational system (1742) by Jean-Jacques Rousseau, in his "Projet concernant de nouveaux signes pour la musique"

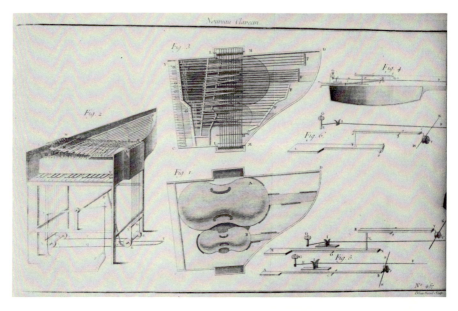

10. Engraving of the *clavecin organisé* (1742) by Jean Le Voir

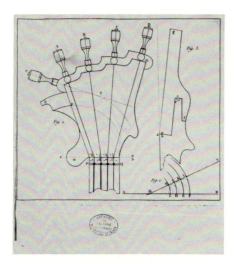

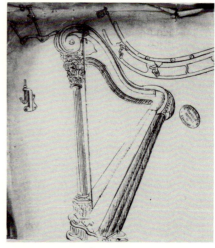

11. Ink drawing from "La préférence des vis aux chevilles, pour les instrumens de musique" (1756) by Jean-Baptiste Domenjoud

12. Detail of ink drawing (1782) of improvements to the harp by Georges Cousineau

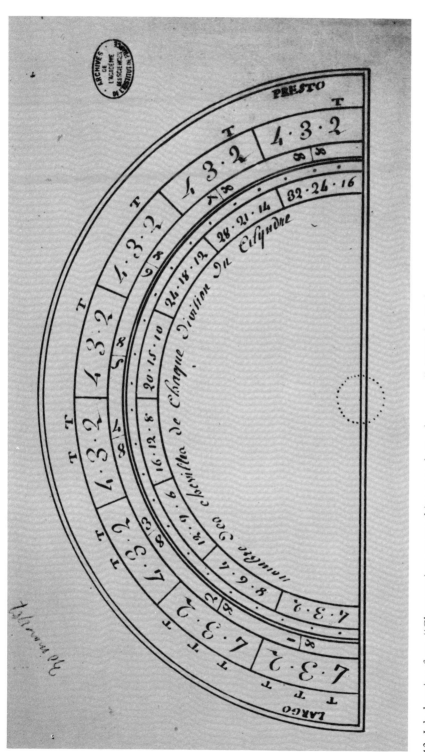

13. Ink drawing from "Chronomètre ou machine pour battre la mesure" (1786) by Dubos

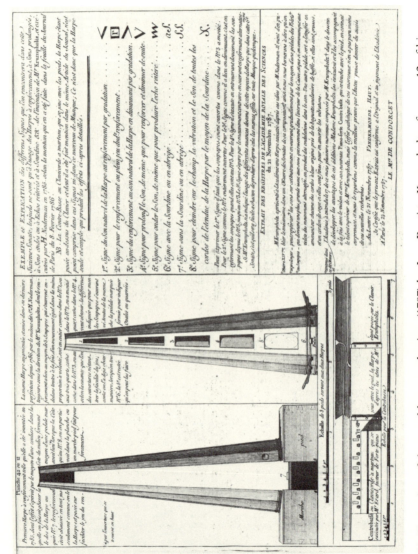

14. Engraving of the novel harp mechanism (1787) by Jean-Baptiste Krumpholtz, from p. 12 of his Op. 14, *Les deux dernières sonates*

Later that same year, Fournier published a *Traité historique et critique sur l'origine et les progrès des caractères de fonte pour l'impression de la musique* (Bern and Paris: Barbou, 1765), an essay that was requested by the referee of the court in Parlement at the time of the resolution of his case.[127] In it, he accuses "Gando père et fils" with plagiarism in the work they submitted to the Academy. The Gandos responded with their own attack on Fournier, *Observations sur le Traité historique et critique de Monsieur Fournier le jeune* (Bern and Paris: Moreau, 1766), a copy of which was submitted to the Academy.[128] Fournier counter-attacked with a *Réponse à un Mémoire publiée en 1766 par MM. Gando au sujet des caractères de fonte pour la musique*, found appended to his *Manuel typographique* (Paris, 1764–1766).[129]

The quarrel appears to have ended with the death of Fournier in 1768. In the detailed review of his work by H. E. Poole, his methods are described as novel and comparable to those of Breitkopf, and his results as "rational in design and graceful in execution."[130] It seems clear that Fournier was the leading innovator in musical typography in eighteenth-century France.

Finally, mention should be made of the several innovations brought to the attention of the Academy early in the century by the Parisian dancing master Des Hayes. For the most part, these were devices intended to assure proper body positions of children, presumably as aids in the teaching of dance. In 1716,[131] he presented a corset (called *somamorphose*)[132] designed to compel a child "to hold his body erect"; and in 1733,[133] he proposed two new inventions, both of which received the Academy's endorsement:

---

[127] A letter by Fournier to M. d'Hémery, Inspecteur de la Librairie, attached to the copy of the *Traité* in BN, Rés. V. 1793, clarifies the nature of the request.

[128] Presentation: 5 juillet 1766 (Reg., T. 85, f. 224-224v). No committee was assigned to review the work.

[129] II, 288-306. The *Traité*, the *Observations*, and the *Réponse* are available in a facsimile ed. by Minkoff in Geneva, 1972.

[130] Poole, "New Music Types: Invention in the Eighteenth Century, II," *Journal of the Printing Historical Society*, II (1966), 37.

[131] Presentation: 27 mai 1716 (Reg., T. 35, f. 173-173v). No committee was assigned to review the innovation.

[132] MGG, III, col. 214.

[133] Report (Winslow and J.-L. Petit): 13 juin 1733 (Reg., T. 52, f. 120-120v; original [dated 10 juin 1733] in *pochette de séance*).

a chin strap to insure that children hold their heads upright, and a device enabling those with pigeon toes "to turn their feet outward."

Des Hayes also had interest in the then-developing choreographic notation for dance. In 1729,[134] he submitted a MS entitled "Chorégraphie" in which, however, the examining committee found only one novel feature—its use of special signs, added to the notational symbols described by Pierre Rameau,[135] "to mark the pitch of the musical note that corresponds to the dance step." Des Hayes had earlier (1721) received a Privilege for the printing of "quelques ouvrages de chorégraphie,"[136] but this MS does not appear to have been published.[137]

[134] Report (Mairan and Maupertuis): 21 mai 1729 (Reg., T. 48, f. 102-102v).

[135] Pierre Rameau, *Abbrégé de la nouvelle méthode dans l'art d'écrire ou de tracer toutes sortes de danses de ville* (Paris: the author, 1725; repr., Farnborough: Gregg, 1972). The novel feature of Des Hayes's notation is described in Borin's *L'Art de la danse* (Paris: J.-B.-C. Ballard, 1746), p. 19, where it is referred to as comprising symbols "très ingénieux et très utiles." (I am grateful to Elisabeth Rebman for calling my attention to this reference.)

[136] See Brenet, "La librairie musicale," p. 427.

[137] Des Hayes may further be identified with the "Dezais" who published several collections of dances and participated in the 1713 ed. of Feuillet's *Chorégraphie*. See the listings in RISM, B VI, 1 (1971), p. 314; A I, 2 (1972), p. 374.

❧ IV ❧

THEORY AND PRACTICE:
MUSIC AS SYSTEM

Early Contributions

WHILE THE NATURE, production, and perception of sound occupied the Academy in much of its work with music, the organization of that sound into patterns that were meaningful to the human ear and mind also became a growing concern of the group. In part, this was a result of the general interest in applying the discoveries of experimentation to practical ends, which gained favor at the Academy early in its development; and, in part, this reflected a change in the aesthetic of the time, in which music theory was viewed increasingly as subordinate to, and dependent upon, practice for its meaning.

Musical systems were proposed to the Academy throughout its activity, but this was especially so in the eighteenth century. Few were comprehensive in scope, and most limited their attention to pitch organization in music: tuning and temperament, harmony, modality, and the construction of scale patterns. As the century unfolded, many related these systems directly to the composition of music and to its performance.

Although discussions of pitch derivation and organization in music are readily found in early papers on acoustics at the Academy, the first attempt there to establish a comprehensive system of pitch is found in the work of Joseph Sauveur. Based on an octave divided into forty-three equal parts (*mérides*), each of which was capable of undergoing yet further division, Sauveur's system provided a mathematical means for describing and comparing all musical intervals, scales, or tuning systems.

Maxham notes that "Sauveur was endeavoring to achieve a tempered system which would preserve, within the conditions he set

(79)

down, the pure diatonic system of just intonation."[1] Sauveur's conditions are identified as follows: establishing limits for the ratio between the minor semitone and the comma (intervals basic to his system); adopting an octave division that is precise yet simple to use; and limiting choices of consonant intervals to those that "do not offend the ear."

Having considered and rejected other multiple divisions of the octave for that of forty-three,[2] Sauveur proceeded to describe how the system can be applied to practice. Already mentioned were his use of the *échomètre* as an aid to the measurement of temperament and to the tuning of instruments, and his design of special solmization syllables. In addition, he recommended a novel method of "reciprocal intervals" that made it possible for performers to adapt a given temperament to changes in pitch-final, and he provided a classification of vocal ranges based on numerical considerations (nineteen possible voice ranges were identified).[3] Although Sauveur's pitch system was not generally adopted by musicians, it influenced the work of theorists later in the century.[4]

During the first quarter of the century, however, except for the ongoing work of Sauveur and Carré, little of consequence was presented to the Academy regarding musical systems. In fact, only two proposals were recorded in the *Registres*, and both were rejected. Of the first, "un nouveau système de musique," presented in 1704, the *procès-verbaux* note: "M. Carré a dit qu'il n'y avoit nulle idée de sistème dans l'écrit de M. Guichard sur la musique."[5] The second was a presentation, in 1708, by "Mr. Durand avocat au parlement . . . de nouvelles vûes sur la musique," which the examining committee judged to be faulty ("pleine d'erreurs").[6]

[1] Maxham, *The Contributions*, p. 61.

[2] For a historical review of multiple division tuning systems, see J. Murray Barbour, *Tuning and Temperament*, 2d ed. (East Lansing: Michigan State College Press, 1953; repr., New York: Da Capo Press, 1972), Chap. VI.

[3] Both novelties are discussed in Sauveur's *Système général* of 1701; see the analysis in Maxham, *The Contributions*, pp. 85-93.

[4] See Barbour, *Tuning and Temperament*, p. 125.

[5] Presentation: 12 avril 1704 (Reg., T. 23, f. 97): "M. Carré said that there was no notion of system in the writing of Guichard on music." The *plumitif* in BN, MS fr.n.a. 5148, f. 66v, spells the author's name as "Guicher."

[6] Presentation: 25 avril 1708 (Reg., T. 27, f. 132v); Report (Parent and Reneaume): 2 mai 1708 (Reg., T. 27, f. 135-135v). An earlier publication of Durand, *La musique naturelle* (Paris: Rebuffé, 1700), proposes a new notation for music, described by Brossard (*Catalogue*, p. 275) as "une idée des plus chimériques."

It was at this very time that the Academy's authority to approve the scientific writings of its members for printing privilege (granted by the royal statutes of 1699) was extended to include non-members.[7] This served both to broaden the base of contributors and to bring outside interests into the academic forum. The opportunity to propose novel ideas to the Academy proved attractive to many theorists and musicians, and beginning with the second quarter of the century, a large variety of musical systems were presented for approval.

Among the earliest of these was a "Traité manuscrit sur l'harmonie," dedicated to the Academy and sent from Italy in 1733, by Charles Hébert, described as "Professeur en Philosophie à Padoüe." An examining committee was appointed to review the treatise, but no report was filed.[8] The manuscript, however, survives (currently at the British Library),[9] and it provides additional information about the author. Hébert is identified on its title page as "Lecteur honoraire de philosophie dans l'Université de Boulogne." In the dedication (dated 25 février 1733), he speaks of his participation in meetings of the Academy in Bologna, and of his having left France ("ma patrie") to work in Italy ("depuis vingt-trois ans"). The title reads: "Traité de l'harmonie des sons et de leurs rapports, ou la musique théorique et pratique ancienne et moderne examinée dès son origine." The treatise provides a comprehensive, although conservative and retrospective view, of music history and theory, founded largely on earlier authorities, but also often on conjecture. Hébert's "modern" practice is based primarily on the work of seventeenth-century figures—for theory: Stancari, Descartes, Mariotte, Dodart, Du Verney, and Sauveur; for practice (i.e., counterpoint): Colonna, Penna, Kircher, and Bononcini. The author appears to be unaware of important new thought on "harmonie" developed just prior to his work, especially by Rameau; and his use of the term reflects an earlier meaning. Since the Traité is neither innovative nor even current, it is

[7] See Hahn, The Anatomy, pp. 61-63. The review process was essentially the same as that for granting patent privileges.

[8] Presentation (Melchior de Polignac): 22 mai 1733 (Reg., T. 52, f. 108); committee named: Mairan, Maupertuis, and Fouchy.

[9] London, British Library, MS Add. 6137; in-4°, 360 fols. An inscription on a prefatory page reads: "purchased with the library of M.P.L. Ginguené." The MS is listed in Catalogue des livres de la bibliothèque de feu M. P.-L. Ginguené (Paris: Merlin, 1817), p. 36, no. 531; it is not known how Ginguené acquired it.

not difficult to conjecture on possible reasons for the absence of a committee report on Hébert's proposal.

Rameau and Later Figures

If the work of Sauveur dominated musical thought at the Academy early in the eighteenth century, that of the composer-theorist Jean-Philippe Rameau (1683-1764) formed an important focus for presentations there throughout the remainder of the century. For through his revolutionary ideas on the nature of harmony and its relationship to the science of sound, Rameau helped to create a climate for the stimulation of new thought and intense debate on the very essence of music and its organization. Throughout all of Europe, theorists and practitioners, scientists and musicians, participated in this activity, with many bringing the results of their work to the Academy for review.[10]

First among these was Rameau, himself, who had earlier startled the musical world through the publication of his influential treatise *Traité de l'harmonie* (1722),[11] in which he formulated principles of harmony derived from the mathematical and physical bases of a vibrating body. Rameau argued the essential unity of harmony and developed basic concepts dealing with harmonic generation, harmonic inversion, and the fundamental bass. These and related ideas were to mature in his later works, where he sought to provide additional scientific support for his proposals, while demonstrating the practical application of his system. Throughout his work, Rameau remained primarily a musician who favored "bon goût" and "le jugement de l'oreille" in solving difficult problems of theory.

Rameau first appeared before the Paris Academy in 1737 with a treatise dedicated to the group, *Génération harmonique*. In it, he restates his earlier ideas, newly deals with the psychological effects of harmony, and seeks rational justification for both the minor

[10] The principal source for Rameau's theoretical works is Erwin R. Jacobi (ed.), *The Complete Theoretical Writings of Jean-Philippe Rameau (1683-1764)*, 6 vols. (Rome: American Institute of Musicology, 1967-1972), which contains facsimile reproductions of all of Rameau's treatises, as well as extensive documentation on their history. Also of note is Michaela Maria Keane, *The Theoretical Writings of Jean-Philippe Rameau* (Washington, D.C.: Catholic Univ. of America Press, 1961).

[11] See the English ed. by Philip Gossett (New York: Dover, 1971).

mode and the sub-dominant sonority in his system. More pertinent, however, is his application of the physical principle of the
elasticity of air (reported to the Academy earlier by Mairan)[12] in
the development of his theories. Jacobi believes that this "first
clear indication of his personal ambitions for a closer connection"
with the Academy, manifest through his "striving . . . to raise
music to the level of scientific discipline," strongly influenced the
evolution of Rameau's later work.[13]

The examining committee's report, which is short and compli-
mentary,[14] commends Rameau for having developed a reasoned
set of theories for an understanding of harmony based on scientific
considerations. The *Génération* was published shortly thereafter,[15]
and it provoked strong reaction from supporters and critics alike.[16]

Some twelve years later, in 1749, Rameau returned to the Academy to present his *Démonstration du principe de l'harmonie*. The *Registres* note that materials related to "un nouveau système de musique de Mons. Rameau" were distributed on 13 août 1749[17] in
preparation for a lecture, which was delivered in November of the
same year.[18] The *Démonstration* presents little that is new, but it is
generally conceded to be the most mature statement of Rameau's
theories, as well as the best written (Denis Diderot is believed to
have been his collaborator in the treatise).[19] Of special note in the
work are his clear description of the triple progression as a gen-

[12] See *Histoire*, 1720, pp. 11-12; reproduced in Jacobi, *The Complete Theoretical Writings*, VI, 107-109.

[13] Jacobi, *The Complete Theoretical Writings*, III, p. XIX.

[14] Report (Réaumur, Mairan, and Gamaches): 12 janvier 1737 (Reg., T. 56, f. 3-3v; original in *Dossier Rameau*, AdS). Report reproduced in Jacobi, *The Complete Theoretical Writings*, VI, 110.

[15] Publ., Paris: Prault fils, 1737, with the committee report attached. See Jacobi, *The Complete Theoretical Writings*, III, 1-150, for a reprint of the treatise, and pp. XI-XXIX, for bibliographical and historical information. See also, Deborah Hayes, *Rameau's Theory of Harmonic Generation: An Annotated Translation and Commentary of* Génération harmonique *by J.-P. Rameau* (Ph.D. dissertation, Stanford Univ., 1968).

[16] For a review of resulting polemics, together with reprints of pertinent documents, see Jacobi, *The Complete Theoretical Writings*, III, pp. XXI-XXIX, and VI, 105-183.

[17] Reg., T. 68, p. 369: "a new musical system by Mons. Rameau."

[18] Presentation: 19 novembre 1749 (Reg., T. 68, p. 474; original *mémoire* in *Dossier Rameau*; summarized in *Histoire*, 1750, pp. 160-165).

[19] Jacobi, *The Complete Theoretical Writings*, III, pp. XXXIX-XL.

erating principle for harmony, and his discussion of tuning systems, among which equal temperament is clearly favored.

The lengthy committee report, filed in December of 1749 (and seemingly drafted by d'Alembert),[20] reviews in great detail the material presented by Rameau in the treatise. It recalls the favorable impression made on the Academy by his earlier presentation, and confirms the group's continued approbation of his work, noting that, through Rameau's efforts, harmony had truly become a science ("l'harmonie . . . est devenue . . . une Science"). The *Démonstration* was approved for publication by the Comité de librairie on 7 janvier 1750,[21] and on the following 18 février,[22] Rameau personally presented the Academy with a printed copy of the work.[23] Publication of the *Démonstration*, as with his earlier works, met with considerable debate, mostly favorable (at least at first). D'Alembert, for one, became a strong advocate of Rameau's ideas. He paid him an exceptional tribute in the "Discours préliminaire" (1751) to the first volume of the *Encyclopédie*. He also helped spread his theories widely, especially through his *Elémens de musique, théorique et pratique, suivant les principes de M. Rameau*, published in 1752, which underwent many subsequent editions.[24]

The decade that followed was not kind to Rameau, for he became directly involved in the bitter *Querelle des bouffons*. Initially it was provoked by the writings of Rousseau, but later it was sustained by the leading *Encyclopédistes*—almost all of whom eventually broke with Rameau, including d'Alembert. To be sure, the

[20] Report (Nicole, Mairan, and d'Alembert): 10 décembre 1749 (Reg., T. 68, pp. 495-506; original in *Dossier Rameau*).

[21] MS *Registre du Comité de librairie, 1749-1770* (AdS), p. 5.

[22] Reg., T. 69, p. 34.

[23] Publ., Paris: Durand and Pissot, 1750 (repr., New York: Broude Bros., 1965), with the complete committee report appended. See Jacobi, *The Complete Theoretical Writings*, III, 153-246, for a reprint of the treatise, and pp. XXXI-L, for its publication history; copies of contemporary documents pertaining to the *Démonstration* are found in VI, 189-224. See also, Roger L. Briscoe, *Rameau's* Démonstration du principe de l'harmonie *and* Nouvelles réflexions de M. Rameau sur sa démonstration du principe de l'harmonie: *An Annotated Translation and Commentary of Two Treatises by Jean-Philippe Rameau* (Ph.D. dissertation, Indiana Univ., 1976).

[24] See Jacobi, *The Complete Theoretical Writings*, III, pp. LI-LIII. Rameau also submitted both the *Génération* and the *Démonstration* to the Royal Society of London for approbation; see London, British Library, Sloan MS 4055, f. 159, and Add. MS 4445, f. 1.

"quarrel" was essentially one of aesthetics rather than of theory, but the issues tended to be blurred, and consequently Rameau's theories came under sharp attack.[25] It was during this period that Rameau paid a final visit to the Academy, on 4 avril 1759, to read his *mémoire* "[Nouvelles] Réflexions sur le principe sonore," an essay intended to be appended to his *Code de musique pratique*, then in print. D'Alembert and Lalande were named to examine the work, but no report was issued.[26] Perhaps anticipating a rebuff, Rameau had earlier sent a copy of the work to the Accademia delle Scienze dell' Instituto di Bologna. In April 1759, he began a series of communications with the Accademia in Bologna that ultimately led to the preparation of a critical report on the work by Padre Martini; this did not appear until 1761, by which time the *Nouvelles réflexions* was already in print.[27] The Paris Academy was not to receive additional proposals from Rameau. However, intense interest provoked by his theoretical writings remained clearly evident in the work presented there by others.

Certainly, this is the case with a *mémoire* proposed to the Academy in 1750 by Pierre Estève (1720-after 1779), a member of the Société Royale des Sciences in Montpellier, called "Démonstration du principe de l'harmonie"—a title apparently borrowed from Rameau's treatise of the same name. The report of the examining committee, which commends the *mémoire*, is quick to clarify that despite the similarity in title the two works deal with different matters and are not contradictory in nature. As if to underscore this point, in the *Histoire* for 1750, the Academy's secretary summarizes the contents of both Rameau's *Démonstration* and Estève's, the one coming immediately after the other.[28]

[25] Concerning the *querelle*, the *Encyclopédistes* and Rameau, see Jacobi, *The Complete Theoretical Writings*, III, pp. LXVI-LXVIII; IV, pp. XIII-XVIII (which includes an extensive bibliography); V, pp. XXXV-XLIV; and VI, pp. XXIV-XXV. See also the collection of documents in Denise Launay (ed.), *La querelle des bouffons*, 3 vols. (Geneva: Minkoff, 1973).

[26] Reg., T. 78, f. 353v.

[27] See the detailed study of Rameau's presentation to the Bolognese Academy, in Jacobi, *The Complete Theoretical Writings*, IV, pp. XXXIII-XL, and the pertinent documents reproduced in VI, 353-407; this material is derived from Jacobi's earlier study, "Rameau and Padre Martini," *The Musical Quarterly*, L (1964), 452-475.

[28] Presentation: 9 décembre 1750 (Reg., T. 69, p. 443); Report (Nicole and d'Alembert): 16 décembre 1750 (Reg., T. 69, pp. 453-454; original and extract in *pochette de séance*; summarized in *Histoire*, 1750, pp. 165-167).

The following year, Estève published his essay in an expanded and partially rewritten form, supplied with a different title, *Nouvelle découverte du principe de l'harmonie.*[29] Perhaps misunderstood in the intent of his original *mémoire*, Estève takes direct issue with many of Rameau's theories in the *Nouvelle découverte*, finding them faulty and incomplete. He denies the identity of octaves, rejects Rameau's use of harmonics below the fundamental as relevant to harmony, and questions the designation of the major triad as a completely natural phenomenon. In Estève's view, a comprehension of the basis for the perceptual differences in consonant and dissonant sonorities is more pertinent to the development of the theory of harmony than are the principles adopted by Rameau. He believed that these differences derive from the interrelationship of several factors: the complexity of the sound itself; the physical motion of air particles that convey the sound to the ear; and the degree of aural sensibility of the listener, as well as his inner feelings ("âme"). This theory links physical with metaphysical processes.[30]

In the Introduction to the *Nouvelle découverte*, Estève states that he reserved discussion of the practical applications of his "discovery" to two *mémoires*, to be published by the Paris Academy.[31] This discussion appears in a two–part *mémoire* presented in 1751, "Recherches sur le meilleur système de musique harmonique, et sur son tempérament."[32] In the first part, Estève establishes primacy for the diatonic scale of just intonation, and in the second, he determines that a ¼-comma meantone tuning is the temperament best suited to performance of music in that scale system. Although approved for publication in the Academy's *Mémoires de mathématique et de physique, présentés à l'Académie Royale des Sciences, par divers savans, & lûs dans ses assemblées,*[33] the *mémoire* was judged to be incomplete and but the beginning of a larger and more in-

[29] Publ., Paris: Huart et Moreau fils, Durand, 1751; S. Jorry, 1752. A critique of Rameau's *Démonstration* and Estève's *Nouvelle découverte* appears in *Journal de Trévoux*, juin 1751 (pp. 1368-1384); reproduced in Jacobi, *The Complete Theoretical Writings*, VI, 218-224.

[30] See Jacobi, *The Complete Theoretical Writings*, VI, pp. XVIII-XIX.

[31] *Nouvelle découverte*, pp. xii-xiii.

[32] Presentation: 10 mars 1751 (Reg., T. 70, p. 258); Report (Mairan and d'Alembert): 31 mars 1751 (Reg., T. 70, pp. 284-285; original in *pochette de séance*). The *mémoire* is listed as approved for publication in *Histoire*, 1750, p. 172.

[33] Vol. II (Paris: l'Imprimerie Royale, 1755), 113-136.

clusive study, which Estève was encouraged to pursue. However, except for essays written in contention with ideas expressed by Romieu, a fellow-member in the Montpellier Société,[34] Estève largely abandoned his interest in the theory of harmony in his later work, favoring studies in aesthetics and literature.[35]

Estève's "Recherches" is but one among many treatises proposed to the Academy during the eighteenth century concerned with the tuning and tempering of musical scales, especially on keyboards and other fixed-pitch instruments. Increased use of remote keys in the music of the time impelled musicians and theorists to seek a tuning system that would accommodate itself to performance in those keys, while remaining true to what was generally understood to be the acoustical laws governing the organization of sound. These concerns form a central consideration in the systems developed by both Sauveur and Rameau, and their discussions of tuning form an important base for the works of other theorists later in the century.

One of these works was the *mémoire* presented to the Academy in 1742 by André Barrigue de Montvallon (1678-after 1773), "Conseiller au Parlement d'Aix en Provence" and an amateur musician.[36] Entitled "Nouveau système [de musique][37] sur les intervales des tons et sur les proportions des accords," it proposes a tuning for keyboard instruments founded on several assumptions: the natural and principal tuning for music is just intonation; there is a need to preserve as closely as possible the variety and expression of different modes derived from that tuning, while providing an adjustment that permits instrumentalists to perform music in transposed keys; *ut* is the fundamental pitch in music, to which all others are related; and a tuning adjustment larger than a comma is perceived as dissonant by the human ear. Based on these as-

---

[34] See the listings in Jos. Berthelé (ed.), *Répertoire numérique des Archives départmentales de l'Hérault, Série D* (Montpellier: Lauriol, 1925), pp. 40 and 43.

[35] Further on Estève, see DBF, XIII, cols. 89-90.

[36] Presentation: 5 mai 1742 (Reg., T. 61, p. 196; original *mémoire* in *pochette de séance*); Report (Nicole and Fouchy): 1 septembre 1742 (Reg., T. 61, pp. 384*-387*; original in *pochette de séance*; summarized in *Histoire*, 1742, pp. 117-124). An earlier presentation by Montvallon, made on 8 mai 1720 (Reg., T. 39, f. 155), "un écrit . . . sur la transposition du clavecin," was assigned to Mairan for examination, but no report survives.

[37] The words "de musique" of the title appear, not in the original *mémoire*, but in the *Histoire*, 1742, p. 117.

sumptions, Montvallon considers and rejects temperaments proposed by others (especially by Sauveur), instead recommending the adoption of his own system, believed by him to be best suited to the requirements of keyboard instruments. Furthermore, a practical method for tuning those instruments to the desired temperament is provided in this study.

Montvallon's tuning (which Romieu later characterized as just intonation with but a slight adjustment of *ut#* and *sol#*)[38] proves to be perhaps less novel than he suggested. It approximates very closely temperaments proposed, for example, by Ramos de Pareja in the sixteenth century and Kepler in the seventeenth; Barbour considers that it "follows a more familiar order in the selection of notes" than did one offered by his contemporary Euler.[39] In arriving at an assessment of Montvallon's proposal, the Academy's examining committee undertook tuning a harpsichord to his system (reasoning, "comme l'oreille est le premier et principal juge de ces matières");[40] they found the resultant harmony to be "très regulière," and the entire proposal "ingénieux et utile."

In 1749, the Academy heard a presentation of "Règles nouvelles de la musique, suivant l'ancien principe de Pitagoras," devised by "le Sr. Tremolet, curé du Tartre Gaudran."[41] The principle described is the derivation of a "natural"musical scale through the systematic division of a string into its aliquot parts (that is, by $\frac{1}{2}$, $\frac{1}{3}$, $\frac{1}{4}$, etc.), a process attributed to Pythagoras. It is found not only that each resultant interval has a proportion different from every other one in the system, but also that a "natural" division of the octave into a usable scale of 9 notes takes place with the numbers, 8, 9, 10, 11, 12, 13, 14, 15, 16, to which the author assigns the solmization syllables, *ut, re, mi, fa, sol, la, za, si, ut.* The note added to the usual 8-note scale, *za,* is not to be considered a *si*[b], but a note equal in importance to all the others. Tremolet demonstrates how the new scale can be adapted to the vio-

---

[38] *Mémoires,* 1758, pp. 486–487.

[39] See the description of "Montvallon's monochord" (derived from Romieu, ibid.) in Barbour, *Tuning and Temperament,* pp. 101-102; comparative tables of temperaments by Ramos, Kepler, and Euler are given on pp. 90, 97-98, and 101.

[40] Reg., T. 61, p. 387★: "since the ear is the first and principal judge of these matters." See further on Montvallon, Michaud (ed.), *Biographie universelle,* XXIX, 205; Fétis, *Biographie universelle,* VI, 188; and DBF, V, col. 608.

[41] Presentation: 12 mars 1749 (Reg., T. 68, p. 156; engraved table, inscribed, "Se vend à Paris, chez Bailleul, le jeune," in *pochette de séance*).

lin. The committee report rejects the system as evolving a scale that is "très fausse," not useful to practice, and not novel in its derivation.[42]

Later in the century, two additional proposals were made describing essentially the same system, on neither of which a committee report was issued. In 1767, T. Jamard (b.c. 1720), "chanoine régulier de Ste.-Geneviève, prieur de Roquefort, membre de l'Académie des Sciences, Belles-lettres et Arts de Rouen," presented a *mémoire*, "Sur la théorie de la musique," which was subsequently withdrawn by its author.[43] Later published, with the title, *Recherches sur la théorie de la musique*,[44] and displaying approval by the Academy in Rouen,[45] the work describes the very system proposed earlier by Tremolet, with some slight modifications. Twenty years afterward, in 1787, l'Abbé Jean-Etienne Feytou (1742-1816), a parish priest from Haute-Marne who contributed articles on music theory to the *Encyclopédie méthodique*,[46] appeared before the Academy to read a "mémoire sur le système harmonique de Pythagore."[47] The *Registres* are silent as to action taken on the proposal. Although the work was not published, it is probable that the description of Feytou's system found in the *Encyclopédie méthodique* formed the basis of his proposal to the Academy.[48] Fundamentally, it is the one described earlier by Tremolet and Jamard.

[42] Report (d'Alembert and Mairan): 19 mars 1749 (Reg., T. 68, p. 175; original in *pochette de séance*). A "second mémoire sur la musique" was presented by Tremolet on 15 mai 1751 (Reg., T. 70, p. 353), examined by Mairan and d'Alembert, and rejected ("rapport verbal" made on 19 mai 1751; Reg., T. 70, p. 356).

[43] Presentation: 28 janvier 1767 (Reg., T. 86, f. 13v). The inscription, "retiré par l'auteur," is found in the *Liste des Commissions données en 1767* and in the *Registre du Comité de librairie, 1749-1770* (p. 161), both MSS in AdS.

[44] Publ., Paris: Jombert and Mérigot, and Rouen: Machuel, 1769. The publication is given favorable review in *Journal encyclopédique*, 1 avril 1770 (III, i, 48-55).

[45] An *extrait* from the *Registres* of the Academy in Rouen is appended to the print; the date of presentation is given as 15 mars 1769. It should be noted that Jamard attributes work by the theorist Charles-Louis-Denis Ballière (1729-1800) as the source for his ideas; Ballière was secretary of the Rouen Academy at the time, and a member of the committee assigned to judge Jamard's proposal (Fétis, *Biographie universelle*, IV, 419-420, compares the ideas of Jamard and Ballière). See the description of Jamard's system in *Encyclopédie méthodique: Musique*, II (Paris: veuve Agasse, 1818; repr., New York: Da Capo Press, 1971), 462-467.

[46] See DBF, XIII, col. 1270.

[47] Presentation: 23 mai 1787 (Reg., T. 106, f. 190).

[48] *Encyclopédie méthodique: Musique*, I, 480-485, 658; and II, 467-474. The "Dis-

IV. THEORY AND PRACTICE

The mathematician Jean-Edme Gallimard (1685-1771), a follower of Rameau, presented a *mémoire* to the Academy in 1754 entitled "La théorie des sons, applicable à la musique, où l'on démontre dans une exacte précision, les rapports de tous les intervales diatoniques et chromatiques de la gamme."[49] The essay derives in a systematic way the ratios of all intervals in the diatonic and chromatic scales of just intonation. The examining committee considered that the work contained little that was different from the treatment of the subject in Rameau's *Démonstration*; however, it judged the *mémoire* as "utile," chiefly for its tables.[50] *La théorie des sons* was published shortly afterward,[51] as was another work by Gallimard, *Arithmétique des musiciens*,[52] which proves to be the more innovative, both for its proposals of irregular tuning systems and for its use of logarithms in describing those systems.[53] Gallimard returned to the Academy ten years later, in 1764, to present "une nouvelle manière d'exécuter [chanter] la musique." The work does not survive, and although a committee was named to examine the proposal, no report was issued.[54]

Somewhat more comprehensive in its treatment of tuning systems than the work of either Montvallon or Gallimard is the "Mémoire théorique et pratique sur les systèmes tempérés de musique" by the physicist-lawyer, Jean-Baptiste Romieu (1723-1766),

cours préliminaire" to the work (I, vi) supplies the following information: "Au commencement de 1788 comme on imprimoit les premières feuilles de ce Dictionnaire, M. l'Abbé Feytou, annonça un cours de musique dans lequel il exposoit un nouveau système, ou peut-être le plus ancien de tous, celui de la nature, celui que Pythagore avoit ou inventé, ou receuilli dans ses voyages en Asie. . . ."

[49] Presentation: 11 mai 1754 (missing from the *Registres*, but listed in the *Liste des Commissions* for that date; original *mémoire* in *pochette de séance*).

[50] Report (d'Alembert and Le Roy): 28 juin 1754 (Reg., T. 73, pp. 383-384; extract in *pochette de séance*).

[51] Publ., Paris: Ballard, Bauche, Saugrain fils, and the author, 1754; an *extrait* of the committee report is appended.

[52] *Arithmétique des musiciens, ou essai qui a pour objet diverses espèces de calcul des intervalles, le développement de plusieurs sistèmes de sons de la musique . . .* (Paris: [Duperron], 1754). The printing privilege, dated 24 décembre 1754, is cited in Brenet, "La librairie musicale," p. 449.

[53] See the description of Gallimard's tuning in Barbour, *Tuning and Temperament*, pp. 136-137 and 140.

[54] Presentation: 29 août 1764 (Reg., T. 83, f. 337): "a new manner to perform [sing] music"; committee named: Mairan and Fouchy. Further on Gallimard, see Fétis, *Biographie universelle*, III, 391.

a member of the Société Royale des Sciences in Montpellier. The paper was read before the Société in 1754;[55] in 1762, it was sent by that body to the Paris Academy for inclusion among its printed *Mémoires*[56]—exercising a privilege accorded the Montpellier Society in 1706 by royal statute.[57] While the *mémoire* was not read to the Academy, it did undergo committee examination[58] and, subsequently, was published among the *Mémoires* for 1758.[59]

In his *mémoire*, Romieu analyzes proposals for tempering the tuning of keyboard instruments offered by various theorists—including Salinas, Zarlino, Mersenne, Kircher, Huygens, Montvallon, Euler, Sauveur, and Rameau. He finally recommends adoption of a $1/6$-comma meantone tuning, which he calls "tempérament anacratique," as best serving the needs of musicians. This temperament, not new with Romieu, "was in use for well over a century," according to Barbour.[60] The examining committee approved the *mémoire* and considered it worthy of publication by the Academy.

Although Romieu's paper provoked some controversy in Montpellier,[61] it was another work of his—not presented to the Academy—that stirred interest in Paris. On 16 décembre 1751, at an *assemblée publique* of the Montpellier Society, Romieu presented his "Nouvelle découverte des sons harmoniques graves dont la résonance est très-sensible dans les accords des instruments à vent," in which he describes the discovery and characteristics of combination tones (more specifically, difference tones), identified as lower harmonics ("des sons harmoniques graves").[62] Romieu recognized the value of these tones to harmony, noting that their

---

[55] Read: 29 août 1754 (noted in *Mémoires*, 1758, p. 483).

[56] Presentation: 22 décembre 1762 (Reg., T. 81, f. 318); reconsideration: 12 janvier 1763 (Reg., T. 82, f. 6v).

[57] See Francisque Bouillier, "Les affiliations des académies de province avec l'Académie Française et l'Académie des Sciences," in *Séances et travaux de l'Académie des sciences morales et politiques*, XXXIX (1879), pp. 270-274.

[58] Report (Mairan and d'Alembert): 19 janvier 1763 (Reg., T. 82, f. 16v; original in *pochette de séance*).

[59] Printed in *Mémoires*, 1758, pp. 483-519.

[60] Barbour, *Tuning and Temperament*, p. 43.

[61] Estève and Romieu exchanged "réflexions" on the *mémoire* in 1756; see Berthelé (ed.), *Répertoire numérique*, pp. 40 and 43.

[62] See the edition by Edouard Roche, *Notice sur les travaux de J.-B. Romieu* (Montpellier: Boehm et fils, 1879), pp. 21-26.

presence supports Rameau's theory of inversion and the identity of octaves. Although published in 1752, the paper did not attract immediate attention, and it was only ten years later that his discovery was first acknowledged in print, in the "Discours préliminaire" to the reedition of d'Alembert's *Elémens de musique théorique et pratique* (1762).[63]

The acknowledgment is made in context of a reexamination of Giuseppe Tartini's *Trattato di musica* of 1754,[64] cited earlier by d'Alembert as being the first work to describe combination tones. Not only is this claim discredited by reference to Romieu's paper, but, also, Tartini's treatise is generally described in a derogatory manner. Since d'Alembert served on the committee (together with Mairan) appointed to examine a French translation of Tartini's system, brought to the Academy in 1759 (of which no report was filed),[65] one wonders if his remarks do not reflect the Academy's judgment of that work.

A different response greeted the work of Tartini's fellow countryman Giovenale Sacchi (1726-1789), who sent a copy of his *Del numero e delle misure delle corde musiche e loro corrispondenze* (1761) to the Academy, shortly after its publication. A member of the Barnabite monastic order, Sacchi was active in several learned societies and was a productive writer on music. The treatise is essentially a study of the physico-mathematical bases for musical scales and intervals, derived from vibrating strings, in which the question of tuning keyboard instruments is also considered. An oral report made on the work judged it to be "bon," and expressed the Academy's appreciation for its receipt.[66]

[63] D'Alembert, *Elémens de musique théorique et pratique* (Lyon: J.-M. Bruyset, 1762), pp. xix-xx; reproduced in Jacobi, *The Complete Theoretical Writings*, VI, 469. D'Alembert made a presentation of this edition to the Académie Française on 12 décembre 1761; see the reference in Institut de France, *Les Registres de l'Académie Françoise, 1672-1793*, 4 vols. (Paris: Firmin-Didot, 1895-1906), III, 154.

[64] Giuseppe Tartini, *Trattato di musica secondo la vera scienza dell' armonia* (Padova: Stamperia del seminario, 1754; repr., New York: Broude Bros., 1966, and Padua: CEDAM, 1973).

[65] Presentation (Malesherbes): 20 janvier 1759 (Reg., T. 78, p. 61): "Une traduction françoise de l'abrégé Italien du système de M. Tartini, sur le vrai principe de l'harmonie."

[66] Presentation: 23 mai 1761 (Reg., T. 80, f. 94v); Report (Mairan): 27 mai 1761 (Reg., T. 80, f. 100). The work was published in Milan: G. Mazzucchelli, 1761. Further on Sacchi, see Fétis, *Biographie universelle*, VII, 359-360; and the listing of his musical publications in RISM, B VI, 2, pp. 743-745.

Several additional proposals specifically on tuning systems were made to the Academy later in the century. In 1769, "M. Dupéron" (not otherwise identified) presented "plusieurs [cinq] mémoires sur la musique" for approbation.[67] In his *mémoires*, Dupéron favors reduction of all tuning systems to two, which he believes are more "natural" than all others proposed by theorists: the ¼-comma and ²/₇-comma meantone temperaments, both of which were propounded in the sixteenth century by Gioseffo Zarlino.[68] He further recommends a new notation to describe tempered notes, as well as the use of logarithms in calculating different tunings. Although the examining committee contested details of his proposals, it generally considered the set of essays to be a useful contribution "to the perfection of the science of music" and worthy of approval. Dupéron returned to the Academy two years later, in 1771, with yet another proposal "sur la musique," but neither his *mémoire* nor a report survives.[69]

The mathematician and music theorist Jean–Baptiste Mercadier de Belesta (1750-1816), a correspondent of the scientific societies in both Montpellier and Toulouse, presented a "Mémoire sur les rapports des sons musicaux" to the Paris Academy in 1783.[70] In the *mémoire*, Mercadier seeks to demonstrate that, although the ratios of consonant intervals expressed in lengths of vibrating strings are theoretically correct, the resultant ratios must be understood as only approximate variables. He argues that in practice, no two strings can ever be physically identical to one another, and, consequently, theoretically correct ratios cannot be derived directly from any strings; they must be tuned by ear to the intervals expressed by the ratios. The committee report expresses reservations regarding the propositions of Mercadier, but it judges the work to be based on sound experiments, meriting approval.[71]

[67] Presentation I: 25 novembre 1769 (Reg., T. 88, f. 367); Presentation II ("un supplément"): 13 décembre 1769 (Reg., T. 88, f. 386); Report (Mairan and Pingré): 7 février 1770 (Reg., T. 89, f. 25-32v; original in *pochette de séance*).

[68] See the description of these temperaments in Barbour, *Tuning and Temperament*, pp. 32-33.

[69] Presentation: 17 avril 1771 (Reg., T. 90, f. 88v); Report (Fouchy and Pingré): 5 juin 1771 (recorded in *plumitif* of 1771, AdS).

[70] Presentation: 23 juillet 1783 (Reg., T. 102, f. 159); Report (Fouchy, d'Alembert, and Pingré): 3 septembre 1783 (Reg., T. 102, f. 199v-202; original *rapport* and *mémoire* [dated 14 juillet 1783], together with a letter requesting an audience [dated 1 août 1783], are in the *pochette de séance*).

[71] Mercadier subsequently presented this very *mémoire* to the Montpellier Société

IV. THEORY AND PRACTICE

Mercadier had earlier approached the Academy, in 1776, with an "Exposition sommaire d'un nouveau système de musique";[72] this was essentially an excerpt from a larger work of his that had received approval from the Toulouse Academy in 1773 and was subsequently published, prior to its presentation to the Paris Academy.[73] No committee assignment was made to review the "Exposition."

A practical proposal for dividing the octave into twelve equal parts was sent in a communication to the Academy in 1778 by Pierre-Joseph Joubert de La Salette (1762?-1832), a captain in the Corps Royal de l'Artillerie from Grenoble.[74] It was based on the projection of a slightly-flat "just" fourth, which the author derived from a pure fifth on a monochord, as its "true" inversion.[75] A committee was named to review the proposal, but no report

---

in November of 1783 (see the listing in Berthelé, *Répertoire numérique*, p. 43, where additional *mémoires* read by Mercadier to the Société are cited). Reference to both the Montpellier and the Paris presentations is made in his publication "Mémoire sur l'accord du clavecin, & sur le système de M. de Boisgelou, concernant les intervalles musicaux," read before the academy in Toulouse on 27 avril 1780, and printed in vol. 3 of the *Histoire et Mémoires de l'Académie Royale des Sciences, Inscriptions et Belles-Lettres de Toulouse*, III (Toulouse: D. Desclassan, 1788), pp. 139-168 (references are on p. 140). See Barbour, *Tuning and Temperament*, pp. 168-169, for a description of Mercadier's irregular tuning system.

[72] Presentation: 20 novembre 1776 (Reg., T. 95, f. 298; original *mémoire* in *pochette de séance*).

[73] An "Extrait des registres de l'Académie Royale des Sciences, Inscriptions et Belles-Lettres de Toulouse," dated 29 juillet 1773, is appended to Mercadier's *Nouveau système de musique théorique et pratique* (Paris: Valade, 1776; Valade and Laporte, 1777), pp. 302-304; the work received a printing privilege on 8 juin 1776 (see Brenet, "La librairie musicale," p. 462). The "Exposition" is derived principally from parts 3 and 4 of the *Nouveau système*. On Mercadier, see Fétis, *Biographie universelle*, VI, 90.

[74] Presentation: 18 novembre 1778 (Reg., T. 97, f. 315; original proposal, dated 1 octobre 1778, in *pochette de séance*). In view of La Salette's accomplishments by 1778, his generally accepted birth date of 1762 must be called into question.

[75] La Salette's interest in his new system of tuning persisted into the nineteenth century; the system reappears in contributions by him to the proceedings of the Académie des Beaux-Arts (see Marcel Bonnaire [ed.], *Procès-verbaux de l'Académie des Beaux-Arts*, III [Paris: Armand Colin, 1943], pp. 159 and 161-162), and in his *Considérations sur les divers systèmes de la musique ancienne et moderne, et sur le genre enharmonique des Grecs*, 2 vols. (Paris: Gaujon, 1810), passim, in which he argues for the adoption of the interval of the fourth as fundamental to both ancient and modern music; in the work, he is identified as "Ancien Général de Brigade, Inspecteur d'Artillerie, Membre résidant de la Société académique de Grenoble."

survives.[76] Four years later, in 1782, a proposal was brought to the group by the brothers Robert, instrument makers in Paris, "pour prouver que le tempérament doit être exclus du clavier sans rien changer au doigté";[77] no report was issued.

A final paper devoted to scale systems and tuning was brought to the Academy in 1792 by Antoine Suremain de Missery (1767-1852), a military man who published works in philosophy and mathematics, as well as in music, and who was a member of the Academy in Dijon.[78] In the paper entitled "Théorie acoustico-musicale" (and subsequently published),[79] Suremain de Missery seeks to derive interval ratios for all known scales described by theorists, and to combine them into one, all-inclusive system. Among those tunings defined, he clearly favored equal temperament ("l'accord égal"). The committee report notes that there is little new in the work, but that it merits the Academy's approval for its comprehensiveness and organization.

Less concerned with tuning and temperament, and more with scale systems and their application to the practice of harmony, was the theorist-composer, Charles-Henri de Blainville (1711-after 1777); he made three petitions to the Academy over a period of twenty years. The first of these, presented in 1751, was entitled "Essay sur un troisième mode,"[80] and it appears to have made a

---

[76] Committee named: Fouchy and Vandermonde.

[77] Presentation: 20 juillet 1782 (Reg., T. 101, f. 137v): "to prove that temperament ought to be [capable of being] excluded from keyboard [instruments] without affecting the fingering at all"; committee named: Bochart de Saron, Laplace, and Vandermonde. The brothers Robert had earlier produced a "buffet d'orgue" capable of dynamic change, reported in *Almanach musical*, 1778 (IV, 32).

[78] Presentation: 4 août 1792 (Reg., T. 109B, p. 236); Report (Vandermonde and Haüy [Monge was named to the committee, but did not participate in the report]): 1 septembre 1792 (Reg., T. 109B, pp. 255-260; original in *pochette de séance*). An earlier *mémoire*, "sur la musique," presented by Suremain on 19 décembre 1789 (Reg., T. 108, f. 239v; committee named: Vandermonde and Haüy) had no report; it may well have been rewritten as the later proposal.

[79] *Théorie acoustico-musicale, ou de la doctrine des sons rapportée aux principes de leur combinaison* (Paris: Firmin-Didot, 1793); an *extrait* of the Academy's report is found on pp. [i-vii]. Suremain de Missery is described as a "très-bon musicien & mathématicien profond" in the *Encyclopédie méthodique: Musique* (I, xii), in which he collaborated. Further on him, see Fétis, *Biographie universelle*, VIII, 168.

[80] Presentation: 16 juin 1751 (Reg., T. 70, p. 365; original *mémoire* in *pochette de séance*); Report (Mairan and Fouchy): 17 juillet 1751 (Reg., T. 70, pp. 441-443; original in *pochette de séance*).

stir among his contemporaries. In it, Blainville proposes the establishment of a third mode in music, which he calls "mode mixte"
because it combines qualities of the other two, major and minor.
The new mode arranges the seven notes of the diatonic scale beginning on *mi*, so that the semitones occur between steps 1-2 and
5-6, the others being whole-tones. Critics of the system argue that
the recommended mode is hardly new, having existed in music
for centuries, and that, harmonically, the mode has little individuality, since it is heard as either major or minor by listeners. The
Academy's examining committee, having audited a musical work
by Blainville written in the new mode and judging its harmony to
be "très bonne," approved the proposal for publication[81] and commended him for uncovering a new resource for music. The composition in question was a "Simphonie," first performed at the
Concert spirituel in Paris on 30 mai 1751, which provoked a controversy on the new mode in publications of the time.[82]

Blainville's second presentation to the Academy, made in 1765,
was a *mémoire* entitled "De l'enharmonique," in which he proposes
readoption of the quarter-tone in music.[83] Because of its
"délicatesse," he favors its use melodically by voices and bowed
string instruments, recommending its insertion in a series of semi-
tones, preferably accompanied by a chord of either the diminished

---

[81] *Essay sur un troisième mode présenté et aprouvé par Mrs. de l'Académie des Sciences,
joint la Simphonie exécutée au concert du Château des Thuilleries, 30 may 1751* (Paris:
the author, Ve. Boivin, Le Clerc, Mlle. Castagnery, 1751). An *extrait* of the committee report is appended.

[82] The controversy was waged principally in the *Mercure de France* in letters by
Rousseau (juin 1751, II, 174-178), Serre (septembre 1751, pp. 166-170; janvier
1752, I, 160-173, which forms the basis for the "deuxième essai" in Serre's *Essais
sur les principes de l'harmonie* [Paris: Prault fils, 1753; repr., New York: Broude Bros.,
1967], pp. 19-99), and Blainville (novembre 1751, pp. 120-124; mai 1752, pp. 137-
147). Rousseau describes the new mode in his *Dictionnaire* (1768), pp. 291-292,
where he refers to Blainville as "un homme d'esprit . . . un musicien très-versé
dans les principes de son art." Later in the century, Roussier takes issue with the
new mode in *Mémoire sur la musique des anciens* (Paris: Lacombe, 1770; repr., New
York: Broude Bros., 1966), pp. 175-182, and Laborde in *Essai*, III, 577-585. Concerning the "Simphonie," see DBF, VI, cols. 562-563. See further, MGG, I, cols.
1889-1891.

[83] Presentation: 17 août 1765 (Reg., T. 84, f. 352; original *mémoire* in *pochette de
séance*); Report (Mairan and Pingré): 4 septembre 1765 (Reg., T. 84, f. 371v-375v;
original in *pochette de séance*).

seventh, or the augmented sixth, or the diminished third (which he calls "septième sousdiminuée"). The committee report approves the proposal, although it questions adding harmonic instability, by use of the quarter-tone, to already unstable seventh chords.[84] A final presentation of Blainville's work was made in 1770, with consideration of his "nouveau système d'harmonie." A committee was appointed to review the work, but no report was made.[85]

The principles of harmony formed an area for study late in the century by Alexandre-Théophile Vandermonde (1735-1796), who was appointed to the Academy as a geometer in 1771 and became one of its most active members in musical matters just prior to the Revolution. Trained initially for a career in music (he appears to have been a violinist), and turning afterward to mathematics, Vandermonde is said to have been considered a mathematician by musicians, and a musician by mathematicians. Notwithstanding this latter view, his contributions to mathematics, while small in number, have been judged to be significant and influential.[86] Those to music, however, have not; they reside in one major paper, "Système d'harmonie applicable à l'état actuel de la musique," presented in two parts to the Academy, in 1778[87] and 1780,[88] and published in the *Journal des Sçavans*.[89]

Seemingly disturbed by the direction of "la musique moderne," Vandermonde notes that great liberties are taken by musicians in

[84] The *mémoire* does not appear to have been published. However, Blainville's *Histoire générale, critique et philologique de la musique* (Paris: Pissot, 1767; repr., Geneva: Minkoff, 1972), devotes a section to discussion of "l'enharmonique" (pp. 167-171), as well as one to "mode mixte" (pp. 119-122).

[85] Presentation: 29 août 1770 (Reg., T. 89, f. 240v). Committee named: Pingré and d'Alembert; Fouchy replaced Pingré on 18 décembre 1771 (Reg., T. 90, f. 250v-251).

[86] DSB, XIII, 571.

[87] Presentation I ("paquet cacheté"): 8 août 1778 (Reg., T. 97, f. 271); Presentation II: 14 novembre 1778 (*assemblée publique*; reported in *Histoire*, 1778, p. 51); reread 9 décembre 1778 (Reg., T. 97, f. 326).

[88] Presentation: 15 novembre 1780 (*assemblée publique*, Reg., T. 99, f. 250).

[89] *Journal des Sçavans*, décembre 1778, pp. 885-862 (part one); janvier 1781, pp. 92-119, and février 1781, pp. 273-300 (part two). Both parts are summarized in *Histoire*, 1778 (publ. 1781), pp. 51-55. See also, Lacepède's *éloge*, in *Mémoires de l'Institut national des sciences et arts, pour l'an IV de la République*, I (Paris: Baudouin, Thermidor An VI [1798]), pp. xxiii-xxiv.

following the natural principles of harmony derived from physics and mathematics, and questions whether music can actually have a "theory." He writes,

> Les Systèmes sont tombés en discrédit . . . . Le Juge Suprême est une oreille exercée; tout le monde en convient. . . . La fonction unique de cette science [musique] est de diriger le plaisir de l'oreille.

> [Systems have fallen into disrepute . . . . The Supreme Judge is a trained ear; everyone agrees . . . . The unique function of this science (music) is to guide the pleasure of the ear.]

Vandermonde rejected systems of harmony proposed by others, and sought fundamental laws that govern "le jugement de l'oreille"—laws that, while based on natural principles, adapt these principles to the requirements of "l'oreille et le goût." To his mind, the laws can be reduced to two, the first of which governs chord succession in music, and the second, part-writing.[90] At the root of both are Vandermonde's contentions that the "accord parfait" (the major or minor triad) on a given tonic (which he calls the "base d'harmonie") is central to all music; that chords should be built on fixed notes in the mode (altered chords are considered substitutes for diatonic ones), of which the tonic and dominant are the most important; and that the ideal music is simple, chordal, and tuneful. In truth, neither of his two laws is "fundamental" in any sense; rather, they both describe elementary, restrictive procedures for succession and part-writing of neighboring chords. Vandermonde proposed to provide tables illustrating these laws (which he, himself, describes as mechanical in nature)—comprising a "dictionnaire d'harmonie" of special value to students. His promise to publish the tables (once approved by "excellens compositeurs"), as well as to prepare a separate, more developed exposition of his ideas, was never realized.[91] In fact, little interest was shown in his system by contemporaries, some of whom were critical of Vandermonde's views.[92]

[90] Vandermonde mentions the "grands musiciens" Philidor, Gluck, and Piccinni as endorsing his ideas.

[91] The MS tables survive in *Dossier Vandermonde*, AdS.

[92] See the critical review in Laborde, *Essai*, III, 690-700. Jacqueline Hecht, "Un exemple de multidisciplinarité: Alexandre Vandermonde (1735-1796)," in *Population*, 26/4 (1971), 646, suggests that Laborde's review may have lacked objectivity,

Shortly afterward, in 1781, the noted German composer and theorist Georg Joseph Vogler (1749-1814) sent "un livre manuscrit" to the Academy for review, entitled "Précis d'un nouveau système musical ou accord mutuel des principes de la musique, de leur application et de leurs effets, démontré et rendu sensible, visible et palpable, sur un instrument appellé Tonomètre."[93] The MS has not survived, but the Academy's report refers to it as an "abrégé" of the German treatises published by Vogler over a period of years, in which his musical system is described. Three parts of the system were dealt with in the MS: intonation—an explanation of the major and minor modes, and of scale systems used in music; harmony—the derivation of chord structures, including those of the seventh built on each of the diatonic scale degrees; and the rules of composition. The examining committee judged the first and second parts to be largely subjective in nature, lacking adequate explanation or demonstration; it found the third the most interesting, but did not consider its subject matter appropriate to academic review. Of special interest to the committee was Vogler's description of his *tonomètre*, an eight-string monochord supplied with bridges, used to demonstrate interval ratios to both the ear and the eye ("aux yeux").[94] Although the work

owing to his displeasure with Vandermonde's critical "observations" on essays published (together with Roussier's rebuttal) in Laborde's *Mémoires sur les proportions musicales* (Paris: P.-D. Pierres, 1781), pp. 42-70. See further, the disparaging description of Vandermonde's system in Alexandre-Etienne Choron and François-J.-M. Fayolle, *Dictionnaire historique des musiciens*, 2d ed. (Paris: Chimot, 1817), I, 82; and the milder criticism in Fétis, *Biographie universelle*, VIII, 303-304.

[93] Presentation: 25 juillet 1781 (Reg., T. 100, f. 159v); Report (d'Alembert and Vandermonde): 5 septembre 1781 (Reg., T. 100, f. 213-215v; original in *pochette de séance*). The work is listed among *mémoires* approved for printing, in *Histoire*, 1781, p. 52. In his *Choral-System* (Copenhagen: N. Christensen, 1800), pp. 3-5, Vogler refers to the presentation of his system to the Academy. He also refers to one before the president of the Royal Society of London, Joseph Banks, in 1783; but according to J. H. Mee, "The records of the Royal Society afford no trace of communication from Vogler or anything else bearing on the question" (*Grove's Dictionary of Music and Musicians*, 5th ed. [1954], X, 39). However, a letter from Vogler to Banks, dated 30 May 1783 and requesting an audience, does survive (British Library, MS Add. 8095, f. 235; see the listing in *The Banks Letters*, ed. W. R. Dawson [London: Trustees of the British Museum, 1958], p. 847).

[94] The *tonomètre* is described in *Journal des Sçavans*, mars 1782 (pp. 165-168), and *Almanach musical*, 1783 (VIII, 58). It appears similar to the "octochord" illustrated in MGG, XIII, cols. 1895-1896, also attributed to Vogler.

was judged worthy of printing, it does not appear to have seen publication.

Two other theorists concerned with the development of musical systems should be mentioned briefly, as having brought their work to the Academy. In both cases, presentation was made of material already published, of which the Academy acknowledged receipt but did not undertake written evaluation. The first of these is Pierre-Joseph Roussier (1716 or 1717-1792), whose name appears several times in documents at the Academy related to presentations by others (i.e., Laborde, Goermans, and Cousineau). In each instance, he is described as a proponent of a musical temperament based on pythagorean tuning of earlier times, on which he wrote extensively. A book and two printed *lettres*, dealing basically with the same subject, were presented by him to the Academy in 1770 and 1771. These are his *Mémoire sur la musique des anciens* (1770)[95] and "Lettre[s] . . . touchant la division du zodiaque, et l'institution de la semaine planétaire, relativement à une progression géométrique, d'où dépendent les proportions musicales," from the *Journal des beaux-arts et des sciences* (1770-1771).[96]

The second of the two theorists is Anton Bemetzrieder (1739-after 1808), an Alsatian musician who established himself in Paris (where Diderot became his patron)[97] and later made his home in London. In 1781, the *Registres* note that Bemetzrieder made a presentation of "la collection de ses oeuvres sur la musique"[98] (Vandermonde reported on the set),[99] and in 1783, two additional works of his were received.[100] Neither entry indicates titles. How-

---

[95] Presentation: 4 avril 1770 (Reg., T. 89, f. 109v-110).

[96] Presentation (*lettre* I): 28 novembre 1770 (Reg., T. 89, f. 284), publ. in *Journal*, issue of novembre-décembre 1770. Presentation (*lettre* II): 31 juillet 1771 (Reg., T. 90, f. 179v), publ. in *Journal*, issue of août 1771. Further on Roussier, see Richard D. Osborne, *The Theoretical Writings of Abbé Pierre-Joseph Roussier* (Ph.D. dissertation, Ohio State Univ., 1966).

[97] Diderot was a collaborator in Bemetzrieder's most successful work, *Leçons de clavecin*, (1771). See further, Robert Niklaus, "Diderot and the *Leçons de clavecin et principes d'harmonie* par Bemetzrieder (1771)," in *Modern Miscellany presented to Eugène Vinaver* (Manchester: Manchester Univ. Press, 1969), pp. 180-194; and Jean-Michel Bardez, *Diderot et la musique* (Paris: Champion, 1975).

[98] Presentation: 19 mai 1781 (Reg., T. 100, f. 119): "the collection of his works on music."

[99] On 23 mai 1781 (recorded in the *plumitif* for 1781, AdS).

[100] Presentation: 3 mai 1783 (Reg., T. 102, f. 114).

ever, in the inventory of the Academy's library made in 1784,[101] four works by Bemetzrieder are listed: *Le tolérantisme musical* (1779), *Nouvel essai sur l'harmonie* (1779), *Exemples des principaux élémens* (1780), and *Méthode et réflexions sur les leçons de musique* (1781).[102] Whether or not these comprised the entire set of works presented to the Academy by this productive author is not known.[103]

Musical Pedagogy

Although the larger part of the writings on music proposed to the Academy for approbation concerned the development of new concepts and systems, a smaller but not minor literature devoted to musical pedagogy also evolved there. Throughout its work in the theory of music, the Academy continued to show interest in the application of that theory, as well as in the teaching of it to the uninitiated. Methods of instruction, especially for beginners in music, began to be brought to the Academy from about the mid-eighteenth century, and central to most all of them are the novel musical ideas developed in writings of the time.

Early among these is the "Tour du clavier" presented to the Academy in 1745 by Louis-Antoine Dornel (c. 1685-1765), organist at "l'abbaye Royale de Ste.-Geneviève de Paris."[104] It is a short, practical manual intended to demonstrate to the student accompanist at the keyboard how to modulate in all the major and minor keys, around the circle of fifths. This is accomplished principally by means of two charts that contain model modulatory progres-

[101] BI, MS 1826, f. 38; also listed in MS 1385 (another catalogue of the Academy's library), p. 495.

[102] See the inventory of his writings in RISM, B VI, 1, pp. 132-136; and in MGG, I, cols. 1619-1621.

[103] Mention should be made of yet another printed work received by the Academy on which no report was made (probably because its subject matter did not lie within the Academy's purview), the *Mémoire au roi, concernant l'exploitation du privilège de l'opéra* (dated in Paris, 29 avril 1789), by the celebrated violinist Giovanni Battista Viotti (1753-1824). Presentation was made on 9 mai 1789 (Reg., T. 108, f. 125) and the work is listed among "Livres présentés à l'Académie par des académiciens ou par savans étrangers" (BI, MS 1827, p. 30).

[104] Presentation: 31 mars 1745 (Reg., T. 64, p. 91; original *mémoire* in *pochette de séance*); Report (Fouchy): 19 mai 1745 (Reg., T. 64, p. 145; original and extract in *pochette de séance*).

(101)

sions notated in figured bass symbols, to which is appended a table that classifies the principal chords used in accompaniment according to their relative consonance or dissonance. Although the committee report takes issue with the classification of several chords in the table, it generally endorses the work as worthy of its author's reputation.[105]

A later aid to the keyboardist, similar in format to Dornel's *Tour du clavier*, was presented in 1768 by François-Guillaume Vial (b.c. 1730), a Parisian musician (nephew of the violinist Jean-Marie Leclair).[106] Entitled *Arbre généalogique de l'harmonie*, the work is composed primarily of tables that provide fundamental harmonic progressions in all the major and minor keys; rules for modulation, for building chords, and for harmonic succession (harmonic motion by fifths and thirds are favored); and general guides to "l'art de préluder." The short committee report approves the work as useful, especially to those who are learning to compose.[107]

Two other aids for the performer were proposed to the Academy in the 1760s: "un mémoire contenant un nouveau système pour faciliter l'étude et l'exécution de la musique" by "M. le Chevalier de Roubin" in 1764,[108] and "un écrit contenant des

---

[105] The work was published in a slightly expanded version later that same year (Paris, "au Mont-Parnasse," 1745); its approval by the Academy is prominently displayed on the title page, as is a copy of the *extrait* of the committee report at the end.

[106] Presentation: 7 mai 1768 (Reg., T. 87, f. 72v); Report (d'Alembert and Le Roy): 20 mai 1768 (Reg., T. 87, f. 107-107v; original in *pochette de séance*).

[107] Publ., Paris: the author, [1766]. The royal printing privilege was issued on 26 novembre 1766 (cited in Brenet, "La librairie musicale," p. 456). Contemporary references in *Annonces*, 4 décembre 1766 (p. 926): *L'Avantcoureur*, 1 décembre 1766 (pp. 755-756), 23 janvier 1769 (p. 49). Further on Vial, see Fétis, *Biographie universelle*, VIII, 338; and Lionel de La Laurencie, *L'Ecole française de violon de Lully à Viotti* (Paris: Delagrave, 1922-1924; repr., Geneva: Minkoff, 1971), I, 300-302.

[108] Presentation: 28 novembre 1764 (Reg., T. 83, f. 409): "a memoir concerning a new system to facilitate the study and performance of music." Some nine years later, in a letter dated "au pont St-Esprit ce 21ᵉ aoust 1773" and addressed to d'Alembert (BI, MS 2466, f. 196-199), Roubin describes a new simplified notation for music, not unlike others proposed to the Academy at about this time (reviewed above, Chap. III, Other Musical Inventions). It replaces notes with initials of solmization symbols, dispenses with use of clefs and staves, and employs dots, slashes, lines, and commas, variously placed, to indicate rhythm, range, mode, and accidentals in the music. In the letter, Roubin requests d'Alembert's judgment before formally presenting the system to the Academy; so far as is known, that presentation never took place.

règles d'accompagnement et de composition" by "M. Mignard" in 1767.[109] No report was filed for either work, nor do the *mémoires* survive.

Afterward, in 1774, the mechanician Doinet presented his "Manière de se servir des tons fixes, et de leur utilité pour accorder les clavecins et les épinettes," in which he proposes the use of a set of metal bars, tuned to the consecutive pitches of the chromatic scale, to enable harpsichordists (especially beginners, and those "without ears") to tune their instruments "sans maître . . . par le seul sens de la vüe."[110] This is achieved by placing a small, circular wire (of pewter or iron) around each string. When a given bar is struck and brought close to the bridge-end of the string to be tuned, the wire vibrates, being most agitated when the string and bar arrive exactly at the unison. In this way, the eye is said to determine "the point of perfect consonance." The review committee considered the method practicable and worthy of approval; however, this approval did not extend to Doinet's recommendation for specific temperaments to be adopted for tuning the metal bars, which the committee judged to lie outside the intended objectives of the principal proposal.

Some ten years later, in 1784, a proposal was brought to the Academy on teaching the practice of harmony by Jean-François Espic, chevalier de Lirou (1740-1806), a "passionate amateur of music and poetry."[111] In an extended work, entitled "Explication du système de l'harmonie par le cercle," Lirou seeks to clarify principles of harmonic motion developed by Rameau. This is done primarily by means of a circular chart, around the circumference of which note-names are arranged to show the processes of harmonic generation (limited to chord generation by thirds) and chord succession (restricted to contrary motion). The committee report questions some of the limitations on these processes adopted

[109] Presentation: 5 septembre 1767 (Reg., T. 86, f. 234v): "a written work containing rules of accompaniment and of composition."

[110] Presentation: 13 juillet 1774 (Reg., T. 93, f. 194v; original *mémoire* in *pochette de séance*); Report (Vandermonde and Fouchy): 17 août 1774 (Reg., T. 93, f. 244v-246; original in *pochette de séance*): "without a teacher . . . by the exclusive use of sight." Contemporary reference in *Almanach musical*, 1775 (I, 35-36). A review of other, non-musical devices proposed by Doinet in 1780 is found in *Dossier Monge* (AdS).

[111] Fétis, *Biographie universelle*, V, 316. Presentation: 11 décembre 1784 (Reg., T. 103, f. 256v-257); Report (Vandermonde and Fouchy): 12 février 1785 (Reg., T. 104, f. 31-32; original in *pochette de séance*).

(103)

IV. THEORY AND PRACTICE

by Lirou, and it recommends the addition of illustrative examples, needed particularly by beginners. However, it generally applauds the enthusiasm ("zèle éclairé") of the author and exhorts him to continue his musical research. The "Explication," published soon afterward, has several plates of examples appended that illustrate the text; these are not mentioned in the Academy's report, and may well have been added in response to the Committee's recommendation.[112]

The first of several proposals to the Academy for training in the elements of music was made in 1747 by Richardo de La Main, a member of the Jesuit order residing in Mexico.[113] Writing in Spanish, the author requests a review of his printed prospectus (also in Spanish) for a new publication on music, based on over thirty years of teaching experience, and intended primarily for the training of choir members in church. The projected work is in two books, the first devoted to music of the service, and the second to art music and to accompaniment. In his letter, La Main expresses unhappiness at being assigned duty "en las Indias," and exhorts the Academy to approve his proposal, thereby making possible his return to Europe ("la tierra de promesa") to oversee publication of his books. La Condamine, who was assigned to translate and to report on La Main's work, is severely critical of the proposal, which he rejects.[114] He notes that the author is current with neither the literature nor the theory of music, that the form of the work is unacceptable, and that its writing style is obscure, forced, and unintelligible.

The fate of La Main's proposal was hardly that which awaited the presentation in 1759 of Henri-Louis Choquel (d. 1767), a lawyer at the Parlement of Provence, of "La musique rendue sensible par la méchanique, ou nouveau système pour apprendre [facile-

[112] Publ. as *Explication du système de l'harmonie, pour abréger l'étude de la composition, et accorder la pratique avec la théorie* (London and Paris: Mérigot, Bailly, Bailleux, Boyer, 1785). After the Revolution, "le citoyen Lirou" presented the work to the Académie des Beaux-Arts in Paris (30 août 1797); see Bonnaire (ed.), *Procès-verbaux de l'Académie des Beaux-Arts*, I, 81.

[113] Presentation: 18 novembre 1747 (Reg., T. 66, p. 529; original letter [dated "Abril 19 de 1747"] and *prospectus* in *pochette de séance*).

[114] Report: 20 mars 1748 (Reg., T. 67, pp. 122-124; original in *pochette de séance*). The similarity of name between this author and the seventeenth-century English mathematician Richard Delamain should be noted (on the latter, see DSB, IV, 13). It is not known if they belonged to the same family.

ment] la musique soy-même."[115] The work is a rudimentary tutor in music intended to provide a means for teaching oneself to sing in tune and in time. It is through use of the monochord and the chronometer that Choquel hoped to achieve this end, systematically leading the student from elementary to more advanced problems. The committee report acknowledges that neither the rules given for solmization and transposition, nor the recommendations for the use of the monochord or the chronometer are new, but it commends the author for his clear and methodical presentation of how to apply these instruments to facilitate learning how to sing. The work was published shortly afterward and quickly became popular, undergoing several editions.[116]

Another method for teaching the rudiments of singing, this time to children, was presented in 1766 by l'Abbé Joseph Lacassagne (c. 1720–c. 1780), a musician from Marseilles.[117] Entitled *Traité général des élémens du chant*, the method proposes simplifying the reading of music by using only one clef (a movable G-clef) and three time signatures (2, 3, and $\frac{2}{3}$).[118] The examining committee approved the method, citing especially its clear and simple precepts, as well as its examples. The method was not without critics; a controversy concerning the proposals ensued, and they do not appear to have gained general favor.[119]

Several years later, in 1770, the Parisian composer, teacher, and "marchand de musique" Antoine Bailleux (c. 1720–between 1798 and 1801) presented his "Méthode pour apprendre facilement la

[115] Presentation: 29 août 1759 (Reg., T. 78bis, f. 716); Report (Mairan and Fouchy): 5 septembre 1759 (Reg., T. 78bis, f. 726-727; original *rapport* and extract in *pochette de séance*).

[116] Publ., Paris: Ballard, Duchesne, Lambert, and the author, 1759; the *extrait* of the committee report is appended. See the list of later editions in RISM, B VI, 1, p. 222 (ed. of 1762 repr., Geneva: Minkoff, 1972). Contemporary references to the work are numerous; see, for example, *L'Avantcoureur*, 6 mars 1769 (pp. 145-146), 8 mars 1762 (p. 158), and 7 septembre 1772 (pp. 565-566).

[117] Presentation: 14 juin 1766 (Reg., T. 85, f. 200v); Report (Fouchy and d'Alembert): 9 juillet 1766 (Reg., T. 85, f. 225v-226; original *rapport* and extract in *pochette de séance*).

[118] Publ., Paris: the author and veuve Duchesne; Versailles: Fournier, 1766; repr., Geneva: Minkoff, 1972); *extrait* of the committee report is appended. Contemporary references in *Annonces*, 1 décembre 1766 (pp. 914-915); *L'Avantcoureur*, 24 novembre 1766 (pp. 737-739), 11 janvier 1768 (pp. 18-19).

[119] Concerning the controversy, and further on Lacassagne, see MGG, VIII, cols. 22-23; Fétis, *Biographie universelle*, II, 203-204.

musique vocale et instrumentale."[120] Intended for beginners, the "Méthode" is a systematic primer in the elements of music, illustrated by examples.[121] The committee report mentions the restrictive nature of the work and its lack of variety; but it praises the author for his clear explanations, and for the variety and profusion of his examples, making the primer very useful to persons with no background in music.[122]

Certainly, the most unusual instructional method presented to the Academy was the poem *La música*, sent in 1780 shortly after its publication,[123] by the noted Spanish literary figure Tomás de Iriarte y Oropesa (1750-1791).[124] The work is reputed to have aroused attention throughout Europe at the time, and the Academy's commendation was but one of many it received.[125] *La música* is an extended poem consisting of a prologue, five cantos, and copious notes. Its aim is truly didactic, which Iriarte makes clear in his prologue. Indeed, a nineteenth-century commentator refers to the work as "more a treatise than a poem."[126] Its five cantos systematically treat the elements of music, harmony, rhythm, taste, and expression in music, its power to move the senses, and its place in the church, in the theater, and as entertainment.[127] The committee report expresses great appreciation for the work, de-

[120] Presentation: 23 mai 1770 (Reg., T. 89, f. 139-139v); Report (d'Alembert and Pingré): 13 juin 1770 (Reg., T. 89, f. 155-156; original in *pochette de séance*).

[121] Publ., Paris: the author, 1770; an *extrait* of the committee report is appended (p. 127). Contemporary references in *L'Avantcoureur*, 6 août 1770 (pp. 499-500); *Journal de Musique*, I, août 1770 (pp. 62-67). Further on Bailleux, see MGG, I, cols. 1086-1087; and Anik Devriès and François Lesure, *Dictionnaire des éditeurs de musique français*, 2 vols. (Geneva: Minkoff, 1979), I, 19-20.

[122] Mention should be made of a MS entitled "Elémens de musique," found among the papers in the Academy's library left by the astronomer Sédileau (d. 1693) and assigned to Fouchy for review on 14 décembre 1776 (Reg., T. 95, f. 307v). The purpose of the review is unclear; at all events, no report was issued, and the MS is not known to have survived. See the listing in BI, MS 1387, p. 3; and BN, MS fr.n.a. 5150, f. 39v.

[123] Publ., *La música, poema* (Madrid: Imprenta Real de la Gazeta, 1779). The poem underwent many eds.; see the listings in RISM, B VI, 1, pp. 429-430.

[124] Presentation: 31 mai 1780 (Reg., T. 99, f. 140); Report (Le Gentil and Pingré): 29 novembre 1780 (Reg., T. 99, f. 255-257; original in *pochette de séance*).

[125] See R. Merritt Cox, *Tomás de Iriarte* (New York: Twayne, 1972), pp. 32-33.

[126] Quoted ibid., p. 134.

[127] For a summary of the poem, see ibid., pp. 73-77; Fétis, *Biographie universelle*, VIII, 501; MGG, VI, col. 1403. The last-named reference includes information on Iriarte as a musician, as does Cox, *Tomás de Iriarte*, p. 127.

scribing its contents in detail and noting its innovative features.[128]

It should be noted that throughout its work the Academy carefully avoided addressing itself purely to the practice of music, which it considered inappropriate to its objectives as a scientific body. Certainly, musical performances did take place there (and they are often referred to in discussions, above), but these performances were intended primarily to demonstrate the practical application of proposals for musical systems (as well as for instruments) submitted for approval.

Nevertheless, by royal statute of 1701, there was one occasion each year when the Academy was obliged to take charge of the performance of music: the celebration of its annual feast day of St.-Louis, 25 août—an event it shared with the Académie des Inscriptions.[129] Beginning in 1701, the two Academies jointly observed the feast at the Eglise des Pères de l'Oratoire, and a *Te Deum* was traditionally sung, "en réjouissance d'événemens publics."[130] Music for the occasion was directed by a musician appointed by the Academy, with royal approval, named "Maître de musique de l'Académie des Sciences"; costs for the performances were sustained "par une ordonnance particulière sur le Trésor Royal."[131]

Provincial Academies

Although the Paris Academy was generally recognized as the leading forum for the exchange of scientific and technological in-

[128] Deserving of mention is the "exemplaire de son poëme sur l'harmonie" presented to the Academy by "M. Pris" on 7 décembre 1785 (Reg., T. 104, f. 228v); but it does not survive.

[129] Maindron, *L'Académie des Sciences*, pp. 39-40.

[130] Described by Dionis du Séjour in 1777; quoted ibid.: "in rejoicing public events." Records indicate that the event was held certainly until 1790, and probably until the suppression of the Academy (see ibid., pp. 39 and 114-118). At least in 1783, the *Te Deum* was replaced by a plainchant mass (Reg., T. 102, f. 165-165v); "motet" appears in later references.

[131] Maindron, *L'Académie des Sciences*, p. 39: "through a special arrangement with the royal treasury." Information is exceedingly sparse concerning details of the music for the celebration, and only a handful of the *maîtres de musique* are documented: in 1760, Dubousset was replaced by Guilleminot Duguet (Duguay), "Maître de musique de St. Germain de l'Auxerrois" (Reg., T. 79, f. 306-306v, 307v, 336); he, in turn, was succeeded in 1770 by François Giroust, "Maître de musique de St. Innocent" (recorded in *plumitif* for 1770 [18 août 1770] and in *lettre* dated 23 août 1770, in *pochette de séance du 29 août 1770*), and in 1771, by Coquerest (Reg., T. 90, f. 195v-196).

formation in France during most of its activity, it was not alone in serving this function. As frequent references above attest, provincial academies served similar roles throughout the eighteenth century; some used the Paris Academy as an organizational model, but others did not. In fact, the very individuality of many of them—based on regional personalities, customs, and interests—became increasingly clear as the Revolution drew near and the call for local autonomy intensified.[132]

Animated by an attitude that La Laurencie characterizes as ". . . avide d'indépendance et de libre discussion, curieux de toutes choses, épris d'art et de savoir,"[133] provincial academies flourished during most of the eighteenth century: 9 were established in its first decade, 24 by midcentury, and 35 by the time of the Revolution. Roche[134] asserts that they typically and primarily addressed practical issues of immediate value to the community at large, while maintaining a "double conscience": they were humanistic bodies in the Renaissance sense, but championed the freedom of the human spirit as understood in the late eighteenth century. Also, since they were composed of representatives from various strata of the existing social order (nobility, clergy, scientists, teachers, bourgeoisie), they tended to serve as important regional political bodies. Barrière[135] believes that the academies slowly replaced the universities as centers for the diffusion of knowledge in the provinces, and Chartier,[136] who classifies most of the provincial academicians as having but average intellects ("de mentalités moyennes"), nevertheless acknowledges the value of their contributions to the greater social good.

[132] For a listing of provincial academies, together with pertinent bibliographical references, see Gustave Lanson, *Manuel bibliographique de la littérature française moderne*, new ed. (Paris: Hachette, 1939), pp. 545-550.

[133] Lionel de La Laurencie, *L'Académie de musique et le concert de Nantes* (Paris: Société française d'imprimerie et de librairie, 1906; repr., Geneva: Minkoff, 1972), p. 4: ". . . eager for independence and for free discussion, curious about everything, absorbed by art and by knowledge." See also, the description in Daniel Mornet, *Les origines intellectuelles de la révolution française (1715-1787)* (Paris: A. Colin, 1933), pp. 298-305.

[134] Daniel Roche, "Milieux académiques provinciaux et société des lumières," in *Livre et société dans la France du XVIIIᵉ siècle* (Paris and La Haye: Mouton, 1965), pp. 96 and 102-108.

[135] Barrière, *L'Académie de Bordeaux*, p. 4.

[136] Roger Chartier, "L'Académie de Lyon au XVIIIᵉ siècle, 1700-1793, étude de sociologie culturelle," in *Nouvelles études lyonnaises* (Geneva: Droz, 1969), p. 133.

Generally speaking, music appears to have played only a minor role in the eighteenth-century provincial academies, in spite of the broad base of topics normally addressed by those bodies—topics that combined sciences with arts and letters. Exceptions are found in the academies of Bordeaux and Lyon, where rich musical traditions combined with the interests of important members of those groups to provide an impetus for the production of a varied literature dealing with music, as both science and art; concerts, too, were sponsored by these two academies.[137]

Contributions to musical theory are known also to have been made to the academies in Montpellier, Dijon, Toulouse, Rouen, and Nancy.[138] Except for Montpellier (with which, as noted earlier, the Paris Academy had a special statutory relationship), contact between the academies in these cities and the scientific academy in Paris was usually governed by the interests of individual members or petitioners.

[137] For music at the Academy in Bordeaux (est. 1712), see Barrière, *L'Académie de Bordeaux*, pp. 177-178, 338-341, and passim; at the Academy in Lyon (est. 1700), see Léon Vallas, *La musique à Lyon au dix-huitième siècle*, T. I: *La musique à l'Académie de Lyon au dix-huitième siècle* (Lyon: Editions de la Revue Musicale, 1908).

[138] Concerning contributions to these academies, see: Junius Castelnau, *Mémoire historique et biographique sur l'ancienne Société Royale des Sciences de Montpellier* (Montpellier: Boehm, 1858), pp. 179-180, 211-218; Roger Tisserand, *Au temps de l'Encyclopédie, l'Académie de Dijon de 1740 à 1793* (Vesoul: Imprimerie nouvelle, and Paris: Boivin, 1936), p. 47; *Table alphabétique des matières contenues dans les seize premiers tomes des Mémoires de l'Académie Impériale des sciences, inscriptions et belles-lettres de Toulouse*, ed. Auguste Larrey (Toulouse: J.-M. Douladoure, 1854), pp. 16, 42, 58; Pierre-L.-G. Gosseaume, *Précis analytique des travaux de l'Académie Royale des sciences, belles-lettres et arts de Rouen*, 5 vols. (Rouen: P. Periaux, 1814-1821), II, 193-196, III, 172-173, V, 263-264; *Mémoires de la Société Royale des sciences, et belles-lettres de Nancy*, IV (Nancy: Haener, 1759), pp. 82-108, 121-122. See also, Christian Desplat, *L'Académie Royale de Pau au XVIIIᵉ siècle* (Pau: Société des sciences, lettres et arts, 1971), pp. 57-61.

CONCLUSION

THE FRENCH ROYAL ACADEMY of Sciences in Paris—by accepting music as a valid discipline for scientific study, by recognizing the importance of the *arts et métiers* in the pursuit of its work, and by assuming the task of adjudicating machines, inventions, and scientific writings for Royal Privilege—played a conspicuous role in innovative musical developments throughout the period of its activity, and especially in the eighteenth century.

The early Academy embraced music in the tradition of humanism, applying to it the same nature of inquiry that generally characterized its work in experimental science. To be sure, such inquiry was initially reserved for the theory of music, which for centuries formed part of the mathematical and physical sciences. Yet in time, musical practice, too, became of increasing concern to the Academy, at least as it confirmed the theory. This concern was expressed notably in the Academy's growing involvement with the technological innovation in musical instruments; in its recognition of the role played by the psychology of perception in deriving theoretical principles for music; in its acceptance of aural proof as final confirmation of those principles; and in its novel interest in musical pedagogy. These and similar factors served to blur the clear separation of theory and practice characteristic of an earlier time. Music was viewed increasingly as a discipline with a unified body of learning, in which the practice—that is, the impact that organized sound made on the ear and, subsequently, on the mind and emotion of the listener—justified the theory.

The period of the Academy's most active interest in music roughly spans the first three-quarters of the eighteenth century. It was a time that largely coincided with one in French cultural history during which the styles and aesthetics of the art, as well as its purpose, were undergoing severe scrutiny and reappraisal; this was

(110)

true not only among musicians and theorists, but especially among the *littéraires* and *philosophes* whose intense debates characterized so much of eighteenth-century intellectual life in France. The central issue of this dialectic initially involved a comparison of French and Italian musical styles (notably of opera) early in the century. But it soon developed into a confrontation, not so much about different styles of music, as attitudes expressed by those styles. Music that reflected the tradition of *le grand siècle*—a noble art that was elaborate, absolute, aristocratic, reserved, and grand in manner—was contrasted with music that broke with the tradition and expressed a new spirit spreading throughout the nation—an affective art that was popular, descriptive, emotional, and free, in imitation of nature. In time, these controversies gave way to a new expression for music, one that was at once refined and accessible to all.

The Academy, too, underwent important development during this period, and especially after midcentury, when it began to show signs of the changes brought about by the social forces leading to the Revolution. Although it had contributed greatly to the popularization of science that took place among the literate classes of society during the eighteenth century, it also tended to alienate those very classes by its growing professionalism. The Academy's work was increasingly technical in nature, and its audience—even among academicians—steadily declined. The broad base of interests that characterized the early Academy sharply narrowed during the second half of the century, particularly under pressure of utilitarian demands placed on it by the needs of the times. Eventually, the literate philosopher-scientist of the founding generation gave way to the professional scientist-technician, much as his regard for the universality of knowledge yielded to demands for increased specialization in all fields of inquiry. By the eve of the Revolution, the Academy had become ever more specialized and isolated in its work. The aristocratic elite among its members played a decreasing role in its affairs and was replaced by a new elite, the professional scientist.

With the sciences undergoing intense redefinition, and with deterioration of the literate base for the Academy's work, it is not difficult to understand why music became less viable as an area for scientific investigation by the end of this period of change and ferment. Music had been shown special favor at the Academy when the roots for these changing attitudes first took hold, at the

CONCLUSION

time of its organizational reforms early in the eighteenth century. Central to the Academy's interest in music then was the work of Joseph Sauveur who, while making significant contributions to the science of acoustics, clearly specified the results of his research as intended for application to practice. Indeed, Sauveur viewed music as forming a comprehensive system, the end product of which was performance and the listener's enjoyment. When, in 1778, Vandermonde called for abandonment of musical systems and the universal reliance on a trained musical ear as the basis for musical judgments ("le Juge Suprême"), he was effectively extending Sauveur's argument to its logical conclusion. It was an argument that gained academic support as the century progressed and that, after the Revolution, was fundamental to the assignment of music to the Troisième Classe (Littérature et Beaux-Arts) of the reconstituted Institut National des Sciences et des Arts (1795), rather than to the Première Classe (Sciences physiques et mathématiques). For with its changed aesthetic, by the turn into the nineteenth century, music was no longer considered an integral part of the mathematical and physical sciences as it had been a century before.

It is evident that music—in all its aspects—formed a lively area for scientific investigation at the Paris Academy throughout most of its activity. That the innovations brought to its attention reflected changing interests and tastes of the time in France is clear. But it is also clear that the Academy exerted influence in the formation of those interests and tastes. As its judgments grew to have the strength of unassailable authority, its voice became ever more audible among the multitude of those seeking to reshape existing attitudes for a new age to come.

Appendices

Appendix I. Presentations by Joseph Sauveur on Music and Acoustics

A. *Principal Papers Published by the Academy*

"Système général des intervalles des sons, et son application à tous les systèmes et à tous les instrumens de musique," *Mémoires*, 1701, pp. 299-366.

"Application des sons harmoniques à la composition des jeux d'orgues," *Mémoires*, 1702, pp. 308-328.

"Méthode générale pour former les systèmes temperés de musique, et du choix de celui qu'on doit suivre," *Mémoires*, 1707, pp. 203-222.

"Table générale des systèmes temperés de musique," *Mémoires*, 1711, pp. 307-315.

"Rapport des sons des cordes d'instruments de musique, aux flèches des cordes; et nouvelle détermination des sons fixes," *Mémoires*, 1713, pp. 324-350.

B. *References Recorded in the Registres*

"Système général de musique," 17 novembre 1696 (Reg., T. 15bis, f. 203); cont. 24 novembre and 15 décembre 1696, 5 janvier 1697 (Reg., T. 15bis, f. 207v and 229, 250v). Reference to an additional presentation in février 1697 is found in Du Hamel, *Regiae*, p. 478.

"Préface d'un Traité sur la découverte qu'il a faite du son fixe," 13 mars 1700 (Reg., T. 19, f. 111v-114v; summarized in *Histoire*, 1700, pp. 134-143); cont. 8 mai (Reg., T. 19, f. 179-182v).

"Propositions d'acoustique," 5 février 1701 (Reg., T. 20, f. 44-46v); cont. 12 and 26 février, 2 and 5 mars (Reg., T. 20, f. 51-60v and 75v, 76 and 77-83v).

"Discours sur les noeuds des ondulations," 6 avril 1701 (*assemblée publique*, Reg., T. 20, f. 115v); reread 9 avril (Reg., T. 20, f. 123-125).

"L'échomètre," 22 décembre 1703 (Reg., T. 22, f. 387v).

"Sistème des orgues," 14 juin 1704 (Reg., T. 23, f. 170); cont. 21 juin (Reg., T. 23, f. 178).

(115)

"Ecrit sur une nouvelle manière d'écrire sa musique. Il l'appelle musique colorée. Il va imprimer cet écrit," 23 janvier 1706 (Reg., T. 25, f. 25).

"Ecrit sur les sistèmes temperez de musique," 25 juin 1707 (Reg., T. 26, f. 236v); cont. 2 juillet (Reg., T. 26, f. 255-255v).

"Réflexions nouvelles sur son sistème de musique, comparé à celuy de Mr. Huguens [!]," 9 juillet 1707 (Reg., T. 26bis, f. 281).

"Réponse qu'il a faite à M. Henfling, auteur allemand qui a attaqué son sistème de musique," 18 novembre 1711 (Reg., T. 30, f. 409-409v); cont. 21, 25, and 28 novembre (Reg., T. 30, f. 411, 413, and 415). Henfling's letter appears in *Miscellanea berolinensia ad incrementum scientiarum*, I (Berlin: J. C. Papenii, 1710), 265-294.

"Remarques sur le nouveau sistème pour les claviers des instrumens de musique, inventé par Michel Bulyowski de Dulycz, Conseiller de Bâle . . . inseré dans le Journal des Sçavans du 2 may 1712," 16 juillet 1712 (Reg., T. 31, f. 271-274).

"Propositions d'acoustique," 1 juillet 1713 (Reg., T. 32, f. 225); cont. 5 and 8 juillet, 20 décembre (Reg., T. 32, f. 227 and 229-233v, 361).

"Nouvelle détermination du son fixe," 23 décembre 1713 (Reg., T. 32, f. 363-366).

"Ecrit sur le centre d'oscillation des cordes sonores," 16 mai 1714 (Reg., T. 33, f. 166-166v); cont. 19 mai, 2 and 6 juin (Reg., T. 33, f. 167, 171 and 173).

"Rapport d'un pendule simple," 9 juin 1714 (Reg., T. 33, f. 177v-184v).

"Ecrit sur les cordes sonores," 11 août 1714 (Reg., T. 33, f. 315v); cont. 18 août (Reg., T. 33, f. 321-325).

Appendix II. Proposals in Music Assigned to Committee Review, 1704-1792

A. *Types of proposals, arranged chronologically*

| Years | Writings | Machines et Inventions | | Total |
		Instruments	Other	
1704-1722	4	4	0	8
1723-1732	0	3	2	5
1733-1742	3	1	3	7
1743-1752	12	1	2	15
1753-1762	8	7	1	16
1763-1772	14	8	2	24
1773-1782	9	9	3	21
1783-1792	8	15	2	25
Grand Totals	58	48	15	121

B. *Committee Actions*

| Action | Writings | Machines et Inventions | | Total |
		Instruments	Other	
Approved	34	38	10	82
Not Approved	5	0	0	5
No Report	19	10	5	34
Grand Totals	58	48	15	121

C. *Academic Members Assigned to Committees*

Name	Number of Assignments	Inclusive Years
d'Alembert	21	1748-1783
Berthollet	2	1782-1785
Bézout	1	1761
Bochart de Saron	4	1779-1785
Brancas de Lauraguais	1	1759
Brisson	3	1783-1788
Camus	1	1759
Carré	2	1704-1707
Cassini de Thury	1	1738

C. *Academic Members Assigned to Committees (cont.)*

Name	Number of Assignments	Inclusive Years
Daubenton	2	1783-1784
Delambre	1	1792
Deparcieux	2	1759-1763
Des Billettes	1	1708
Desmarest	1	1785
Dietrich	2	1788
Dodart	1	1707
Dufay	1	1738
Duhamel du Monceau	3	1763-1772
Ferrein	2	1743-1753
Fouchy	49	1733-1785
Gamaches	1	1737
Haüy	14	1785-1792
Hellot	2	1742
Jussieu	1	1753
La Condamine	1	1747
Lagrange	1	1792
La Hire	1	1708
Lalande	2	1759-1775
Laplace	3	1779-1790
Lassone	3	1743-1756
Le Gendre	1	1785
Le Gentil	1	1780
Le Monnier	2	1754-1761
Le Roy	10	1754-1790
Macquer	1	1768
Mairan	38	1720-1769
Maupertuis	6	1726-1734
Monge	1	1792
Montalembert	1	1772
Montigny	2	1754-1762
Morand	1	1752
Nicole	4	1742-1750
Parent	1	1708
Perronet	1	1775
Petit	1	1733
Pingré	14	1759-1792
Portal	1	1785
Réaumur	2	1737-1745
Reneaume	2	1708-1721
Rochon	1	1785
Sabatier	6	1779-1790
Sage	1	1785
Sauveur	2	1716

C. *Academic Members Assigned to Committees (cont.)*

Name	Number of Assignments	Inclusive Years
Sébastien (= Truchet)	2	1716
Tenon	1	1768
Terrasson	2	1716
Vaillant	1	1721
Vandermonde	35	1773-1792
Vaucanson	5	1748-1775
Vicq d'Azyr	3	1778-1784
Winslow	2	1733-1743
Total Nominations	281	

APPENDIX III. MUSICAL INSTRUMENTS AT THE PARIS ACADEMY, A CHECKLIST OF PROPOSALS, 1678–1792

Year	Name	Topic
1678	J.-B. Cartois	Nouvelle invention pour les sautereaux des clavessins
1696	J.-B. Cartois	Un roüet à filer
avant 1699	L. Carré	Un monochorde [de quatre sautereaux] pour accorder toutes sortes d'instruments
1699	E. Loulié	Le sonomètre . . . pour accorder le clavecin . . . [et] Un autre sonomètre
1700	J. Marius	Un clavessin brisé
1701	J. Sauveur	"Système général des intervalles des sons, et son application à tous les systèmes et à tous les instrumens de musique"
1702	J. Sauveur	"Application des sons harmoniques à la composition des jeux d'orgues"
1708	J. Marius	Une manière d'appliquer les sautereaux au clavessin sans registre
1708	F. Cuisinié	Un nouveau clavessin . . . ou de vielle réduite en clavessin
1716	J. Marius	Un nouveau clavessin à maillets . . . [quatre] nouvelles manières de substituer des maillets aux sautereaux ordinaires
1716	J. Marius	Une orgue à soufflet
1721	[A.?] L'Epine	Un nouvel instrument à clavier [no report]
1724	P.-L. M. de Maupertuis	"Sur la forme des instrumens de musique [à cordes]"
1727	Thevenard	Un clavecin de nouveaux sautereaux
1732	L.-C. Bellot	Un clavecin dont le grand chevalet d'unisson est construit . . . [à] procurer . . . une plus grande uniformité d'harmonie
1734	F. Cuisinié	Une espèce de vielle, ou petite épinette à jeu de viole
1738	J. de Vaucanson	Le flûteur automate

APPENDIX III

Year	Name	Topic
1742	J. Le Voir	Un nouveau clavecin composé d'une quinte de violon et d'un violoncelle
1748	J.-B. Micault	Un petit buffet d'orgue contenant un jeu de flûte ordinaire . . . aussi un violon
1756	Joinville	Un buffet d'orgue portatif
1756	J.-B. Domenjoud	Une nouvelle construction de têtes pour les manches des violons et autres instrumens à cordes
1756	L. Lagette (Lagetto)	Une addition aux violons [*no report*]
1759	L. Lagette	Une violon à éclisses bombées [*no report*]
1759	Puisieux	Une orgue hydrolique [*no report*]
1759	Weltman (A. Veltman?)	Un nouveau clavessin susceptible d'un grand nombre de changements
1760	Thierri	Un manuscrit sur "L'art de la facture d'orgue" [*no report*]
1762	D. Le Gay	Un nouvel instrument de musique à clavier, monté en cordes à boyau
1763-1778	F. Bedos de Celles	"L'Art du facteur d'orgues"
1765	J.-A. Berger	Un nouveau clavecin organisé . . . on peut enfler et diminuer les sons
1766	Virbès (Virebez)	Un nouveau clavecin à plusieurs jeux
1768	H. Joubert	Une vielle organisée
1769	N. Gosset	Une guitare et . . . une nouvelle division du manche des instrumens à cordes
1770	Obert	Un clavessin vertical organisé
1772	A. de L'Epine	Un forté-piano organisé
1773	J. Delaine	Un violon-vielle
1774	P. Musset	Un violon à touches
1775	F. Rigi	Une lettre sur la proportion des diamètres des tuyaux d'orgues
1776	C. Chyquelier II	Un clavier à double feuilles et sur un cilindre [*no report*]
1776	F.-A. D. Philidor	Un piano-forté dont les dessus sont montés en cordes de fer bleüi
1779	J. Delaine	Un [autre] violon-vielle
1779	F.-B. Péronard	Un clavecin, qui a un clavier de pédales
1782	G. Cousineau	La harpe . . . un nouveau mécanisme
1782	J. Germain, with J.-B. de Laborde & P.-J. Roussier	Le nouveau clavecin chromatique
1784	Bosch	Un piano-forté [*no report*]
1785	Beyer	Un instrument en forme de forté-piano . . . à cordes des lames de glace
1787	J.-B.Krumpholtz, with J.-H. Naderman	Une harpe . . . [un nouveau] mécanisme
1788	A.C.G. Deudon	Les deffauts de l'armonica . . . corrigés

(121)

APPENDIX III

Year	Name	Topic
1788	Lami	Un instrument de musique . . . [qui] réunit le piano-forté et la harpe
1788	P.-J. Taskin	Un forté-piano en forme de clavecin
1789	Schmitz	Un clavecin organisé [*no report*]
1790	Beyer	Un harmonica à lame de verre qu'on fait jouer avec un archet [*no report*]
1790	J. J. Schnell, with Tschirszcki	Un nouvel instrument de musique à clavier, dont le son est . . . produit par l'action de l'air sur les cordes
1791	Schmidt (Smith?)	Un moyen mécanique . . . relativement à la construction du forté-piano
1792	Langevin	Un instrument de musique à touches dont les cordes sont situées verticalement
1792	A. Montu	Un violon harmonique en forme de clavecin
1792	F. Pelletier	Une nouvelle méthode de perfectionner les instruments à vent [*no report*]
1792	P.-J. Taskin	Un clavecin et un forté-piano . . . où les unissons sont rendus par une même corde

Bibliography

The bibliography includes all printed sources cited in the text, as well as others not cited but pertinent to the subject. Manuscript sources are not listed, nor are individual articles or *mémoires* published by the Academy in its various series. For a comprehensive listing of the latter, the reader is referred to Albert Cohen and Leta E. Miller, *Music in the Paris Academy of Sciences, 1666-1793, A Source Archive in Photocopy at Stanford University: An Index* (Detroit: Information Coordinators,1979).

Abrégé du Journal de Paris, Années 1777-1781. 2 vols. Paris, 1789.

Accademia del Cimento. *Saggi di naturali esperienze fatte nell' Accademia del Cimento.* Florence: G. Cocchini, 1667.

Alembert, Jean Le Rond d'. *Elémens de musique théorique et pratique.* 2d ed., Lyon: J.-M. Bruyset, 1762; new ed., 1766. Reprint of 1752 ed., New York: Broude Bros., 1966.

———. *Oeuvres et correspondances inédites de d'Alembert,* ed. Charles Henry. Paris: Didier, Perrin, 1887. Reprint ed., Geneva: Slatkine, 1967.

———. *Preliminary Discourse to the Encyclopedia of Diderot,* trans., Richard N. Schwab. Indianapolis: Bobbs-Merrill Educational Publ., 1963.

Almanach Dauphin, ou tablettes Royales du vrai mérite des artistes célèbres, Année 1777. Paris: Lacombe, Edme, and the author [1777].

Almanach musical. 10 vols. Paris, 1775-1789 (vols. 9-10 entitled *Calendrier musical universel*). Reprint ed., Geneva: Minkoff, 1972.

Annonces, affiches et avis divers (from 1783, *Affiches, annonces et avis divers*). Paris, 1762-1784.

Art du faiseur d'instruments de musique et lutherie. Vol. IV, pt. 1, of *Arts et métiers mécaniques,* in *Encyclopédie méthodique.* Paris, 1785. Reprint ed., Geneva: Minkoff, 1972.

Audin, Marius. *Les livrets typographiques des fonderies françaises créées avant 1800.* Amsterdam: G. T. van Heusden, 1964.

Auger, Léon. "Les apports de J. Sauveur (1653-1716) à la création de l'acoustique," *Revue d'histoire des sciences,* I (1947-1948), 323-336.

———. *Un savant méconnu: Gilles Personne de Roberval.* Paris: A. Blanchard, 1962.

L'Avantcoureur, feuille hebdomadaire. Paris, 1759-1773.

Bailleux, Antoine. *Méthode pour apprendre facilement la musique vocale et instrumentale.* Paris: the author, 1770.

BIBLIOGRAPHY

Banks, Joseph. *The Banks Letters*, ed. W. R. Dawson. London: Trustees of the British Museum, 1958.

Barber, William H. *Leibniz in France, from Arnauld to Voltaire. A Study in French Reactions to Leibnizianism, 1670-1760.* Oxford: Clarendon Press, 1955.

Barbour, J. Murray. *Tuning and Temperament.* 2d ed., East Lansing: Michigan State College Press, 1953. Reprint ed., New York: Da Capo Press, 1972.

Bardez, Jean-Michel. *Diderot et la musique.* Paris: H. Champion, 1975.

Barrière, Pierre. *L'Académie de Bordeaux.* Paris and Bordeaux: Bière, 1951.

Bayle, Antoine L.-J., and Auguste J. Thillaye. *Biographie médicale.* 2 vols. Paris: A. Delahays, 1855.

Bedos de Celles, François. *L'Art du facteur d'orgues.* 4 vols. Paris: L. F. Delatour, 1766-1778. Reprint ed. by C. Mahrenholz, Kassel: Baerenreiter, 1963-1966. English trans. by C. Ferguson, 2 vols., Raleigh, N.C.: Sunbury Press, 1977.

Bell, Arthur E. *Christian Huygens and the Development of Science in the Seventeenth Century.* London: E. Arnold, 1947.

Berthe, Léon-Noël. *Dictionnaire des correspondants de l'Académie d'Arras au temps de Robespierre.* Arras: the author, 1969.

Bertrand, Joseph-L.-F. *L'Académie des Sciences et les académiciens de 1666 à 1793.* Paris: J. Hetzel, 1869.

———. "Quelques pages inédites de Jean-Jacques Rousseau," *Journal des Savants,* avril 1880, pp. 222-231.

Biographie universelle ancienne et moderne, ed. J.-F. Michaud. New ed. 45 vols. Paris: C. Desplaces, 1854-1865.

Blainville, Charles-Henri de. *Essay sur un troisième mode présenté et aprouvé par Mrs. de l'Académie des Sciences, joint la Simphonie exécutée au concert du Château des Thuilleries, 30 may 1751.* Paris: the author, Ve. Boivin, Le Clerc, Mlle. Castagnery, 1751.

———. *Histoire générale, critique et philologique de la musique.* Paris: Pissot, 1767. Reprint ed., Geneva: Minkoff, 1972.

Blondel, Nicolas-François. *Cours d'architecture enseigné dans l'Académie Royale d'Architecture.* 3 vols. Paris: P. Auboin, F. Clouzier, N. Langlois, and the author, 1657-1683.

———. *Cours de mathématique.* 2 vols. Paris: the author and N. Langlois, 1683.

Boalch, Donald H. *Makers of the Harpsichord and Clavichord, 1440-1840.* 2d ed., Oxford: Clarendon Press, 1974.

Borin. *L'Art de la danse.* Paris: J.-B.-C. Ballard, 1746.

Bouillier, Francisque. "Les affiliations des académies de province avec l'Académie Française et l'Académie des Sciences," in *Séances et travaux de l'Académie des sciences morales et politiques,* XXXIX (1879), 246-278.

Brémond, François de. *Table des mémoires imprimés dans les Transactions philosophiques*. Paris: Piget, 1739.

Brenet, Michel. "La librairie musicale en France de 1653 à 1790," *Sammelbände der Internationalen Musikgesellschaft*, VIII (1906-1907), 401-466.

―――. *Les concerts en France sous l'ancien régime*. Paris: Fischbacher, 1900. Reprint ed., New York: Da Capo Press, 1970.

Bricqueville, Eugène de. *Les ventes d'instruments de musique au XVIIIᵉ siècle*. Paris: Fischbacher, 1908.

Briscoe, Roger L. *Rameau's* Démonstration du principe de l'harmonie *and* Nouvelles réflexions de M. Rameau sur sa Démonstration du principe de l'harmonie: *An Annotated Translation and Commentary of Two Treatises by Jean-Philippe Rameau*. Ph.D. dissertation, Indiana Univ., 1976.

Brown, Harcourt. *Scientific Organizations in Seventeenth Century France (1620-1680)*. Baltimore: Wilkins and Wilkins, 1934.

Brugmans, Henri-L. *Le séjour de Christian Huygens à Paris*. Paris: P. André, 1935.

Brunet, Pierre. *Maupertuis*; T. II: *L'Oeuvre et sa place dans la pensée scientifique et philosophique du XVIIIᵉ siècle*. Paris: A. Blanchard, 1929.

Bruni, Antonio B. *Un inventaire sous la terreur*, ed. J. Gallay. Paris: Chamerot, 1890.

Carpenter, Nan C. *Music in the Medieval and Renaissance Universities*. Norman: Univ. of Oklahoma Press, 1958. Reprint ed., New York: Da Capo Press, 1972.

Castelnau, Junius. *Mémoire historique et biographique sur l'ancienne Société Royale des Sciences de Montpellier*. Montpellier: Boehm, 1858.

Caullery, Maurice. "Les sciences biologiques du milieu du XVIIᵉ à la fin du XVIIIᵉ sièle," in *Histoire de la science*, ed. M. Daumas. Vol. 5 of *Encyclopédie de la Pléiade* (Paris: Gallimard, 1957), pp. 1178-1203.

Chapuis, Alfred. *Histoire de la boîte à musique et de la musique mécanique*. Lausanne: Scriptar, 1955.

Chartier, Roger. "L'Académie de Lyon au XVIIIᵉ siècle, 1700-1793, étude de sociologie culturelle," in *Nouvelles études lyonnaises* (Geneva: Droz, 1969), pp. 131-250.

Chastel, Anne. "Etude sur la vie musicale à Paris à travers la presse pendant le règne de Louis XVI," in *"Recherches" sur la musique française classique*, ed. N. Dufourcq. Vol. XVI (Paris: A. and J. Picard, 1976), 37-70.

Choquel, Henri-Louis. *La Musique rendue sensible par la méchanique, ou nouveau système pour apprendre facilement la musique soy-même*. Paris: Ballard, Duchesne, Lambert, and the author, 1759. Reprint of 1762 ed., Geneva: Minkoff, 1972.

BIBLIOGRAPHY

Choron, Alexandre-Etienne, and François-J.-M. Fayolle. *Dictionnaire historique des musiciens.* 2 vols. Paris: Valade, 1810-1811. 2d ed., Paris: Chimot, 1817. Reprint of 1st ed., Hildesheim: G. Olms, 1971.

Chouquet, Gustave. *Le musée du conservatoire national de musique, Catalogue raisonné des instruments de cette collection.* Paris: Firmin-Didot, 1875.

Cohen, Albert. "Etienne Loulié as a Music Theorist," *Journal of the American Musicological Society*, XVIII (1965), 70-72.

———. "Music in the French Scientific Academy before the Revolution," *Stanford French Review*, I/1 (1977), 29-37.

———. "*Musique* in the *Dictionnaire mathématique* (1690) of Jacques Ozanam," *The Music Review*, 36/2 (1975), 85-91.

———, and Leta E. Miller. *Music in the Paris Academy of Sciences, 1666-1793. A Source Archive in Photocopy at Stanford University: An Index.* Detroit Studies in Music Bibliography No. 43. Detroit: Information Coordinators, 1979.

Cohen, John M. *The Confessions of Jean-Jacques Rousseau.* London: Penguin, 1953.

Collection académique, ed. Jean Berryat. 13 vols. Dijon: F. Desventes, 1755-1779.

Condorcet, Marie-Jean-Antoine-Nicolas Caritat de. *Oeuvres de Condorcet*, ed. A. C. O'Connor and F. Arago. 12 vols. Paris: Firmin-Didot, 1847-1849.

Conservatoire national des Arts et Métiers. *Catalogue du Musée, Section Z: Automates et mécanismes à musique.* Paris, 1973.

Cornereau, Armand. *Tables générales et particulières des travaux contenus dans les Mémoires (1769-1913), Académie des sciences, arts et belles-lettres de Dijon.* Dijon: Nourry, 1915.

Costabel, Pierre. "La participation de Malebranche au mouvement scientifique," in *Malebranche, l'homme et l'oeuvre, 1638-1715*, publ. Centre international de synthèse (Paris: J. Vrin, 1967), pp. 75-101.

Couperin, Armand-Louis. *Selected Works for Keyboard, Part I: Music for Two Keyboard Instruments*, ed. David Fuller. Madison: A-R Editions, 1975.

Cousin, Jean. *L'Académie des sciences, belles-lettres et arts de Besançon, deux cents ans de vie comtoise (1752-1952).* Besançon: Jean Ledoux, 1954.

Cox, R. Merritt. *Tomás de Iriarte.* New York: Twayne, 1972.

Curtis, Alan. "Dutch Harpsichord Makers," *Tijdschrift van der Vereniging voor Nederlandse Muziekgeschiedenis*, XIX (1960-1961), 44-66.

Dainville, François de. "Foyers de culture scientifique dans la France méditerranéenne du XVIᵉ au XVIIIᵉ siècle," *Revue d'histoire des sciences*, I (1947-1948), 289-300.

Daumas, Maurice. *Les instruments scientifiques aux xviiᵉ et xviiiᵉ siècles.* Paris:

BIBLIOGRAPHY

Presses Universitaires de France, 1953. Trans. by Mary Holbrook, *Scientific Instruments of the Seventeenth and Eighteenth Centuries.* New York: Praeger, 1972.

———. "Les sciences physiques aux xvie et xviie siècles," in *Histoire de la science,* ed. M. Daumas. Vol. 5 of *Encyclopédie de la Pléiade* (Paris: Gallimard, 1957), pp. 837-882.

Demoz, Jean-François. *Méthode de musique selon un nouveau système.* Paris: P. Simon, 1728.

———. *Méthode de plein-chant selon un nouveau système.* Paris: G.-F. Quillau fils, 1728.

Desaguliers, John T. *An Account of the Mechanism of an Automaton.* London: T. Parker, 1742.

Descriptions des Arts et Métiers faites ou approuvées par MM. de l'Académie Royale des Sciences. 84 monographs in 27 vols. Paris, 1761-1789.

Description des machines et procédés consignés dans les brevets d'invention, de perfectionnement et d'importation. Table des quarants premiers volumes, ed. Cunin-Gridaine. Paris: veuve Bouchard-Huzard, 1843.

Desplat, Christian. *L'Académie Royale de Pau au XVIIIe siècle.* Pau: Société des sciences, lettres et arts, 1971.

Deville, Etienne. *Index du Mercure de France, 1672-1832.* Paris: Jean Schemit, 1910.

Devriès, Anik, and François Lesure. *Dictionnaire des éditeurs de musique français.* 2 vols. Geneva: Minkoff, 1979.

Dictionary of Scientific Biography, ed. C. C. Gillispie. 16 vols. New York: Scribner, 1970-1980.

Dictionnaire de Biographie Française, ed. J. Balteau, M. Barroux, and M. Prévost. Paris, 1933—.

Domenjoud, Jean-Baptiste. *De la préférence des vis aux chevilles, pour les instrumens de musique.* Paris: Thiboust, 1757. Reprint ed., Geneva: Minkoff, 1972.

Dornel, Louis-Antoine. *Le tour du clavier.* Paris, "au Mont-Parnasse," 1745.

Doyon, André, and Lucien Liaigre. *Jacques Vaucanson, mécanicien de génie.* Paris: Presses Universitaires de France, 1966.

Dufourcq, Norbert. *Le livre de l'orgue français, 1589-1789.* Vol. I, *Les sources.* Paris: A. and J. Picard, 1971.

Du Hamel, Jean-Baptiste. *Regiae scientiarum academiae historia.* Paris: S. Michallet, 1698. 2d ed., Paris: J.-B. Delespine, 1701.

Dunken, Gerhard. *Die deutsche Akademie der Wissenschaften zu Berlin in Vergangenheit und Gegenwart.* 2d ed. Berlin: Akademie-Verlag, 1960.

Durand. *La musique naturelle.* Paris: Rebuffé, 1700.

Du verney, Joseph-Guichard. *Traité de l'organe de l'ouïe.* Paris: E. Mi-

challet, 1683, and Leyden: J. A. Langerak, 1731; Latin ed., Nurnberg: J. Ziegeri, 1684; English editions, London: S. Baker, 1737
and 1748.

*Encyclopédie, ou Dictionnaire raisonné des sciences, des arts et des métiers, par
une société de gens de lettres,* ed. D. Diderot and J. Le Rond
d'Alembert. 17 vols. Paris, 1751-1765.
Encyclopédie méthodique: Musique. 2 vols. Paris: Panckoucke, 1791, and
veuve Agasse, 1818. Reprint ed., New York: Da Capo Press, 1971.
Estève, Pierre. *Nouvelle découverte du principe de l'harmonie.* Paris: Huart et
Moreau fils, Duran, 1751; S. Jorry, 1752.

Favier, Justin. *Table alphabétique des publications de l'Académie de Stanislas
(1750-1900).* Nancy: Berger-Levrault, 1902.
Fétis, François-Joseph. *Biographie universelle des musiciens.* 2d ed. 8 vols.
Paris: Firmin-Didot, 1873-1875. Suppl., ed. Arthur Pougin, 2 vols.
Paris: Firmin-Didot, 1878-1880. Reprint ed., 10 vols., Brussels:
Culture et civilisation, 1963 and 1972.
Fontenelle, Bernard Le Bovier de. *Lettres galantes,* ed. Daniel Delafarge.
Paris: Société d'édition "Les belles lettres," 1961.
————. *Eloges des académiciens.* 2 vols. La Haye: Isaac vander Kloot, 1740.
Reprint ed., Brussels: Culture et civilisation, 1969.
Fournier, Pierre-Simon, le jeune. *Fournier on Typefounding. The Text of the
Manuel Typographique (1764-1766) translated into English,* ed. Harry
Carter. London: Soncino Press, 1930.
————. *Manuel typographique.* 2 vols. Paris: Fournier, 1764-1766.
————. *Traité historique et critique sur l'origine et les progrès des caractères de
fonte pour l'impression de la musique.* Bern and Paris: Barbou, 1765.
Reprint ed., Geneva: Minkoff, 1972.
Franklin, Benjamin. *Oeuvres de M. Franklin, . . . traduites de l'anglois sur la
quatrième édition, par M. Barbeu Du Bourg.* 2 vols. Paris: Quillau,
Esprit, and the author, 1773.

Gallimard, Jean-Edme. *Arithmétique des musiciens, ou essai qui a pour objet
diverses espèces de calcul des intervalles, le développement de plusieurs
systèmes de sons de la musique . . .* Paris: [Duperron], 1754.
————. *La théorie des sons applicable à la musique.* Paris: Ballard, Bauche,
Saugrain fils, and the author, 1754.
Gando, Nicolas and Pierre-François. *Observations sur le Traité historique et
critique de Monsieur Fournier le jeune.* Bern and Paris: Moreau, 1766.
Reprint ed., Geneva: Minkoff, 1972.
Gauja, Pierre. "L'Académie Royale des Sciences (1666-1793)," *Revue
d'histoire des sciences,* II (1949), 293-310.

BIBLIOGRAPHY

————. "Les origines de l'Académie des Sciences de Paris," in Institut de France, *Académie des Sciences, Troisième centenaire, 1666-1966* (Paris: Gauthier-Villars, 1971), I, 1-51.

Gazette et Avantcoureur de littérature, des sciences et des arts. Paris: J.-G. Clousier, 1774.

Geoffroy, Etienne-Louis. *Dissertation sur l'organe de l'ouïe de l'homme, des reptiles, et des poissons.* Amsterdam and Paris: Cavelier, 1778.

Gerber, Ernst Ludwig. *Historisch-biographisches Lexicon der Tonkünstler.* 2 vols. Leipzig: Breitkopf, 1790-1792.

Gille, Bertrand. *Histoire des techniques.* Vol. 41 of *Encyclopédie de la Pléiade.* Paris: Gallimard, 1978.

Gillispie, Charles C. "The Natural History of Industry," in *Science, Technology, and Economic Growth in the Eighteenth Century*, ed. A. E. Musson (London: Methuen, 1972), pp. 121-135.

Gillmor, C. Stewart. *Coulomb and the Evolution of Physics and Engineering in Eighteenth-Century France.* Princeton: Princeton Univ. Press, 1971.

Gillot, Hubert. *La querelle des anciens et des modernes en France.* Paris: H. Champion, 1914. Reprint ed., Geneva: Slatkine, 1968.

Ginguené, Pierre-Louis. *Catalogue des livres de la bibliothèque de feu M. P.-L. Ginguené.* Paris: Merlin, 1817.

Gosseaume, Pierre-L.-G. *Précis analytique des travaux de l'Académie des sciences, belles-lettres et arts de Rouen.* 5 vols. Rouen: P. Periaux, 1814-1821.

Grimsley, Donald. *Jean d'Alembert.* Oxford: Clarendon Press, 1963.

Grove's Dictionary of Music and Musicians, 5th ed., ed. E. Blom. 10 vols. London: Macmillan, 1954. 6th ed., ed. S. Sadie. 20 vols. London: Macmillan, 1980.

Guigard, Joannis. *Indicateur du Mercure de France, 1672-1789.* Paris: Librairie Bachelin-Deflorenne, 1869.

Gunther, Robert W. T. *Early Science in Oxford.* Vol. VIII. Oxford: the author, 1931.

Hahn, Roger. *The Anatomy of a Scientific Institution: The Paris Academy of Sciences, 1666-1803.* Berkeley: Univ. of California Press, 1971.

————. "The Application of Science to Society: the Societies of Arts," in *Studies on Voltaire and the Eighteenth Century*, XXV (1963), 829-836.

————. "L'Autobiographie de Lacépède retrouvée," *Dix-Huitième Siècle*, VII (1975), 49-85.

Hallays, André. *Les Perrault.* Paris: Perrin, 1926.

Handschin, Jacques. *Der Toncharakter, eine Einführung in die Tonpsychologie.* Zürich: Atlantis Verlag, 1948.

Hankins, Thomas L. *Jean d'Alembert, Science and the Enlightenment.* Oxford: Clarendon Press, 1970.

(129)

BIBLIOGRAPHY

Hanks, Lesley. *Buffon avant l' "Histoire naturelle."* Paris: Presses Universitaires de France, 1966.

Harding, Rosamond E. M. *Origins of Musical Time and Expression.* Oxford: Oxford Univ. Press, 1938.

———. *The Piano-Forte.* Cambridge: Cambridge Univ. Press, 1933. Reprint ed., New York: Da Capo Press, 1973.

Hayes, Deborah. "Christian Huygens and the Science of Music," in *Musicology at the University of Colorado*, ed. Wm. Kearns, 1977, pp. 17-31.

———. *Rameau's Theory of Harmonic Generation: An Annotated Translation and Commentary of* Génération harmonique *by J.-P. Rameau.* Ph.D. dissertation, Stanford Univ., 1968.

Hauksbee, Francis. *Expériences physico-méchaniques sur différens sujets*, trans. F. de Brémond. 2 vols. Paris: veuve Cavelier et fils, 1754.

Hautefeuille, Jean de. *Problème d'acoustique, curieux et intéressant.* Paris: Varin, 1788.

———. *Recueil des ouvrages de M. de Hautefeuille.* Paris: veuve D. Horthemels, 1694.

Hecht, Jacqueline. "Un exemple de multidisciplinarité: Alexandre Vandermonde (1735-1796)," in *Population*, 26/4 (1971), 641-675.

Herrmann, Wolfgang. *The Theory of Claude Perrault.* London: A. Zwemmer, 1973.

Hirt, Franz Josef. *Stringed Keyboard Instruments, 1440-1880.* Boston: Boston Book and Art Shop, 1968.

Histoire de l'Académie Royale des Sciences, avec les Mémoires de mathématique et de physique tirés des Registres de cette Académie. 114 vols. Paris: 1702-1797.

Histoire générale des sciences, ed. René Taton. 4 vols. Paris: Presses Universitaires de France, 1957-1964. Trans. A. J. Pomerans, *History of Science.* London: Thames & Hudson, [1963-1966].

Hubbard, Frank. "The *Encyclopédie* and the French Harpsichord," *Galpin Society Journal*, IX (1956), 37-50.

———. *Three Centuries of Harpsichord Making.* Cambridge: Harvard Univ. Press, 1965.

Hunt, Frederick V. *Origins in Acoustics.* New Haven: Yale Univ. Press, 1978.

Hutt, Allen. *Fournier, The Compleat Typographer.* Totowa, N.J.: Rowan and Littlefield, 1972.

Huygens, Christian. *Oeuvres complètes.* 22 vols. La Haye: M. Nijhoff, 1888-1950.

Institut de France. *Académie des Sciences, Troisième centenaire, 1666-1966.* 2 vols. Paris: Gauthier-Villars, 1967.

BIBLIOGRAPHY

————. *Index biographique de l'Académie des Sciences.* Paris: Gauthier-Villars, 1979.

————. *Les Registres de l'Académie Françoise, 1672-1793.* 4 vols. Paris: Firmin-Didot, 1895-1906.

Iriarte y Oropesa, Tomás de. *La música, poema.* Madrid: Imprenta Real de la Gazeta, 1779. French trans. by J.B.C. Grainville, Paris: J. J. Fuchs, 1799.

Jacobi, Erwin R. "Rameau and Padre Martini," *The Musical Quarterly,* L (1964), 452-475.

Jacquot, Albert. *La lutherie lorraine et française.* Paris: Fischbacher, 1912.

Jamard, T. *Recherches sur la théorie de la musique.* Paris: Jombert and Mérigot, and Rouen: Machuel, 1769.

James, Philip. *Early Keyboard Instruments.* London: P. Davies, 1930. Reprint ed., London: Tabard Press, 1970.

Jansen, Albert. *Jean-Jacques Rousseau als Musiker.* Berlin: G. Reimer, 1884.

Journal encyclopédique. Paris, 1756-1793.

Journal de Musique. Paris, 1770-1777. Reprint ed., Geneva: Minkoff, 1972.

Journal de Paris. Paris, 1777-1840.

Journal des Sçavans. Paris, 1665-1792.

Juramie, Ghislaine. *Histoire du Piano.* Paris: Editions Prisma, 1947.

Kaplan, Harold M. *Anatomy and Physiology of Speech.* New York: Mc-Graw-Hill, 1960.

Keane, Michaela Maria. *The Theoretical Writings of Jean-Philippe Rameau.* Washington, D.C.: Catholic Univ. of America Press, 1961.

Kempelen, Wolfgang von. *Mechanismus der menschlichen Sprache nebst Beschreibung einer sprechenden Maschine.* Vienna, 1791. Reprint ed., Stuttgart-Bad Cannstatt: Friedrich Frommann Verlag, 1970.

Kiernan, Colm. "The Enlightenment and Science in Eighteenth-Century France," in *Studies on Voltaire and the Eighteenth Century,* LIXA (1973).

Kleinbaum, Abby R. *Jean-Jacques Dortous de Mairan (1687-1771): A Study of an Enlightenment Scientist.* Ph.D. dissertation, Columbia Univ., 1970.

Krumpholtz, Johann-Baptiste. *Les deux dernières sonates de la collection de pièces de différents genres,* Op. 14. Paris: the author and H. Naderman, n.d.

Laborde, Jean-Benjamin de. *Essai sur la musique ancienne et moderne.* 4 vols. Paris: E. Onfroy, 1780. Reprint ed., New York: AMS Press, 1978.

————. *Mémoires sur les proportions musicales.* Paris: P.-D. Pierres, 1781.

Lacassagne, Joseph. *Traité général des élémens du chant.* Paris: the author and veuve Duchesne; Versailles: Fournier, 1766. Reprint ed., Geneva: Minkoff, 1972.

Lagrange, Joseph-Louis de. *Oeuvres de Lagrange*, ed. J.-A. Serret. Vol. I. Paris: Gauthier-Villars, 1867.

La Hire, Philippe de. *Oeuvres diverses*. Paris: Compagnie des Libraires, 1730.

La Laurencie, Lionel de. *L'Académie de musique et le concert de Nantes*. Paris: Société française d'imprimerie et de librairie, 1906. Reprint ed., Geneva: Minkoff, 1972.

———. *L'Ecole française de violon de Lully à Viotti*. 3 vols. Paris: Delagrave, 1922-1924.

Lange, Georg. "Zur Geschichte der Solmisation," *Sammelbände der Internationalen Musikgesellschaft*, I (1899-1900), 535-622.

Lanson, Gustave. *Manuel bibliographique de la littérature française moderne*. New ed., Paris: Hachette, 1939.

La querelle des bouffons, ed. Denise Launay. 3 vols. Geneva: Minkoff, 1973.

La Salette, Pierre-Joseph Joubert de. *Considérations sur les divers systèmes de la musique ancienne et moderne, et sur le genre enharmonique des Grecs.* 2 vols. Paris: Gaujon, 1810.

Lasteyrie, Robert de. *Bibliographie générale des travaux historiques et archéologiques publiés par les sociétés savantes de la France.* 6 vols. Paris: Imprimerie nationale, 1888-1918.

Lautard, Jean-Baptiste. *Histoire de l'Académie de Marseille, depuis sa fondation en 1726 jusqu'en 1826.* 3 vols. Marseille: Achard, 1826-1843.

La Voye-Mignot. *Traité de musique pour bien et facilement apprendre à chanter et composer.* 2d ed., Paris: R. Ballard, 1666. Reprint ed., Geneva: Minkoff, 1972; English ed. by A. Gruber, Brooklyn, N.Y.: Institute of Medieval Music, 1972.

Le Cat, Claude-Nicolas. *Traité des sens*. Rouen, 1740.

Leichtentritt, Hugo. "Mechanical Music in Olden Times," *The Musical Quarterly*, XX (1934), 15-26.

Lenardon, France-A. *Index du Journal encyclopédique, 1756-1793.* Geneva: Slatkine, 1976.

Lenihan, John M. A. "Mersenne and Gassendi, An Early Chapter in the History of Sound," *Acustica*, I/2 (1951), 96-99.

Lindsay, R. Bruce. "The Story of Acoustics," in *Acoustics: Historical and Philosophical Development*, ed. R. B. Lindsay (Stroudsburg, Pa.: Dowden, Hutchinson, and Ross, 1972), pp. 5-20.

Lirou, Jean-François Espic, Chevalier de. *Explication du système de l'harmonie, pour abréger l'étude de la composition, et accorder la pratique avec la théorie.* London and Paris: Mérigot, Bailly, Bailleux, Boyer, 1785.

Lloyd, Ll. S. "Musical Theory in the Early *Philosophical Transactions*," *Notes and Records of the Royal Society of London*, III/2 (1941), 149-157.

BIBLIOGRAPHY

Locy, William A. *The Story of Biology*. New York: Garden City Publ. Co., 1925.

Loulié, Etienne. *Eléments ou principes de musique*. Paris: C. Ballard and the author, 1696. Reissued, Amsterdam: E. Roger, 1698. English ed. by Albert Cohen, *Elements or Principles of Music*. Brooklyn, N.Y.: Institute of Medieval Music, 1965. Reprint of 1696 ed., Geneva: Minkoff, 1971.

————. *Nouveau système de musique ou nouvelle division du monocorde . . . avec la description et l'usage du sonomètre*. Paris: C. Ballard, 1698.

Lütgendorff, Willibald Leo, Freiherrn von. *Die Geigen- und Lautenmacher von Mittelalter bis zum Gegenwart*. Frankfurt a.M.: H. Keller, 1904.

Luynes, Charles-Philippe d'Albert, duc de. *Mémoires du Duc de Luynes sur la cour de Louis XV (1735-1758)*, ed. L. Dussieux and E. Soulié. 17 vols. Paris: Firmin-Didot, 1860-1865.

Machines et Inventions approuvées par l'Académie Royale des Sciences, ed. J.-G. Gallon. 7 vols. Paris, 1735-1777.

McCloy, Shelby T. *French Inventions of the Eighteenth Century*. Lexington: Univ. of Kentucky Press, 1952.

Maindron, Ernest. *L'Académie des Sciences*. Paris: Félix Alcan, 1888.

Marcuse, Sibyl. *A Survey of Musical Instruments*. New York: Harper & Row, 1975.

————. *Musical Instruments, A Comprehensive Dictionary*. Corrected ed., New York: Norton, 1975.

Martinod, Jean. *Répertoire des travaux des facteurs d'orgues*. Paris: Fischbacher, 1970.

Mathias, Peter. "Who Unbound Prometheus? Science and Technical Change, 1600-1800," in *Science, Technology and Economic Growth in the Eighteenth Century*, ed. A. E. Musson (London: Methuen, 1972), pp. 69-96.

Matzke, Hermann. *Unser technisches Wissen von der Musik*. Lindau: Frisch and Perneder, 1949.

Mauclaire, Placide, and C. Vigoureux. *Nicolas-François de Blondel, Ingénieur et Architecte du Roi (1618-1686)*. Paris: A. Picard, 1938.

Maxham, Robert E. *The Contributions of Joseph Sauveur (1653-1716) to Acoustics*. 2 vols. Ph.D. dissertation, Univ. of Rochester, 1976.

Mémoires pour l'histoire des sciences et des beaux-arts (= Journal de Trévoux). Trévoux, 1701-1767. Reprint ed., Geneva: Slatkine, 1974.

Mémoires de l'Institut national des sciences et arts, pour l'an IV de la République. Vol. I. Paris: Baudouin, Thermidor An VI [1798].

Mémoires de mathématique et de physique, présentés à l'Académie Royale des Sciences par divers savans, et lûs dans ses assemblées. 11 vols. Paris, 1750-1786.

(133)

Mémoires de la Société Royale des sciences, et belles-lettres de Nancy. Series 1, 4 vols. Nancy: Haener, 1754-1759.

Mercadier de Belesta, Jean-Baptiste. *Nouveau système de musique théorique et pratique.* Paris: Valade, 1776; Valade and Laporte, 1777.

————. "Mémoire sur l'accord du clavecin, & sur le système de M. de Boisgelou, concernant les intervalles musicaux," in *Histoire et Mémoires de l'Académie Royale des Sciences, Inscriptions et Belles-Lettres de Toulouse* , III (Toulouse: D. Desclassan, 1788), 139-168.

Mercure de France. Paris, 1724-1791,

Mersenne, Marin. *Correspondance du P. Marin Mersenne,* ed. C. de Waard, R. Pintard, B. Rochot, and A. Beaulieu, 1932—.

————. *Harmonie universelle.* 2 vols. Paris: S. Cramoisy and P. Ballard, 1636-1637. Reprint ed., 3 vols., Paris: Centre National de la Recherche Scientifique, 1963.

Middleton, W. E. Knowles. *The Experimenters.* Baltimore: Johns Hopkins Press, 1971.

Miller, Dayton C. *Anecdotal History of the Science of Sound.* New York: Macmillan, 1935.

Milliot, Sylvette. *Documents inédits sur les luthiers parisiens du XVIIIᵉ siècle.* Paris: Heugel, 1970.

Miscellanea berolinensia ad incrementum scientiarum. Vol I. Berlin: J. C. Papenii, 1710.

Montu, Anselme. *Numération harmonique, ou Echelle d'arithmétique, pour servir à l'explication des lois de l'harmonie.* Paris: Colnet, Debrai, and Duprat, n.d.

Montucla, Jean-Etienne. *Histoire des mathématiques.* New ed., 4 vols. Paris: H. Agasse, 1799-1802.

Mornet, Daniel. *Les origines intellectuelles de la révolution française (1715-1787).* Paris: A. Colin, 1933.

Mráček, Jaroslav J. S. *Seventeenth-Century Instrumental Dances in Uppsala IMhs 409.* 2 vols. Ph.D. dissertation, Indiana Univ., 1965.

Musée du Conservatoire National des Arts et Métiers. *Histoire et prestige de l'Académie des Sciences.* Paris, 1966.

Die Musik in Geschichte und Gegenwart, ed. F. Blume. 16 vols. Kassel: Baerenreiter, 1949-1979.

Niderst, Alain. *Fontenelle à la recherche de lui-même (1657-1702).* Paris: A.-G. Nizet, 1972.

Nielsen, Niels. *Géomètres français du dix-huitième siècle.* Copenhagen and Paris: Levin and Munskgaard, 1935.

Niklaus, Robert. "Diderot and the *Leçons de clavecin et principes d'harmonie par Bemetzrieder* (1771)," in *Modern Miscellany presented to Eugène Vinaver* (Manchester: Manchester Univ. Press, 1969), pp. 180-194.

Nollet, Jean-Antoine. *Leçons de physique expérimentale*. 6 vols. Paris: Guérin, 1743-1748.
Nouvelle biographie générale, ed. Jean C.-F. Hoefer. 46 vols. Paris: Firmin-Didot, 1852-1881.

Oldenburg, Henry. *The Correspondence of Henry Oldenburg*, ed. A. R. Hall and M. B. Hall. Madison: Univ. of Wisconsin Press, and London: Mansell, 1965—.
Oliver, Alfred R. *The Encyclopedists as Critics of Music*. New York: Columbia Univ. Press, 1947.
Onsenbray, Louis-Léon Pajot, comte d'. *Catalogue des livres et estampes de la bibliothèque de feu Monsieur Pajot, Comte d'Onsenbray*. Paris: G. Martin and M. Damonneville, 1756.
Ord-Hume, Arthur W.J.G. *Clockwork Music*. New York: Crown, 1973.
Ornstein, Martha. *The Rôle of Scientific Societies in the Seventeenth Century*. Chicago: Univ. of Chicago Press, 1928.
Osborne, Richard D. *The Theoretical Writings of Abbé Pierre-Joseph Roussier*. Ph.D. dissertation, Ohio State Univ., 1966.

Pelletier, [François]. *Hommage aux amateurs des arts*. Saint Germain-en-Laye: the author; and Paris: veuve Thiboust and l'Abbé Lesueur, 1782.
Perrault, Claude. *Essais de physique, ou Recueil de plusieurs traités touchant les choses naturelles*. 4 vols. Paris: J.-B. Coignard, 1680-1688.
Pierre, Constant. *Les facteurs d'instruments de musique*. Paris: Ed. Sagot, 1893. Reprint ed., Geneva: Minkoff, 1971.
Pingaud, Léonce. "Documents pour servir à l'histoire de l'Académie de Besançon (1752-1789), " in Académie des sciences, belles-lettres et arts, *Procès-verbaux et Mémoires, Année 1892* (Besançon: P. Jacquin, 1893), pp. 234-311.
Plantefol, Lucien. "L'Académie des Sciences durant les trois premiers siècles de son éxistence," in Institut de France, *Académie des Sciences, Troisième centenaire, 1666-1966* (Paris: Gauthier-Villars, 1971), I, 53-139.
Pontécoulant, Adolphe Le Doulcet de. *Organographie, Essai sur la facture instrumentale*. 2 vols. Paris: Castel, 1861. Reprint ed., Amsterdam: Frits Knuf, 1972.
Poole, H. Edmund. "New Music Types: Invention in the Eighteenth Century," *Journal of the Printing Historical Society*, I (1965), 21-38, and II (1966), 23-44.
Pougin, Arthur. *Jean-Jacques Rousseau, musicien*. Paris: Fischbacher, 1901.
Procès-verbaux de l'Académie des Beaux-Arts, ed. Marcel Bonnaire. 3 vols. Paris: Armand Colin, 1937-1943.
Procès-verbaux des séances de l'Académie des Sciences. 10 vols. Hendaye: Impr.

de l'Observatoire d'Abbadia, 1910-1922. *Tables générales alphabétiques.* Paris: Imprimerie Nationale, 1979.

Protz, Albert. *Mechanische Musikinstrumente.* Kassel: Bärenreiter, 1940.

Rameau, Jean-Philippe. *The Complete Theoretical Writings of Jean-Philippe Rameau (1683-1764),* ed. Erwin. R. Jacobi. 6 vols. Rome: American Institute of Musicology, 1967-1972.

———. *Démonstration du principe de l'harmonie.* Paris: Durand and Pissot, 1750. Reprint ed., New York: Broude Bros., 1965.

———. *Génération harmonique.* Paris: Prault fils, 1737.

———. *Traité de l'harmonie.* Paris J.-B.-C. Ballard, 1722. English trans. by Philip Gossett, New York: Dover, 1971.

Rameau, Pierre. *Abbrégé de la nouvelle méthode dans l'art d'écrire ou de tracer toutes sortes de danses de ville.* Paris: the author, 1725. Reprint ed., Farnborough: Gregg, 1972.

Raugel, Félix. *Recherches sur quelques maîtres de l'ancienne facture d'orgues française.* Paris: H. Hérelle, Fortemps, [1925?].

Ravetz, Jerome R. "Vibrating Strings and Arbitrary Functions," in *The Logic of Personal Knowledge: Essays Presented to Michael Polanyi on his Seventieth Birthday* (London: Routledge & Kegan Paul, 1961), pp. 71-88.

Rensch, Roslyn. *The Harp.* New York: Praeger, 1969.

Répertoire international des sources musicales. B VI, 1 and 2, *Ecrits imprimés concernant la musique,* ed. Fr. Lesure. Munich: G. Henle, 1971.

Répertoire numérique des Archives départmentales de l'Hérault, Série D, ed. Jos. Berthelé. Montpellier: Lauriol, 1925.

Ripin, Edwin M. "Expressive Devices Applied to the Eighteenth-Century Harpsichord," *The Organ Yearbook,* I (1970), 65-80.

Robinet, André. *Malebranche de l'Académie des Sciences, l'oeuvre scientifique, 1674-1715.* Paris: J. Vrin, 1970.

Roche, Daniel. "Milieux académiques provinciaux et société des lumières," in *Livre et société dans la France du XVIIIᵉ siècle* (Paris and La Haye: Mouton, 1965), pp. 93-184.

Roche, Edouard. *Notice sur les travaux de J.-B. Romieu.* Montpellier: Boehm et fils, 1879.

Roger, Jacques. *Les sciences de la vie dans la pensée française du XVIIIᵉ siècle.* Paris: Armand Colin, 1963.

Rohault, Jacques. *Traité de physique.* Paris: veuve de Charles Savreux, 1671.

Rousseau, Jean-Jacques. *Correspondance complète de Jean Jacques Rousseau,* ed. R. A. Leigh. Geneva: Institut et Musée Voltaire, and Oxford: The Voltaire Foundation, 1965—.

———. *Correspondance générale de J.-J. Rousseau,* ed. Théophile Dufour. 20 vols. Paris: Armand Colin, 1924-1934.

————. *Dictionnaire de musique*. Paris: veuve Duchesne, 1768. Reprint ed., Hildesheim: G. Olms, 1969.

————. *Dissertation sur la musique moderne*. Paris: G.-F. Quillau, 1743.

————. *Les Confessions*, ed. Jacques Voisine. Paris: Garnier frères, 1964.

————. *Oeuvres complètes*, ed. Michel Launay. 3 vols. Paris: Editions du Seuil, 1967-1971.

Roussier, Pierre-Joseph. *Mémoire sur la musique des anciens*. Paris: Lacombe, 1770. Reprint ed., New York: Broude Bros., 1966.

————. *Mémoire sur la nouvelle harpe de M. Cousineau*. Paris: Lamy, 1782. Reprint ed., Geneva: Minkoff, 1972.

————. *Mémoire sur le nouveau clavecin chromatique de M. de Laborde*. Paris: P.-D. Pierres, 1782. Reprint ed., Geneva: Minkoff, 1972.

Royal Society of London. *Philosophical Transactions*. London, 1665/66-1886.

Rozier, François. *Nouvelle Table des articles contenus dans les volumes de l'Académie Royale des Sciences de Paris depuis 1666 jusqu'en 1770*. 4 vols. Paris: Ruault, 1775-1776.

Ruffey, Richard de. *Histoire secrète de l'Académie de Dijon (de 1741 à 1770)*. Paris: Hachette, 1909.

Russell, Raymond. *The Harpsichord and Clavichord*. 2d ed. New York: W. W. Norton, 1973.

Sacchi, Giovenale. *Del numero e delle misure delle corde musiche e loro corrispondenze*. Milan: G. Mazzucchelli, 1761.

Sachs, Curt. *Real-Lexicon der Musikinstrumente*. Berlin: J. Bard, 1913. New ed., New York: Dover, 1964.

Salomon-Bayet, Claire. "Un préambule théorique à une Académie des Arts," *Revue d'histoire des sciences*, XXIII (1970), 229-250.

Samoyault-Verlet, Colombe. *Les facteurs de clavecins parisiens*. Paris: Heugel, 1966.

Scherchen, Hermann. *Vom Wesen der Musik*. Winterthur: Mondial, 1946. English trans. by W. Mann, *The Nature of Music*. London: H. Regnery, 1950.

Schier, Donald S. *Louis-Bertrand Castel, Anti-Newtonian Scientist*. Cedar Rapids, Iowa: Torch Press, 1941.

Schneider, Herbert. *Die französische Kompositionslehre in der ersten Hälfte des 17. Jahrhunderts*. Tutzing: Hans Schneider, 1972.

Semmens, Richard T. *Etienne Loulié as Music Theorist: An Analysis of Items in Ms. Paris*, fonds fr. n.a. 6355. Ph.D. dissertation, Stanford Univ., 1980.

Serre, Jean-Adam. *Essais sur les principes de l'harmonie*. Paris: Prault fils, 1753. Reprint ed., New York: Broude Bros., 1967.

Sigerist, Henry E. "The Story of Tarantism," in *Music and Medicine*, ed.

BIBLIOGRAPHY

D. M. Schullian and M. Schoen (New York: H. Schuman, 1948), pp. 96-116.

Société philomathique de Paris. *Bulletin des sciences*. Ser. 1, vols. 1-3. Paris, 1791-1805.

Souberbielle, Léon. *La théorie Louisquatorzienne du plein-jeu de l'orgue français*. Sévres: the author, 1971.

Spink, John S. *French Free-Thought from Gassendi to Voltaire*. London: Univ. of London, 1960.

Stimson, Dorothy. *Scientists and Amateurs, A History of the Royal Society*. New York: H. Schuman, 1948.

Suite de la clef, ou Journal historique sur les matières du tems. Paris, 1717-1776.

Suremain de Missery, Antoine. *Théorie acoustico-musicale, ou de la doctrine des sons rapportée aux principes de leur combinaison*. Paris: Firmin-Didot, 1793.

Table alphabétique (générale) des matières contenues dans l'Histoire et les Mémoires de l'Académie Royale des Sciences, ed. L. Godin, P. Demours, and L. Cotte. 10 vols. Paris: Compagnie des Libraires and Bachelier, 1734-1809.

Table alphabétique des matières contenues dans les seize premiers tomes des Mémoires de l'Académie Impériale des sciences, inscriptions et belles-lettres de Toulouse, ed. Auguste Larrey. Toulouse: J.-M. Douladoure, 1854.

Table générale des matières contenues dans le Journal des Savans, de l'édition de Paris, depuis l'année 1665 qu'il a commencé, jusqu'en 1750 inclusivement. 10 vols. Paris, 1753-1764.

Tableau général, raisonné et méthodique des ouvrages contenus dans le recueil des Mémoires de l'Académie Royale des Inscriptions et Belles-Lettres, depuis sa naissance jusques et compris l'année 1788, ed. C.C.F. de L'Averdy. Paris: P. Didot l'aîné, 1791.

Tartini, Giuseppe. *Trattato di musica secondo la vera scienza dell' armonia*. Padova: Stamperia del seminario, 1754. Reprint editions, New York: Broude Bros., 1966, and Padua: CEDAM, 1973.

Tassin, René P. *Histoire littéraire de la Congrégation de Saint-Maur*. Brussels and Paris: Humblot, 1770. Reprint ed., Ridgewood, N.J.: Gregg Press, 1965.

Taton, René. "Inventaire chronologique de l'oeuvre de Lagrange." *Revue d'histoire des sciences*, XXVII (1974), 2-36.

―――. *Les origines de l'Académie Royale des Sciences*. Paris: Univ. de Paris, 1966.

Thibaut, Geneviève, Jean Jenkins, and Josiane Bran-Ricci. *Eighteenth Century Musical Instruments: France and Britain*. London: Eyre and Spottiswoode, 1973.

Tisserand, Roger. *Au temps de l'Encyclopédie, l'Académie de Dijon de 1740 à 1793*. Vesoul: Imprimerie nouvelle, and Paris: Boivin, 1936.

BIBLIOGRAPHY

Torlais, Jean. *Un physicien au siècle des lumières, l'Abbé Nollet, 1700-1770.* Paris: Sipuco, 1954.

Truesdell, Clifford A. "The Rational Mechanics of Flexible or Elastic Bodies, 1638-1788," Intro. to *Leonhardi Euleri Opera Omnia*, series 2, vol. 11, pt. 2. Zurich: O. Füssli, 1960.

Vallas, Léon. *La musique à Lyon au dix-huitième siècle.* T. I: *La musique à l'Académie de Lyon au dix-huitième siècle.* Lyon: Editions de la Revue Musicale, 1908.

Vannes, René. *Dictionnaire universel des luthiers.* 2d ed. Brussels: Les amis de la musique, 1951.

Vaucanson, Jacques de. *Le mécanisme du flûteur automate.* Paris: Guérin, 1738. Reprint ed., Amsterdam: Frits Knuf, 1979.

Vial, François-Guillaume. *Arbre généalogique de l'harmonie.* Paris: the author, [1766].

Vicq d'Azyr, Félix. *Oeuvres de Vicq-d'Azyr*, ed. J.-L. Moreau. 6 vols. Paris: L. Duprat-Duverger, an XIII-1805.

Viotti, Giovanni Battista. *Mémoire au roi, concernant l'exploitation du privilège de l'opéra.* Paris, 1789.

Vogler, Georg Joseph. *Betrachtungen der Mannheimer Tonschule.* 3 Jahrg., 1778-1781. Reprint ed., Hildesheim: G. Olms, 1974.

———. *Choral-System.* Copenhagen: N. Christensen, 1800.

———. *Tonwissenschaft und Tonsetzkunst.* Mannheim: Khurfürstlichen Hofbuchdruckerei, 1776. Reprint ed., Hildesheim: G. Olms, 1970.

Weld, Charles R. *A History of the Royal Society.* London: J. W. Parker, 1848. Reprint ed., New York: Arno Press, 1975.

Wellek, Albert. "Das Doppelempfinden im 18. Jahrhundert," *Deutsche Vierteljahrsschrift für Literaturwissenschaft und Geistesgeschichte*, V. 14 (1936), 75-102.

———. "Farbenharmonie und Farbenklavier, Ihre Entstehungsgeschichte im 18. Jahrhundert," *Archiv für die gesamte Psychologie*, V. 94 (1935), 347-375.

Wever, Ernest G., and Merle Lawrence. *Physiological Acoustics.* Princeton: Princeton Univ. Press, 1954.

Wolf, Abraham. *A History of Science, Technology, and Philosophy in the 16th and 17th Centuries.* London: G. Allen and Unwin, 1935.

———. *A History of Science, Technology, and Philosophy in the Eighteenth Century.* 2d ed. London: G. Allen and Unwin, 1952.

Wright, Rowland. *Dictionnaire des instruments de musique.* London: Battley Bros., 1941.

Yates, Frances A. *The French Academies of the Sixteenth Century.* London: The Warburg Institute, 1947.

Index

Académie de Lyon, 109
Académie des Beaux-Arts (Paris), 94, 104
Académie des Belles-Lettres, Sciences et Arts de Bordeaux, 14, 15, 31, 60, 109
Académie des Inscriptions (Paris), 107
Académie des Sciences, Arts et Belles-Lettres de Dijon, 95, 109
Académie des Sciences, Belles-Lettres et Arts de Rouen, 89, 109
Académie Française (Paris), 92
Académie Royale d'Architecture (Paris), 13, 18
Académie Royale de Peinture et de Sculpture (Paris), 18
Académie Royale des Sciences (Paris), archives, 7; character, 3, 17-18; early history, 3-4, 6-7, 17-18; founding, 6, 8, 12, 16; publications, 44-45; relations with other academies, 6; reorganization, 17, 18
Académie Royale des Sciences, Inscriptions et Belles-Lettres de Toulouse, 37, 62, 93, 94, 109
academies, general, 3; provincial, 107-109
Accademia del Cimento (Florence), 6, 8
Accademia delle Scienze dell'Instituto di Bologna, 81, 85
Accademia Filarmonica di Bologna, 55
accompaniment, 74, 101, 103, 104
acoustics, as field, 6, 18-19, 23, 27, 29, 46, 50, 112; experiments in, 23, 26-27, 37, 93, 115, 116; origin of term, 24, 26; see also sound
aesthetics, general, 10, 18, 87; musical, 48, 53, 79, 85, 98, 110, 112
air, elasticity of, 9-10, 31, 83, 86
Aix en Provence, 87

Alembert, Jean le Rond d', 3, 33, 44, 45, 46, 53, 84, 85, 86, 89, 90, 91, 92, 93, 97, 99, 102, 105, 106, 117
allemande (La Voye-Mignot), 7
alphabet (Demoz), 72
Amelot de Chaillou, Jean-Jacques, 54
anémocorde (Schnell and Tschirszcki), 66
Ango, Pierre, 21
architecture, 13, 61
arithmetic, 13, 90
armonica (Franklin), 65; see also harmonica
art, 18, 19
art gammo-graphique (Vausenville), 75
artes liberales (liberal arts), 4-5, 45
Arts et Métiers (arts and crafts), 41-44, 110
arts mécaniques, 42, 45
assemblée publique, 14, 20, 23, 31, 32, 33, 35, 37, 39, 40, 91, 97, 115
astronomy, 4, 14
audition, 12; anatomy of, 9-11, 40; in animals, 11, 36, 39-40; in fish, 11, 36, 37, 38; in humans, 28, 38, 39-40; see also ear, hearing

Bailleux, Antoine, 105
Ballard family, music printers, 76
Ballière, Charles-Louis-Denis, 89
Banks, Joseph, 99
Barbour, J. Murray, 88, 91
Bar-le-Duc, 61
Barrière, Pierre, 108
Beaugrand, Jean de, 5
Bedos de Celles, Dom François, 59-60, 61, 121
Beeckman, Isaac, 5
Bell, Arthur E., 5
Bellot, Louis-Charles, 52, 120
Bemetzrieder, Anton, 100-101

(141)

INDEX

Berger, Joseph-Antoine, 55, 121
Berlin Academy, 34
Bernoulli, Daniel, 31, 33, 34
Berthollet, Claude-Louis, 30, 63, 117
Beyer, 66, 121, 122
Bézout, Etienne, 34, 117
Bianconi, Giovanni Lodovico, 33
Bignon, Jean-Paul, 17, 18, 22, 42, 45
biological sciences, 36
Blainville, Charles-Henri de, 95-97
Blondel, Nicolas-François, 7, 12-13,
   14, 18
Bochart de Saron, Jean-Philippe-Gas-
   pard, 57, 63, 66, 95, 117
Boethius, 24
Boisgelou, François-Paul Roualle de,
   94
Bologna, 33
Bononcini, Giovanni Maria, 81
Bordeaux, 52
Bosch, 59, 121
Bouguer, Pierre, 33
Boulliau, Ismaël, 5
Boulogne-sur-mer, 55
Bouvard, Michel-Philippe, 35-36
Bouvier, 21
Brancas de Lauraguais, Louis-Léon-
   Félicité, 62, 117
Bredeau, Claude, 5
Breitkopf, Johann Gottlob Immanuel,
   76, 77
Brémond, François de, 37
Brisson, Mathurin-Jacques, 39, 67, 68,
   117
British Library, 81
Brossard, Sébastien de, 7, 71, 73, 80
buffet d'orgue, Joinville, 121; Robert, 95
Buffon, Georges-Louis Leclerc, comte
   de, 31-32
Bulyowski de Dulycz, Michel, 116
Buot, Jacques, 7
Burmeister, Joachim, 73

calculus, invention of, 33
Camper, Petrus, 37, 38, 40
Camus, Charles-Etienne-Louis, 61,
   117
carillon, 56

Carré, Louis, 18, 22-24, 45, 49, 80,
   117, 120
Cartesianism, 30
Cartois, J.-B., 49, 120
Cassini de Thury, César-François, 32,
   67, 117
Cassini, Giovanni Domenico, 8, 32
Castel, Louis-Bertrand, 32
céleste (de Virbès), 52
Châlons, 19
Chambéry, 72
Chapotot, 69
Charles, 74
Chartier, Roger, 108
Château de La Rochepot, 19
Chevalier, François, 27
Chladni, Ernst Florenz Friedrich, 23
Choquel, Henri-Louis, 104-105
chords, types and succession of, 96-99,
   102-103
choreography, 78
chronomètre (chronometer), Choquel,
   105; Dubos, 70; Loulié, 68, 69; Sauveur, 68
chronometry, as field, 68
Chyquelier, Christophe II, 53, 121
Clairaut, Alexis-Claude, 34
Clairvaux, 61
clapette (Taskin), 57
clavecin (clavessin), see harpsichord
clavecin acoustique (de Virbès), 52
clavecin à maillets (Marius), 47, 50, 51,
   120
clavecin brisé (Marius), 50, 120
clavecin organisé, Bedos de Celles, 60;
   Berger, 55, 121; Joinville, 61; Le
   Voir, 53-54; Schmitz, 58, 122
clavecin-vielle (Cuisinié), 51, 120
clavichord, 51
clavicordium (Le Gay), 54
clavicytherium, 51
clavier (keyboard), 30, 59, 87, 88, 95,
   101, 120
claviorganum, 55
Clermont, count of, 56
clockwork mechanisms, 15, 67, 68, 70
cloth, waterproofing (Marius), 50
Colbert, Jean-Baptiste, 17, 19, 42

INDEX

Collège Royal (Paris), 18, 26, 27
Colonna, Fabius, 24
Colonna, Giovanni Paolo, 81
combination tones, 91-92
Comité de librairie, 84
comma, in tuning systems, 80, 87, 91, 93
committees, academic, *liste des commissions*, 90; review process, 47-49, 81; statistics, 46-47, 48, 117-119
Communauté des Imprimeurs, 76
comparative anatomy, 11, 35, 36, 38, 39-40
composition, musical, 21, 79, 99, 102, 103
Concert spirituel, 96
Condorcet, Marie-Jean-Antoine-Nicolas Caritat de, 7, 35, 59, 75
Confessions (Rousseau), 72, 74
Conservatoire National des Arts et Métiers (Paris), 44, 67, 69
consonance and dissonance, basis for, 24, 28, 86, 87
contrebasse, see *piano-forté contrebasse*
Coquerest, 107
Corps Royal de l'Artillerie, 94
Corsica, 75
Cosmotheoros (Huygens), 16
Cousineau, Georges, 48, 63, 64, 66, 100, 121
Cuisinié, François, 51, 120

dampers, harp, 64; piano, 56, 57
dance, 21, 77-78
Daubenton, Louis-Jean-Marie, 39, 118
Daumas, Maurice, 41
Delaine, Jean, 61-62, 121
Delamain, Richard, 104
Delambre, Jean-Baptiste-Joseph, 68, 118
Delaunay, 74
Demoz, Jean-François, 71-72, 73
Deparcieux, Antoine, 61, 118
Desargues, Gérard, 5
Des Billettes, Gilles Filleau, 42, 44, 51, 118
Descartes, René, 5, 26, 81

Description des Arts et Métiers, 22, 42, 44, 45, 59
Des Hayes, 77-78
Desmarest, Nicolas, 37, 67, 118
Deudon, A.C.G., 65-66, 121
Diderot, Denis, 44, 45, 83, 100
Dietrich, Philippe-Frédéric, baron de, 29-30, 58, 65, 118
Dionis du Séjour, Achille-Pierre, 107
dissonance, *see* consonance and dissonance
Dodart, Denis, 20, 21, 35, 39, 40, 81, 118
Doinet, 103
Domenjoud, Jean-Baptiste, 62, 121
Dornel, Louis-Antoine, 101-102
Droüyn, l'Abbé, 21
Dubos, 70
Du Bourg, Barbeu, 65
Dubousset, 107
Dufay, Charles-François de Cisternay, 33, 67, 118
Dufourni, 39
Duguet (Duguay), Guilleminot, 107
Du Hamel, Jean-Baptiste, 18
Duhamel du Monceau, Henri-Louis, 38, 44, 59, 60, 76, 118
Dumontier, 56
Dupéron, 93
Du Quet, 14
Durand, 80
Du Verney, Joseph-Guichard, 10-12, 37, 81
dynamics, control of, 50, 52, 54, 55, 56, 57, 59, 62, 64, 65, 95; *see also* expression

ear, artificial, 14; judgment of, 82, 86, 88, 93, 98, 110, 112; structure of, 9, 10-11, 15, 30; *see also* audition, hearing
echo, 15, 19
échomètre (Sauveur), 28, 69, 80, 115
Ecole Royale Militaire, 47
Encyclopédie, 44, 45, 84
Encyclopédie méthodique, 89, 95
engineering, 26, 48
Enlightenment, 3

(143)

INDEX

INDEX

121; folding, see *clavecin brisé*; improvements to, 52, 53, 62, 120-122; jacks, *see* jacks, harpsichord; ocular (Castel), 32; organized, see *clavecin organisé*; pedals, 47, 50, 56, 121; tuning, 23, 49, 88, 94, 103; upright, see *clavicytherium*

Hauksbee, Francis, 37

Hautefeuille, l'Abbé Jean de, 14-15

Haute-Marne, 89

Haüy, René-Just, 55, 58, 64, 65, 66, 67, 70, 95, 118

Hayes, Deborah, 16

hearing, 9-11, 14, 15, 24, 36-37, 39; *see also* audition, ear

hearing trumpet, 14

Hébert, Charles, 81-82

Hellot, Jean, 54, 72-73, 118

Hémery, Joseph d', 77

Henfling, Conrad, 116

Hérissant, François-David, 38-39, 40

Histoire et Mémoires, 44

Hubbard, Frank, 43

humanism, 4, 108, 110

hurdy-gurdy (*vielle*), improvements to, 49, 51, 120; see also *instruments organisés*

Huygens, Christian, 6, 12, 15-16, 18, 21, 91, 116

Huygens, Constantijn, 5, 15

Institut National des Sciences et des Arts, 55, 58, 112

instruments, acoustical, 14, 15

instruments organisés (organized instruments), 48, 53; bowed harpsichord, 50, 53-55, 121, 122; bowed string-organ, 60, 121; harpsichord-organ (*claviorganum*), 53, 55-56, 121; harpsichord-piano, 47, 51, 53, 56-57, 121; harpsichord-*vielle*, 51; keyboard-wind, 66, 122; organ-*vielle*, 47, 60, 121; piano-harp, 64, 122; piano-organ, 59, 121; violin-*vielle*, 61, 62, 121; see also *clavecin-vielle*, *clavecin organisé*, *pneumacorde*, *vielle-organisée*

Iriarte y Oropesa, Tomás de, 106-107

jacks, forte-piano, 57, 64; harpsichord, 49, 50, 52, 54, 56, 120; *vielle*, 62

Jacobi, Erwin R., 83

Jamard, T., 89

Joinville, 61, 121

Joubert, Henri, 47, 60, 121

joueuse de tympanon, 67

Journal des beaux-arts et des sciences, 100

Journal des Sçavans, 19, 97

Jussieu, Bernard de, 38, 118

Kepler, Johannes, 24, 88

keyboard, see *clavier*

Kircher, Athanasius, 81, 91

Kleinbaum, Abby R., 31

knee-levers, harpsichord, see *genouillères*

Krumpholtz, Johann-Baptiste, 47, 64, 121

Laborde, Jean-Benjamin de, 48, 53, 96, 98, 99, 100, 121

La Caille, l'Abbé Nicolas-Louis de, 32

Lacassagne, l'Abbé Joseph, 105

La Charlonye, Gabriel de, 5

La Condamine, Charles-Marie de, 33, 104, 118

La Flèche, Jesuit school at, 26

Lagette (Lagetto), Louis, 62, 121

Lagrange, Joseph-Louis de, 34, 55, 118

La Hire, Laurent de, 18

La Hire, Philippe de, 18-19, 51, 75, 118

Lalande, Joseph-Jérôme Lefrançois de, 61, 85, 118

La Laurencie, Lionel de, 108

La Main, Richardo de, 104

Lami, 64, 122

Landrieu, 47

Langevin de Falaise, 58, 122

Laplace, Pierre-Simon, 57, 67, 95, 118

larynx, 20, 35, 40

La Salette, Pierre-Joseph Joubert de, 94

Lassone, Joseph-Marie-François de, 36, 38, 62, 67, 118

Laurent de Valenciennes, 74

La Voye-Mignot, de, 5, 6-7

Le Cat, Claude-Nicolas, 36-37

(145)

INDEX

INDEX

Library of Congress Cataloging in Publication Data

Cohen, Albert, 1929-
    Music in the French Royal Academy of Sciences.

    Bibliography: p.
    Includes index.
    1.   Music—France—History and criticism.   2.   Académie
des sciences (Paris, France)—History.   I.   Title.
ML270.8.P22A23   781'.09'032   81-47118
ISBN 0-691-09127-7   AACR2

Albert Cohen is Chairman of the Department of Music and the first William H. Bonsall Professor of Music at Stanford University. He specializes in the history and theory of French music in the seventeenth and eighteenth centuries and is the author of numerous scholarly articles and books.